Chemistry revision? CGP has the solution...

No doubt about it, WJEC GCSE Chemistry is tough. Luckily, this CGP book is crammed full of info, from facts and theory to practical skills — plus a generous serving of practice questions to help you sharpen up your science skills.

And of course, it's all matched to the latest Welsh Grade A*-G GCSE exams.

How to access your free Online Edition

This book includes a free Online Edition to read on your PC, Mac or tablet.
To access it, just go to cgpbooks.co.uk/extras and enter this code...

3061 2144 7097 2655

By the way, this code only works for one person. If somebody else has used this book before you, they might have already claimed the Online Edition.

CGP — still the best! ☺

Our sole aim here at CGP is to produce the highest quality books — carefully written, immaculately presented and dangerously close to being funny.

Then we work our socks off to get them out to you
— at the cheapest possible prices.

Contents

What to Expect in the Exams 2

Working Scientifically
The Scientific Method 3
Communication & Issues Created by Science 4
Risk 5
Designing Investigations 6
Collecting Data 7
Processing and Presenting Data 8
Units and Equations 10
Drawing Conclusions 11
Uncertainties and Evaluations 12

Unit 1a — The Nature of Substances and Chemical Reactions
Elements, Compounds and Mixtures 13
Separating Mixtures 14
Chromatography 15
Chemical Formulae 16
Chemical Equations 17
Chemical Reactions 18
Relative Formula Mass 19
The Mole 20
Calculating Masses in Reactions 21
Calculating Formulae from Reacting Masses 22
Revision Questions for Unit 1a 24

Unit 1b — Atomic Structure and the Periodic Table
The Atom 25
Ions, Isotopes and Relative Atomic Mass 26
The Periodic Table 27
Electron Shells 28
Group 1 — The Alkali Metals 29
Reactions of the Alkali Metals 30
Group 7 — The Halogens 31
Reactions of the Halogens 32
Halogen Displacement Reactions 33
Group 0 — The Noble Gases 34
Tests for Ions and Hydrogen 35
Revision Questions for Unit 1b 36

Unit 1c — Water and the Earth
Water Treatment 37
Distillation and Desalination 38
Solubility Curves 39
Investigating Solubility 40
Water Hardness 41
Measuring Water Hardness 42
The Earth's Structure 43
Plate Tectonics 44
Plate Boundaries 45
The Atmosphere 46
Greenhouse Gases and Climate Change 47
Reducing Pollution and Tests for Gases 48
Revision Questions for Unit 1c 49

Unit 1d — Rate of Chemical Change and Thermal Decomposition
Reaction Rates 50
Rate Experiments Involving Gases 51
Rate Experiments Involving Precipitation 52
Calculating Rates 53
Factors Affecting Rate of Reaction 54
More Factors Affecting Rate of Reaction 55
Thermal Decomposition 56
Limestone 57
Revision Questions for Unit 1d 58

Unit 2a — Bonding, Structure and Properties
Metallic Bonding 59
Ionic Bonding 60
Ionic Compounds 61
Simple Molecules 62
Giant Covalent Structures and Fullerenes 63
Nanoparticles 64
Smart Materials 65
Revision Questions for Unit 2a 66

Unit 2b — Acids, Bases and Salts
Acids and Bases 67
Acid and Alkali Strength 68
Reactions of Acids 69
Making Salts 70
Titrations 71
Titration Calculations 72
Revision Questions for Unit 2b 73

Unit 2c — Metals, Extraction and Energy

Metal Ores and The Reactivity Series 74
Extracting Iron 75
Metal Displacement Reactions 76
Electrolysis 77
More on Electrolysis 78
Electrolysis of Aqueous Solutions 79
Uses of Electrolysis 80
Sustainability of Metal Extraction 81
Uses of Metals 82
Transition Metals 83
Endothermic and Exothermic Reactions 84
Bond Energies 85
Revision Questions for Unit 2c 86

Unit 2d — Crude Oil, Fuels and Organic Chemistry

Fractional Distillation of Crude Oil 87
Crude Oil and Cracking 88
Hydrocarbons 89
Burning Fuels 90
Measuring Energy Changes 91
Alkanes 92
Alkenes 93
Naming Other Alkanes and Alkenes 94
Addition Polymers 95
Uses of Plastics 96
Disposing of Polymers 97
Alcohols 98
Uses of Ethanol 99
Testing for Alcohols and Infrared Spectroscopy 100
Revision Questions for Unit 2d 101

Unit 2e — Reversible Reactions and Industrial Processes

Reversible Reactions 102
The Haber Process 103
The Contact Process 104
Uses of Sulfuric Acid 105
Nitrogenous Fertilisers 106
Revision Questions for Unit 2e 107

Practical Skills

Measuring Techniques 108
Measuring Techniques and Safety 109
Setting Up Experiments 110
Heating Substances 111

Answers 112
Index 116
Periodic Table and Formulae of Common Ions 118

Published by CGP
From original material by Richard Parsons

Editors: Dan Chesman, Emily Forsberg, Paul Jordin, Sharon Keeley-Holden, Luke Molloy and Sarah Pattison
Contributors: Paddy Gannon and Mike Thompson

ISBN: 978 1 78908 342 2

Graph to show atmospheric CO_2 concentration and global temperature on page 47 based on data by EPICA community members 2004 and Siegenthaler et al 2005.

With thanks to Duncan Lindsay and Barrie Crowther for the proofreading.

With thanks to Jan Greenway for the copyright research.

Printed by Elanders Ltd, Newcastle upon Tyne.
Clipart from Corel®

Illustrations by: Sandy Gardner Artist, email sandy@sandygardner.co.uk

Text, design, layout and original illustrations © Coordination Group Publications Ltd (CGP) 2019
All rights reserved.

Photocopying more than one section of this book is not permitted, even if you have a CLA licence.
Extra copies are available from CGP with next day delivery • 0800 1712 712 • www.cgpbooks.co.uk

What to Expect in the Exams

Before you get cracking with your revision, here's a handy guide to what you'll have to face in the exams — and the special features of this book that we've included especially to help you. You're welcome.

1) Topics are Covered in Different Papers

For WJEC GCSE Chemistry, you'll sit two exam papers.

You're expected to know the basic concepts in chemistry for both exams.

Paper	Time	No. of marks	Units covered
Unit 1	1 hr 45 mins	80	1a, 1b, 1c and 1d
Unit 2	1 hr 45 mins	80	2a, 2b, 2c, 2d and 2e

2) There are Different Question Types

In each exam, you'll be expected to answer a mixture of structured questions, questions that have short, closed answers as well as open response questions.

For some open response questions, you'll be marked on the overall quality of your answer, not just its scientific content. So, always make sure...

- You answer the question fully.
- You include detailed, relevant information.
- Your answer is clear and has a logical structure.
- You've checked your spelling, punctuation and grammar.

3) You'll be Tested on your Maths...

At least 20% of the total marks for GCSE Chemistry will come from questions that test your maths skills. For these questions, always remember to:

EXAMPLE: Look out for these worked examples in this book — they show you maths skills you'll need in the exam.

- Show your working — you could get marks for this, even if your final answer's wrong.
- Check that the units of your answer are the same as the ones they asked for in the question.
- Make sure your answer is given to an appropriate number of significant figures.

4) ...and on your Practical Skills

Whenever one of the specified practicals crops up in this book, it's marked up like this...

PRACTICAL

...and there's a whole section on Practical Skills on pages 108-111.

- GCSE Chemistry contains 10 specified practicals that you'll do during the course. You might be asked about these, and the practical skills involved in them, in the exams.
- At least 15% of the total marks will be for questions that test your understanding of practical skills.
- For example, you might be asked to comment on the design of an experiment (the apparatus and method), make predictions, analyse or interpret results... Pretty much anything to do with planning and carrying out the investigations.

You'll also do two practical assessments in school. In each assessment you'll have to carry out an experiment to collect some results and then analyse and evaluate your results.

5) You'll need to know about Working Scientifically

Working Scientifically is all about how science is applied in the outside world by real scientists.

For example, you might be asked about ways that scientists communicate an idea to get their point across without being biased, or about the limitations of a scientific theory.

Working Scientifically is covered on pages 3-12.

You need to think about the situation that you've been given and use all your scientific savvy to answer the question. Always read the question and any data you've been given really carefully before you start writing your answer.

Working Scientifically

The Scientific Method

This section isn't about how to 'do' science — but it does show you the way most scientists work.

Scientists Come Up With Hypotheses — Then Test Them

1) Scientists try to explain things. They start by observing something they don't understand.
2) They then come up with a hypothesis — a possible explanation for what they've observed.
3) The next step is to test whether the hypothesis might be right or not. This involves making a prediction based on the hypothesis and testing it by gathering evidence (i.e. data) from investigations. If evidence from experiments backs up a prediction, you're a step closer to figuring out if the hypothesis is true.

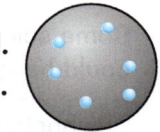

About 100 years ago, scientists hypothesised that atoms looked like this.

Several Scientists Will Test a Hypothesis

1) Normally, scientists share their findings in peer-reviewed journals, or at conferences.
2) Peer-review is where other scientists check results and scientific explanations to make sure they're 'scientific' (e.g. that experiments have been done in a sensible way) before they're published. It helps to detect false claims, but it doesn't mean that findings are correct — just that they're not wrong in any obvious way.
3) Once other scientists have found out about a hypothesis, they'll start basing their own predictions on it and carry out their own experiments. They'll also try to reproduce the original experiments to check the results — and if all the experiments in the world back up the hypothesis, then scientists start to think the hypothesis is true.
4) However, if a scientist does an experiment that doesn't fit with the hypothesis (and other scientists can reproduce the results) then the hypothesis may need to be modified or scrapped altogether.

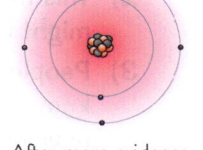

After more evidence was gathered, scientists changed their hypothesis to this.

If All the Evidence Supports a Hypothesis, It's Accepted — For Now

1) Accepted hypotheses are often referred to as theories. Our currently accepted theories are the ones that have survived this 'trial by evidence' — they've been tested many times over the years and survived.
2) However, theories never become totally indisputable fact. If new evidence comes along that can't be explained using the existing theory, then the hypothesising and testing is likely to start all over again.

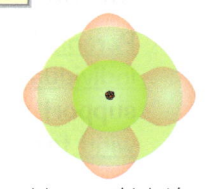

Now we think it's more like this.

Theories Can Involve Different Types of Models

1) A representational model is a simplified description or picture of what's going on in real life. Like all models, it can be used to explain observations and make predictions. E.g. we can use a simplified model to show the arrangement of the nucleus and electrons in an atom (see p.25). It can be used to explain trends down groups in the periodic table.
2) Computational models use computers to make simulations of complex real-life processes, such as climate change. They're used when there are a lot of different variables (factors that change) to consider, and because you can easily change their design to take into account new data.
3) All models have limitations on what they can explain or predict. E.g. ball and stick models (a type of spatial model) can be used to show how ions are arranged in an ionic compound. One of their limitations is that they don't show the relative sizes of ions (see p.61).

Scientists test models by carrying out experiments to check that the predictions made by the model happen as expected.

I'm off to the zoo to test my hippo-thesis...

The scientific method has developed over time, and many people have helped to develop it. From Aristotle to modern day scientists, lots of people have contributed. And many more are likely to contribute in the future.

Communication & Issues Created by Science

Scientific developments can be great, but they can sometimes raise more questions than they answer...

It's Important to Communicate Scientific Discoveries to the General Public

Some scientific discoveries show that people should change their habits, or they might provide ideas that could be developed into new technology. So scientists need to tell the world about their discoveries.

> Technologies are being developed that make use of fullerenes (see p.63). These include drug delivery systems for use in medicine. Information about these systems needs to be communicated to doctors so they can use them, and to patients, so they can make informed decisions about their treatment.

Scientific Evidence can be Presented in a Biased Way

1) Reports about scientific discoveries in the media (e.g. newspapers or television) aren't peer-reviewed.
2) This means that, even though news stories are often based on data that has been peer-reviewed, the data might be presented in a way that is over-simplified or inaccurate, making it open to misinterpretation.
3) People who want to make a point can sometimes present data in a biased way. (Sometimes without knowing they're doing it.) For example, a scientist might overemphasise a relationship in the data, or a newspaper article might describe details of data supporting an idea without giving any evidence against it.

Scientific Developments are Great, but they can Raise Issues

Scientific knowledge is increased by doing experiments. And this knowledge leads to scientific developments, e.g. new technologies or new advice. These developments can create issues though. For example:

Economic issues: Society can't always afford to do things scientists recommend (e.g. investing in alternative energy sources) without cutting back elsewhere.

Personal issues: Some decisions will affect individuals. For example, someone might support alternative energy, but object if a wind farm is built next to their house.

Social issues: Decisions based on scientific evidence affect people — e.g. should fossil fuels be taxed more highly? Would the effect on people's lifestyles be acceptable...

Environmental issues: Human activity often affects the natural environment. For example, building a dam to produce electricity will change the local habitat so some species might be displaced. But it will also reduce our need for fossil fuels, so will help to reduce climate change.

Science Can't Answer Every Question — Especially Ethical Ones

1) We don't understand everything. We're always finding out more, but we'll never know all the answers.
2) In order to answer scientific questions, scientists need data to provide evidence for their hypotheses.
3) Some questions can't be answered yet because the data can't currently be collected, or because there's not enough data to support a theory.
4) Eventually, as we get more evidence, we'll answer some of the questions that currently can't be answered, e.g. what the impact of global warming on sea levels will be. But there will always be the "Should we be doing this at all?"-type questions that experiments can't help us to answer...

> Think about new drugs which can be taken to boost your 'brain power'.
> - Some people think they're good as they could improve concentration or memory. New drugs could let people think in ways beyond the powers of normal brains.
> - Other people say they're bad — they could give you an unfair advantage in exams. And people might be pressured into taking them so that they could work more effectively, and for longer hours.

Tea to milk or milk to tea? — Totally unanswerable by science...

Science can't tell you whether or not you should do something. That's for you and society to decide. But there are tons of questions science might be able to answer, like where life came from and where my superhero socks are.

Working Scientifically

Risk

By reading this page you are agreeing to the risk of a paper cut or severe drowsiness...

Nothing is Completely Risk-Free

1) A hazard is something that could potentially cause harm.
2) All hazards have a risk attached to them — this is the chance that the hazard will cause harm.
3) The risks of some things seem pretty obvious, or we've known about them for a while, like the risk of causing acid rain by polluting the atmosphere, or of having a car accident when you're travelling in a car.
4) New technology arising from scientific advances can bring new risks, e.g. scientists are unsure whether nanoparticles that are being used in cosmetics and suncream might be harming the cells in our bodies. These risks need to be considered alongside the benefits of the technology, e.g. improved sun protection.
5) You can estimate the size of a risk based on how many times something happens in a big sample (e.g. 100 000 people) over a given period (e.g. a year). For example, you could assess the risk of a driver crashing by recording how many people in a group of 100 000 drivers crashed their cars over a year.
6) To make decisions about activities that involve hazards, we need to take into account the chance of the hazard causing harm, and how serious the consequences would be if it did. If an activity involves a hazard that's very likely to cause harm, with serious consequences if it does, it's considered high risk.

People Make Their Own Decisions About Risk

1) Not all risks have the same consequences, e.g. if you chop veg with a sharp knife you risk cutting your finger, but if you go scuba-diving you risk death. You're much more likely to cut your finger during half an hour of chopping than to die during half an hour of scuba diving. But most people are happier to accept a higher probability of an accident if the consequences are short-lived and fairly minor.
2) People tend to be more willing to accept a risk if they choose to do something (e.g. go scuba diving), compared to having the risk imposed on them (e.g. having a nuclear power station built next door).
3) People's perception of risk (how risky they think something is) isn't always accurate. They tend to view familiar activities as low-risk and unfamiliar activities as high-risk — even if that's not the case. For example, cycling on roads is often high-risk, but many people are happy to do it because it's a familiar activity. Air travel is actually pretty safe, but a lot of people perceive it as high-risk.
4) People may over-estimate the risk of things with long-term or invisible effects, e.g. ionising radiation.

Investigations Can be Hazardous

1) Hazards from science experiments might include:
   - Microorganisms, e.g. some bacteria can make you ill.
   - Chemicals, e.g. sulfuric acid can burn your skin and alcohols catch fire easily.
   - Fire, e.g. an unattended Bunsen burner is a fire hazard.
   - Electricity, e.g. faulty electrical equipment could give you a shock.

2) Part of planning an investigation is making sure that it's safe.
3) You should always make sure that you identify all the hazards that you might encounter. Then you should think of ways of reducing the risks from the hazards you've identified. For example:
   - If you're working with sulfuric acid, always wear gloves and safety goggles. This will reduce the risk of the acid coming into contact with your skin and eyes.
   - If you're using a Bunsen burner, stand it on a heatproof mat. This will reduce the risk of starting a fire.

You can find out about potential hazards by looking in textbooks, doing some Internet research, or asking your teacher.

Not revising — an unacceptable exam hazard...

The world's a dangerous place, but if you can recognise hazards, decide how to reduce their risks, and be happy to accept some risks, you can still have fun. Just maybe don't go skydiving with a great white shark on Friday 13th.

Working Scientifically

Designing Investigations

Dig out your lab coat and dust down your badly-scratched safety goggles... it's investigation time.

Investigations Produce Evidence to Support or Disprove a Hypothesis

1) Scientists observe things and come up with hypotheses to explain them (see p.3). You need to be able to do the same. For example:

> Observation: People have big feet and spots. Hypothesis: Having big feet causes spots.

2) To determine whether or not a hypothesis is right, you need to do an investigation to gather evidence. To do this, you need to use your hypothesis to make a prediction — something you think will happen that you can test. E.g. people who have bigger feet will have more spots.

3) Investigations are used to see if there are patterns or relationships between two variables, e.g. to see if there's a pattern or relationship between the variables 'number of spots' and 'size of feet'.

Evidence Needs to be Repeatable, Reproducible and Valid

1) Repeatable means that if the same person does an experiment again using the same methods and equipment, they'll get similar results.
2) Reproducible means that if someone else does the experiment, or a different method or piece of equipment is used, the results will still be similar.
3) If data is repeatable and reproducible, it's reliable and scientists are more likely to have confidence in it.
4) Valid results are both repeatable and reproducible AND they answer the original question. They come from experiments that were designed to be a FAIR TEST...

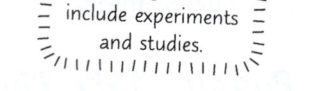

Investigations include experiments and studies.

To Make an Investigation a Fair Test You Have to Control the Variables

1) In a lab experiment you usually change one variable and measure how it affects another variable.
2) To make it a fair test, everything else that could affect the results should stay the same — otherwise you can't tell if the thing you're changing is causing the results or not.
3) The variable you CHANGE is called the INDEPENDENT variable.
4) The variable you MEASURE when you change the independent variable is the DEPENDENT variable.
5) The variables that you KEEP THE SAME are called CONTROL variables.

> You could find how temperature affects reaction rate by measuring the volume of gas formed over time. The independent variable is the temperature. The dependent variable is the volume of gas produced. Control variables include the concentration and amounts of reactants, the time period you measure, etc.

6) Because you can't always control all the variables, you often need to use a control experiment. This is an experiment that's kept under the same conditions as the rest of the investigation, but doesn't have anything done to it. This is so that you can see what happens when you don't change anything at all.

The Bigger the Sample Size the Better

1) Data based on small samples isn't as good as data based on large samples. A sample should represent the whole population (i.e. it should share as many of the characteristics in the population as possible) — a small sample can't do that as well. It's also harder to spot anomalies if your sample size is too small.
2) The bigger the sample size the better, but scientists have to be realistic when choosing how big. For example, if you were studying the effects of a chemical used to sterilise water on the people drinking it, it'd be great to study everyone who was drinking the water (a huge sample), but it'd take ages and cost a bomb. It's more realistic to study a thousand people, with a mixture of ages, gender, and race.

This is no high street survey — it's a designer investigation...

Not only do you need to be able to plan your own investigations, you should also be able to look at someone else's plan and decide whether or not it needs improving. Those examiners aren't half demanding.

Working Scientifically

Collecting Data

You've designed the perfect investigation — now it's time to get your hands mucky and collect some data.

Your Data Should be Repeatable, Reproducible, Accurate and Precise

1) To check repeatability you need to repeat the readings and check that the results are similar. You need to repeat each reading at least three times.
2) To make sure your results are reproducible you can cross check them by taking a second set of readings with another instrument (or a different observer).
3) Your data also needs to be ACCURATE. Really accurate results are those that are really close to the true answer. The accuracy of your results usually depends on your method — you need to make sure you're measuring the right thing and that you don't miss anything that should be included in the measurements. E.g. estimating the amount of gas released from a reaction by counting the bubbles isn't very accurate because you might miss some of the bubbles and they might have different volumes. It's more accurate to measure the volume of gas released using a gas syringe (see p.108).
4) Your data also needs to be PRECISE. Precise results are ones where the data is all really close to the mean (average) of your repeated results (i.e. not spread out).

Beth's result was a curate.

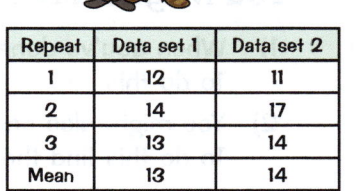

Repeat	Data set 1	Data set 2
1	12	11
2	14	17
3	13	14
Mean	13	14

Data set 1 is more precise than data set 2.

Your Equipment has to be Right for the Job

1) The measuring equipment you use has to be sensitive enough to measure the changes you're looking for. For example, if you need to measure changes of 1 cm^3 you need to use a measuring cylinder or burette that can measure in 1 cm^3 steps — it'd be no good trying with one that only measures 10 cm^3 steps.
2) The smallest change a measuring instrument can detect is called its RESOLUTION. E.g. some mass balances have a resolution of 1 g, some have a resolution of 0.1 g, and some are even more sensitive.
3) Also, equipment needs to be calibrated by measuring a known value. If there's a difference between the measured and known value, you can use this to correct the inaccuracy of the equipment.

You Need to Look out for Errors and Anomalous Results

1) The results of your experiment will always vary a bit because of RANDOM ERRORS — unpredictable differences caused by things like human errors in measuring. The errors when you make a reading from a burette are random. You have to estimate or round the level when it's between two marks — so sometimes your figure will be a bit above the real one, and sometimes it will be a bit below.
2) You can reduce the effect of random errors by taking repeat readings and finding the mean. This will make your results more precise.
3) If a measurement is wrong by the same amount every time, it's called a SYSTEMATIC ERROR. For example, if you measured from the very end of your ruler instead of from the 0 cm mark every time, all your measurements would be a bit small. Repeating the experiment in the exact same way and calculating a mean won't correct a systematic error.

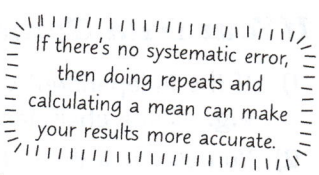

If there's no systematic error, then doing repeats and calculating a mean can make your results more accurate.

4) Just to make things more complicated, if a systematic error is caused by using equipment that isn't zeroed properly, it's called a ZERO ERROR. For example, if a mass balance always reads 1 gram before you put anything on it, all your measurements will be 1 gram too heavy.
5) You can compensate for some systematic errors if you know about them though, e.g. if your mass balance always reads 1 gram before you put anything on it you can subtract 1 gram from all your results.
6) Sometimes you get a result that doesn't fit in with the rest at all. This is called an ANOMALOUS RESULT. You should investigate it and try to work out what happened. If you can work out what happened (e.g. you measured something totally wrong) you can ignore it when processing your results.

Watch what you say to that mass balance — it's very sensitive...

Weirdly, data can be really precise but not very accurate. For example, a fancy piece of lab equipment might give results that are really precise, but if it's not been calibrated properly those results won't be accurate.

Working Scientifically

Processing and Presenting Data

Processing your data means doing some calculations with it to make it more useful. Once you've done that, you can present your results in a nice chart or graph to help you spot any patterns in your data.

Data Needs to be Organised

1) Tables are dead useful for organising data.
2) When you draw a table use a ruler and make sure each column has a heading (including the units).

You Might Have to Process Your Data

1) When you've done repeats of an experiment you should always calculate the mean (average). To do this add together all the data values and divide by the total number of values in the sample.
2) You might also need to calculate the range (how spread out the data is). To do this find the largest number and subtract the smallest number from it.

Ignore anomalous results when calculating these.

EXAMPLE: The results of an experiment to find the mass of gas lost from two reactions are shown below. Calculate the mean and the range for the mass of gas lost in each reaction.

Test tube	Repeat 1 (g)	Repeat 2 (g)	Repeat 3 (g)	Mean (g)	Range (g)
A	28	37	32	(28 + 37 + 32) ÷ 3 = 32	37 − 28 = 9
B	47	51	60	(47 + 51 + 60) ÷ 3 = 53	60 − 47 = 13

Round to the Lowest Number of Significant Figures

The first significant figure of a number is the first digit that's not zero. The second and third significant figures come straight after (even if they're zeros). You should be aware of significant figures in calculations.

1) In any calculation, you should round the answer to the lowest number of significant figures (s.f.) given.
2) Remember to write down how many significant figures you've rounded to after your answer.
3) If your calculation has multiple steps, only round the final answer, or it won't be as accurate.

EXAMPLE: The volume of one mole of gas is 24.0 dm^3 at room temperature and pressure. How many moles are there in 4.6 dm^3 of gas under the same conditions?

No. of moles of gas = 4.6 dm^3 ÷ 24.0 dm^3 = 0.19166... = 0.19 mol (2 s.f.)

2 s.f.　　3 s.f.　　*Final answer should be rounded to 2 s.f.*

If Your Data Comes in Categories, Present It in a Bar Chart

1) If the independent variable is categoric (comes in distinct categories, e.g. alkane chain length, metals) you should use a bar chart to display the data.
2) You also use them if the independent variable is discrete (the data can be counted in chunks, where there's no in-between value, e.g. number of protons is discrete because you can't have half a proton).
3) There are some golden rules you need to follow for drawing bar charts:

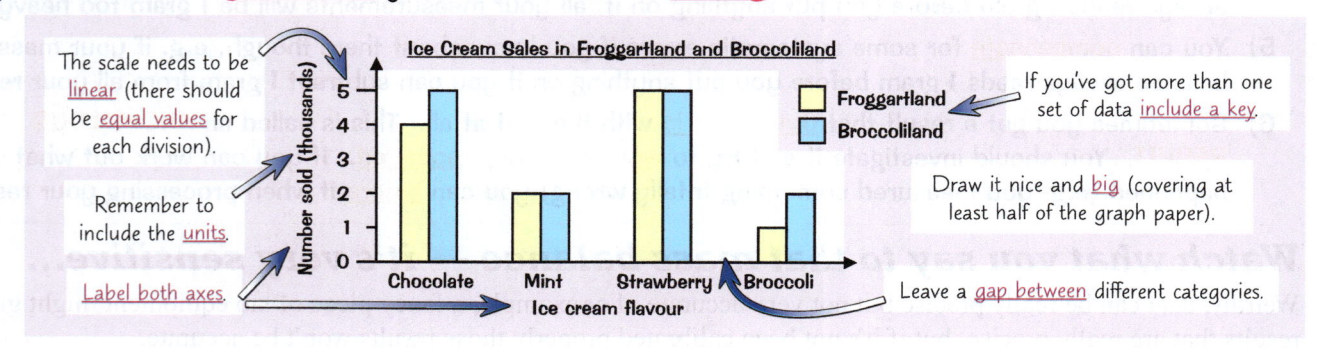

Ice Cream Sales in Froggartland and Broccoliland

- The scale needs to be linear (there should be equal values for each division).
- Remember to include the units.
- Label both axes.
- If you've got more than one set of data include a key.
- Draw it nice and big (covering at least half of the graph paper).
- Leave a gap between different categories.

Working Scientifically

If Your Data is Continuous, Plot a Graph

If both variables are continuous (numerical data that can have any value within a range, e.g. length, volume, temperature) you should use a graph to display the data.

Here are the rules for plotting points on a graph:

Use the biggest data values you've got to draw a sensible scale on your axes. Here, the highest amount of product formed is 8.8 cm³, so it makes sense to label the y-axis up to 10 cm³.

The dependent variable goes on the y-axis (the vertical one).

The independent variable goes on the x-axis (the horizontal one).

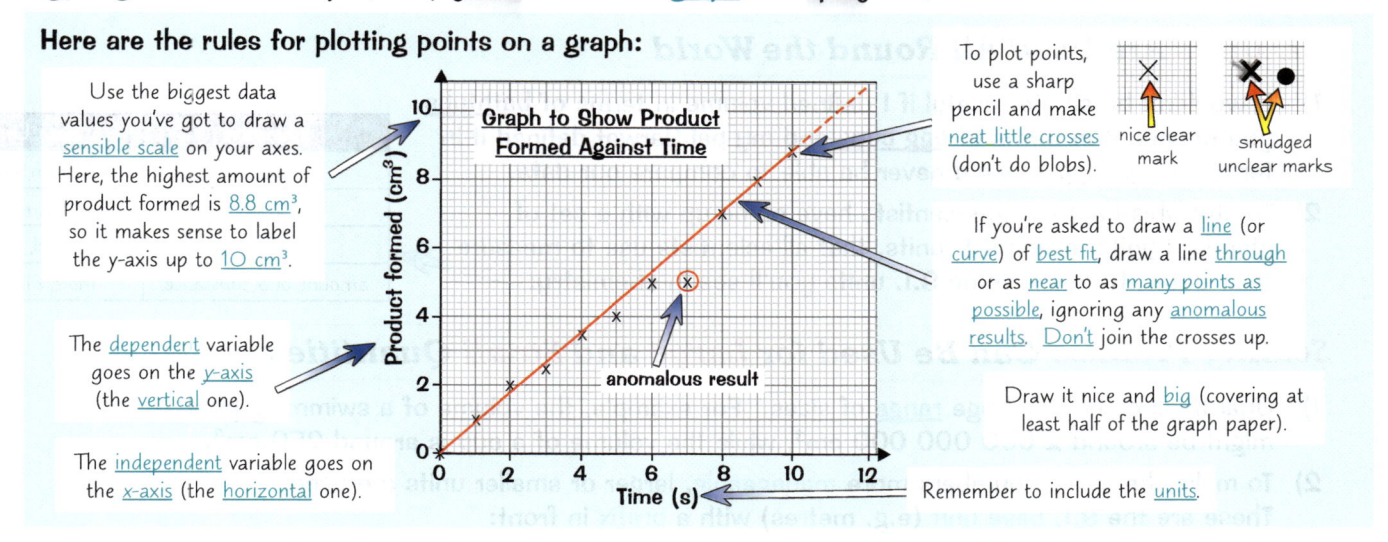

Graph to Show Product Formed Against Time

To plot points, use a sharp pencil and make neat little crosses (don't do blobs). — nice clear mark / smudged unclear marks

If you're asked to draw a line (or curve) of best fit, draw a line through or as near to as many points as possible, ignoring any anomalous results. Don't join the crosses up.

Draw it nice and big (covering at least half of the graph paper).

Remember to include the units.

Graphs Can Give You Information About Your Data

1) The **gradient** (slope) of a graph tells you how quickly the **dependent variable** changes if you change the **independent variable**.

$$\text{gradient} = \frac{\text{change in } y}{\text{change in } x}$$

This graph shows the volume of gas produced in a reaction against time. The graph is linear (it's a straight line graph), so you can simply calculate the gradient of the line to find out the rate of reaction.

1) To calculate the gradient, pick **two points** on the line that are easy to read and a **good distance** apart.
2) **Draw a line down** from one of the points and a **line across** from the other to make a **triangle**. The line drawn down the side of the triangle is the **change in y** and the line across the bottom is the **change in x**.

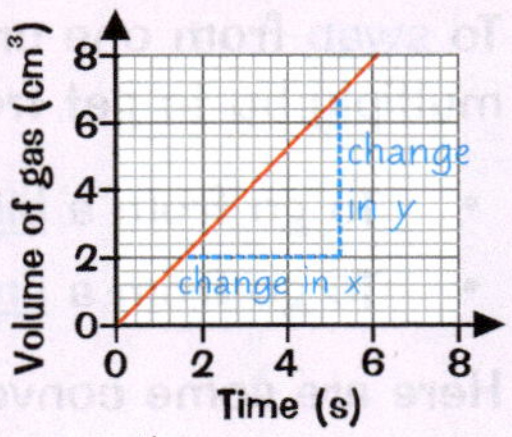

Change in y = 6.8 − 2.0 = 4.8 cm³   Change in x = 5.2 − 1.6 = 3.6 s

$$\text{Rate} = \text{gradient} = \frac{\text{change in } y}{\text{change in } x} = \frac{4.8 \text{ cm}^3}{3.6 \text{ s}} = 1.3 \text{ cm}^3/\text{s}$$

The units of the gradient are (units of y)/(units of x). cm³/s can also be written as cm³ s⁻¹.

You can use this method to calculate other rates from a graph, not just the rate of a reaction. Just remember that a rate is how much something changes over time, so x needs to be the time.

---

2) To find the **gradient of a curve** at a **certain point**, draw a **tangent** to the curve at that point and then find the **gradient of the tangent**. See page 53 for details on how to do this.

3) The **intercept** of a graph is where the line of best fit crosses the **axes**. The **x-intercept** is where the line of best fit crosses the x-axis and the **y-intercept** is where it crosses the y-axis.

Graphs Show the Relationship Between Two Variables

1) You can get **three** types of **correlation** (relationship) between variables:

2) Just because there's correlation, it doesn't mean the change in one variable is **causing** the change in the other — there might be **other factors** involved (see page 11).

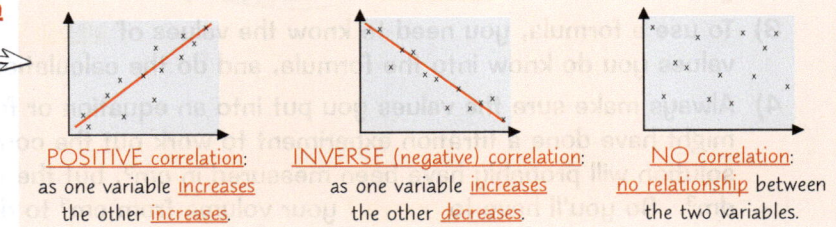

POSITIVE correlation: as one variable increases the other increases.

INVERSE (negative) correlation: as one variable increases the other decreases.

NO correlation: no relationship between the two variables.

3) You can spot these relationships in **tables** too — look at how the data for each variable changes.

I love eating apples — I call it core elation...

Science is all about finding relationships between things. And I don't mean that chemists gather together in corners to discuss whether or not Devini and Sebastian might be a couple... though they probably do that too.

Working Scientifically

Units and Equations

Graphs and maths skills are all very well, but the numbers don't mean much if you can't get the units right.

S.I. Units Are Used All Round the World

1) It wouldn't be all that useful if I defined volume in terms of bathtubs, you defined it in terms of egg cups and my pal Sarwat defined it in terms of balloons — we'd never be able to compare our data.
2) To stop this happening, scientists have come up with a set of standard units, called S.I. units, that all scientists use to measure their data. Here are some S.I. units you'll see in chemistry:

Quantity	S.I. Base Unit
mass	kilogram, kg
length	metre, m
time	second, s
amount of a substance	mole, mol

Scaling Prefixes Can Be Used for Large and Small Quantities

1) Quantities come in a huge range of sizes. For example, the volume of a swimming pool might be around 2 000 000 000 cm^3, while the volume of a cup is around 250 cm^3.
2) To make the size of numbers more manageable, larger or smaller units are used. These are the S.I. base unit (e.g. metres) with a prefix in front:

prefix	tera (T)	giga (G)	mega (M)	kilo (k)	deci (d)	centi (c)	milli (m)	micro (μ)	nano (n)
multiple of unit	10^{12}	10^9	1 000 000 (10^6)	1000	0.1	0.01	0.001	0.000001 (10^{-6})	10^{-9}

The conversion factor is the number of times the smaller unit goes into the larger unit.

3) These prefixes tell you how much bigger or smaller a unit is than the base unit. So one kilometre is one thousand metres.
4) To swap from one unit to another, all you need to know is what number you have to divide or multiply by to get from the original unit to the new unit — this is called the conversion factor.
   - To go from a bigger unit (like m) to a smaller unit (like cm), you multiply by the conversion factor.
   - To go from a smaller unit (like g) to a bigger unit (like kg), you divide by the conversion factor.
5) Here are some conversions that'll be useful for GCSE chemistry:

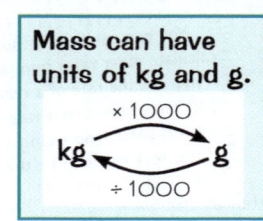

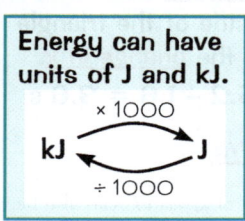

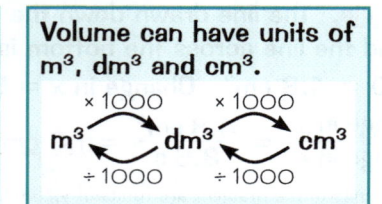

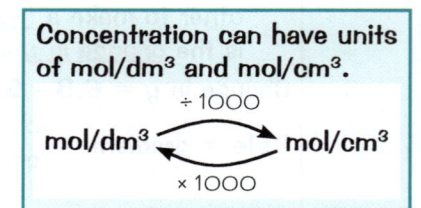

- Mass can have units of kg and g. kg ×1000 / ÷1000 g
- Energy can have units of J and kJ. kJ ×1000 / ÷1000 J
- Volume can have units of m^3, dm^3 and cm^3. m^3 ×1000 / ÷1000 dm^3 ×1000 / ÷1000 cm^3
- Concentration can have units of mol/dm^3 and mol/cm^3. mol/dm^3 ÷1000 / ×1000 mol/cm^3

Always Check The Values Used in Equations Have the Right Units

1) Formulae and equations show relationships between variables.
2) To rearrange an equation, make sure that whatever you do to one side of the equation you also do to the other side.

> You can find the number of moles of something using the equation: moles = mass ÷ molar mass.
> You can rearrange this equation to find the mass by multiplying each side by molar mass to give: mass = moles × molar mass.

3) To use a formula, you need to know the values of all but one of the variables. Substitute the values you do know into the formula, and do the calculation to work out the final variable.
4) Always make sure the values you put into an equation or formula have the right units. For example, you might have done a titration experiment to work out the concentration of a solution. The volume of the solution will probably have been measured in cm^3, but the equation to find concentration uses volume in dm^3. So you'll have to convert your volume from cm^3 to dm^3 before you put it into the equation.
5) To make sure your units are correct, it can help to write down the units on each line of your calculation.

I wasn't sure I liked units, but now I'm converted...

It's easy to get in a muddle when converting between units, but there's a handy way to check you've done it right. If you're moving from a smaller unit to a larger unit (e.g. g to kg) the number should get smaller, and vice versa.

Working Scientifically

Drawing Conclusions

Congratulations — you're nearly at the end of a gruelling investigation, time to draw conclusions.

You Can Only Conclude What the Data Shows and NO MORE

1) Drawing conclusions might seem pretty straightforward — you just look at your data and say what pattern or relationship you see between the dependent and independent variables.

The table on the right shows the rate of a reaction in the presence of two different catalysts:

Catalyst	Rate of reaction (cm^3/s)
A	13.5
B	19.5
No catalyst	5.5

CONCLUSION: Catalyst B makes this reaction go faster than catalyst A.

2) But you've got to be really careful that your conclusion matches the data you've got and doesn't go any further. → You can't conclude that catalyst B increases the rate of any other reaction more than catalyst A — the results might be completely different.

3) You also need to be able to use your results to justify your conclusion (i.e. back up your conclusion with some specific data). → The rate of this reaction was 6 cm^3/s faster using catalyst B compared with catalyst A.

4) When writing a conclusion you need to refer back to the original hypothesis and say whether the data supports it or not: → The hypothesis for this experiment might have been that catalyst B would make the reaction go quicker than catalyst A. If so, the data supports the hypothesis.

Correlation DOES NOT Mean Cause

If two things are correlated (i.e. there's a relationship between them) it doesn't necessarily mean a change in one variable is causing the change in the other — this is REALLY IMPORTANT — DON'T FORGET IT. There are three possible reasons for a correlation:

1) **CHANCE:** It might seem strange, but two things can show a correlation purely due to chance.

   For example, one study might find a correlation between people's hair colour and how good they are at frisbee. But other scientists don't get a correlation when they investigate it — the results of the first study are just a fluke.

2) **LINKED BY A 3RD VARIABLE:** A lot of the time it may look as if a change in one variable is causing a change in the other, but it isn't — a third variable links the two things.

   For example, there's a correlation between water temperature and shark attacks. This isn't because warmer water makes sharks crazy. Instead, they're linked by a third variable — the number of people swimming (more people swim when the water's hotter, and with more people in the water you get more shark attacks).

3) **CAUSE:** Sometimes a change in one variable does cause a change in the other. You can only conclude that a correlation is due to cause when you've controlled all the variables that could, just could, be affecting the result.

   For example, there's a correlation between smoking and lung cancer. This is because chemicals in tobacco smoke cause lung cancer. This conclusion was only made once other variables (such as age and exposure to other things that cause cancer) had been controlled and shown not to affect people's risk of getting lung cancer.

I conclude that this page is a bit dull...

...although, just because I find it dull doesn't mean that I can conclude it's dull (you might think it's the most interesting thing since that kid got his head stuck in the railings near school). In the exams you could be given a conclusion and asked whether some data supports it — so make sure you understand how far conclusions can go.

Working Scientifically

Uncertainties and Evaluations

Hurrah! The end of another investigation. Well, now you have to work out all the things you did wrong.

Uncertainty is the Amount of Error Your Measurements Might Have

1) When you repeat a measurement, you often get a slightly different figure each time you do it due to random error. This means that each result has some uncertainty to it.
2) The measurements you make will also have some uncertainty in them due to limits in the resolution of the equipment you use (see page 7).
3) This all means that the mean of a set of results will also have some uncertainty to it. You can calculate the uncertainty of a mean result using the equation:
4) The larger the range, the less precise your results are and the more uncertainty there will be in your results. Uncertainties are shown using the '±' symbol.

The range is the largest value minus the smallest value (p.8).

$$\text{uncertainty} = \frac{\text{range}}{2}$$

EXAMPLE: The table below shows the results of a titration experiment to determine the volume of 0.5 mol/dm³ sodium hydroxide solution needed to neutralise 25 cm³ of a solution of hydrochloric acid with unknown concentration. Calculate the uncertainty of the mean.

Repeat	1	2	3	mean
Volume of sodium hydroxide (cm³)	20.10	19.80	20.00	19.97

1) First work out the range:
   Range = 20.10 − 19.80
          = 0.30 cm³

2) Use the range to find the uncertainty:
Uncertainty = range ÷ 2 = 0.30 ÷ 2 = 0.15 cm³   So the uncertainty of the mean = 19.97 ± 0.15 cm³

5) Measuring a greater amount of something helps to reduce uncertainty. For example, in a rate of reaction experiment, measuring the amount of product formed over a longer period compared to a shorter period will reduce the percentage uncertainty in your results.

Evaluations — Describe How it Could be Improved

An evaluation is a critical analysis of the whole investigation.

1) You should comment on the method — was it valid? Did you control all the other variables to make it a fair test?
2) Comment on the quality of the results — was there enough evidence to reach a valid conclusion? Were the results repeatable, reproducible, accurate and precise?
3) Were there any anomalous results? If there were none then say so. If there were any, try to explain them — were they caused by errors in measurement? Were there any other variables that could have affected the results? You should comment on the level of uncertainty in your results too.
4) All this analysis will allow you to say how confident you are that your conclusion is right.
5) Then you can suggest any changes to the method that would improve the quality of the results, so that you could have more confidence in your conclusion. For example, you might suggest changing the way you controlled a variable, or increasing the number of measurements you took. Taking more measurements at narrower intervals could give you a more accurate result. For example:

Enzymes have an optimum temperature (a temperature at which they work best). Say you do an experiment to find an enzyme's optimum temperature and take measurements at 10 °C, 20 °C, 30 °C, 40 °C and 50 °C. The results of this experiment tell you the optimum is 40 °C. You could then repeat the experiment, taking more measurements around 40 °C to a get a more accurate value for the optimum.

6) You could also make more predictions based on your conclusion, then further experiments could be carried out to test them.

When suggesting improvements to the investigation, always make sure that you say why you think this would make the results better.

Evaluation — next time, I'll make sure I don't burn the lab down...

So there you have it — Working Scientifically. Make sure you know this stuff like the back of your hand. It's not just in the lab that you'll need to know how to work scientifically. You can be asked about it in the exams as well.

Working Scientifically

Unit 1a — The Nature of Substances and Chemical Reactions

Elements, Compounds and Mixtures

Elements make up everything that we use and see in our everyday lives...

Elements Consist of One Type of Atom Only

1) Quite a lot of everyday substances are elements:

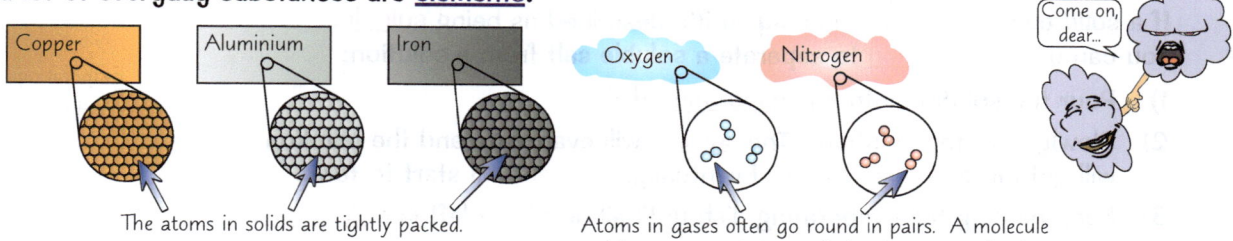

   Copper, Aluminium, Iron — The atoms in solids are tightly packed.

   Oxygen, Nitrogen — Atoms in gases often go round in pairs. A molecule with two atoms in it is called a diatomic molecule.

2) It's impossible to break down an element into a simpler substance.
3) For example, if iron is heated, it produces molten iron. The iron doesn't break down into any other substance.
4) Elements are the building blocks of all other substances, such as compounds.

The melting point of iron is around 1500 °C.

Compounds are Chemically Bonded

1) A compound is a substance that is made of two or more different types of atom which are chemically joined (bonded).
2) For example, carbon dioxide is a compound formed from a chemical reaction. One carbon atom reacts with two oxygen atoms to form a molecule of carbon dioxide, with the formula CO_2.
3) It's very difficult to separate the two original elements out again.

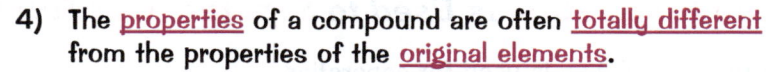

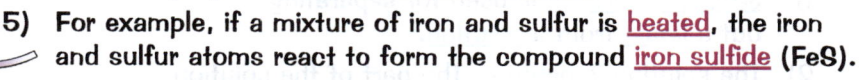

   carbon + oxygen → carbon dioxide

4) The properties of a compound are often totally different from the properties of the original elements.
5) For example, if a mixture of iron and sulfur is heated, the iron and sulfur atoms react to form the compound iron sulfide (FeS).
6) Iron sulfide is not much like iron (e.g. it's not attracted to a magnet), nor is it much like sulfur (e.g. it's not yellow in colour).

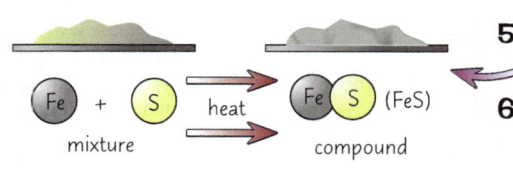

Fe + S (mixture) —heat→ Fe S (FeS) (compound)

Mixtures are Easily Separated — Not Like Compounds

1) Unlike in a compound, there's no chemical bond between the different parts of a mixture. The parts can be separated out by physical methods such as distillation (see page 14).
2) The properties of a mixture are just a combination of the properties of the separate parts. E.g. a mixture of iron filings and sulfur powder will show the properties of both iron and sulfur. It will contain grey magnetic bits of iron and bright yellow bits of sulfur.

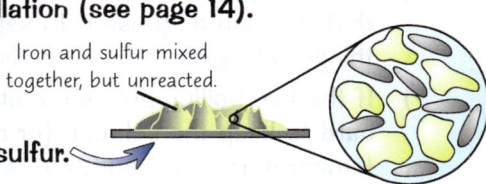

Iron and sulfur mixed together, but unreacted.

Not learning this stuff will only compound your problems...

Sometimes it's easiest to explain things in chemistry using examples. If you understand the difference between the mixture of iron powder and sulfur powder, and the compound iron sulfide, it'll make this stuff easier to remember.

Q1 State whether each of the following is an element, a compound or a mixture:
    a) carbon dioxide gas   b) chlorine gas   c) air   [3 marks]

Unit 1a — The Nature of Substances and Chemical Reactions

Separating Mixtures

Separating mixtures is really easy. All you need is some special scientific equipment and the instructions. Luckily all the instructions you need are here... (Equipment sold separately.)

Evaporation Can Separate Soluble Solids from Solutions

If a solid can be dissolved in a liquid it's described as being soluble.
You can use evaporation to separate a soluble salt from a solution:

1) Pour the solution into an evaporating dish.
2) Slowly heat the solution. The solvent will evaporate and the solution will get more concentrated. Eventually, crystals will start to form.
3) Keep heating the evaporating dish until all you have left is a dry solid.
4) Evaporation is a quick way of separating a soluble salt from a solution, but only if the salt doesn't decompose (break down) when heated.

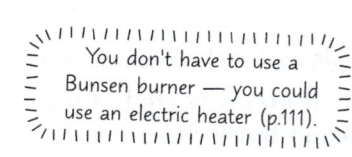

Evaporating dish

You don't have to use a Bunsen burner — you could use an electric heater (p.111).

Filtration is Used to Separate an Insoluble Solid from a Liquid

1) To separate an insoluble solid from a liquid, you can use filtration.
2) This means it can be used in purification. For example, solid impurities can be separated out from a reaction mixture using filtration.
3) All you do is pop some filter paper into a funnel and pour your mixture into it. The liquid part of the mixture runs through the paper, leaving behind a solid residue.

Filter paper folded into a cone shape.
The solid is left in the filter paper.

Simple Distillation is Used to Separate Out Solutions

1) Simple distillation is used for separating out a liquid from a solution.
2) The solution is heated. The part of the solution that has the lowest boiling point evaporates first.
3) The vapour is then cooled, condenses (turns back into a liquid) and is collected.
4) The rest of the solution is left behind in the flask.
5) Distillation can be used to separate a mixture of liquids as well.
6) The problem with simple distillation is that you can only use it to separate things with very different boiling points.
7) If the two boiling points are close together, it's hard to keep the solution (or mixture) at the right temperature to evaporate one but not the other.

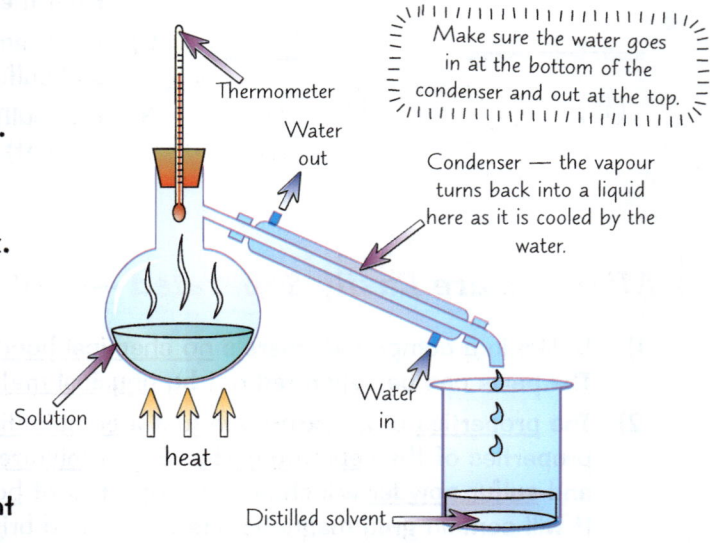

Thermometer, Water out, Condenser — the vapour turns back into a liquid here as it is cooled by the water. Solution, heat, Water in, Distilled solvent

Make sure the water goes in at the bottom of the condenser and out at the top.

There's more on distillation on page 38.

It's impossible to filter the boredom out from revision — sadly...

There is one thing you shouldn't separate from revision, though — practice questions. Oh look, here's some now.

Q1 Which technique could be used to separate a soluble solid from a solution? [1 mark]

Q2 Describe the process of simple distillation. [3 marks]

Unit 1a — The Nature of Substances and Chemical Reactions

Chromatography

Last page on separation, I promise. This one's even got a nice equation for you to learn too — how exciting...

You Need to Know How to Do Paper Chromatography

1) Draw a line near the bottom of a sheet of filter paper — this is the baseline. (Use a pencil to do this — pencil marks are insoluble so won't dissolve in the solvent.)
2) Add spots of different inks to the line at regular intervals.
3) Loosely roll the sheet up and put it in a beaker of solvent, e.g. water.
4) The solvent used depends on what's being tested. Some compounds dissolve well in water, but sometimes other solvents, like ethanol, are needed.
5) Make sure the level of solvent is below the baseline — you don't want the inks to dissolve into the solvent.
6) Place a lid on top of the container to stop the solvent evaporating.
7) The solvent seeps up the paper, carrying the inks with it.
8) Each different dye in the inks will move up the paper at a different rate and form a spot in a different place.
9) When the solvent has nearly reached the top of the paper, take the paper out of the beaker and leave it to dry.
10) The end result is a pattern of spots called a chromatogram.

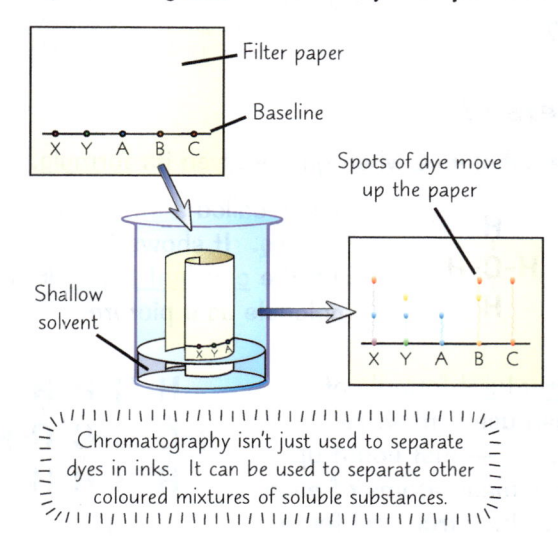

Chromatography isn't just used to separate dyes in inks. It can be used to separate other coloured mixtures of soluble substances.

How Chromatography Separates Mixtures...

1) Chromatography works because different dyes will move up the paper at different rates.
2) Some dyes will be more attracted to the paper so spend more time stuck to it and not travel as far, whilst others will be more soluble in the solvent so will travel further up the paper.
3) The distance the dyes travel up the paper depends on the solvent and the paper you use.

You can Calculate an R_f Value for Each Chemical

1) An R_f value is the ratio between the distance travelled by the substance and the distance travelled by the solvent (the solvent front). You can find R_f values using the formula:

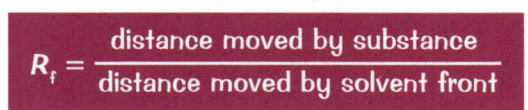

$$R_f = \frac{\text{distance moved by substance}}{\text{distance moved by solvent front}}$$

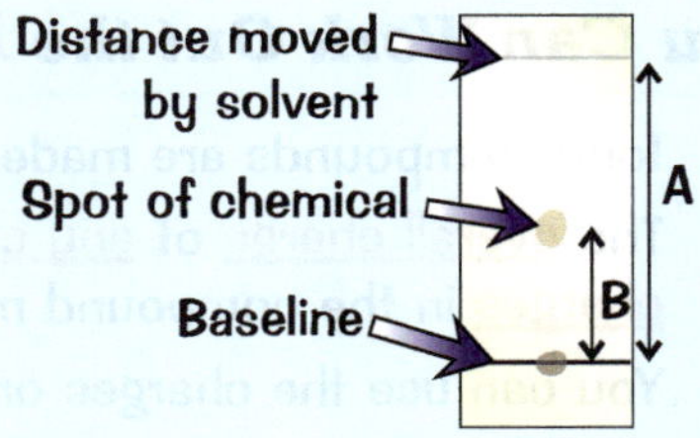

2) To find the distance travelled by the solute, measure from the baseline to the centre of the spot.

R_f value of this chemical = B ÷ A

3) Chromatography is often carried out to see if a certain substance is present in a mixture. You run a pure sample of a substance that you think may be in your mixture alongside a sample of the mixture itself. If the sample has the same R_f value as one of the spots, they're likely to be the same.

I tried dyeing my hair once — it ended up fluorescent green...

... not a good look. You'd look amazing if you could remember this page on chromatography, though. That equation is pretty important, so make sure you know how to use that — examiners really like R_f values.

Q1 A student carries out an investigation using paper chromatography. A spot of dye has moved 2 cm up the paper and the solvent has travelled 6 cm. Calculate the R_f value for this spot. [1 mark]

Unit 1a — The Nature of Substances and Chemical Reactions

Chemical Formulae

I bet you've been dying to know how to write out chemical formulae — you're welcome...

Atoms Can be Represented by Symbols

1) Atoms of each element can be represented by a one or two letter symbol — it's a type of shorthand that saves you the bother of having to write the full name of the element.
2) Some make perfect sense, e.g. C = carbon, O = oxygen, Mg = magnesium
3) Others less so, e.g. Na = sodium, Fe = iron, Pb = lead
4) You'll see these symbols on the periodic table (see page 27).

Most of these odd symbols actually come from the Latin names of the elements.

The Formula of a Molecule Shows the Numbers of Atoms

You can work out how many atoms of each type there are in a substance when you're given its formula.

This is called a molecular formula. It shows the number and type of atoms in a molecule.

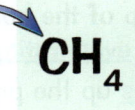

CH_4 — Methane contains 1 carbon atom and 4 hydrogen atoms.

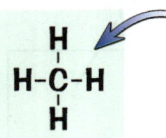

This is called a structural formula. It shows the atoms and the covalent bonds in a molecule as a picture.

Don't panic if a formula has brackets in it — they're easy to deal with.

$CH_3(CH_2)_2CH_3$

For example, the 2 after the bracket here means that there are 2 lots of CH_2. So altogether there are 4 carbon atoms and 10 hydrogen atoms.

If you have the structural formula of a molecule, you can use it to write the molecular formula — just count up and write down how many atoms of each element there are in the structural formula.

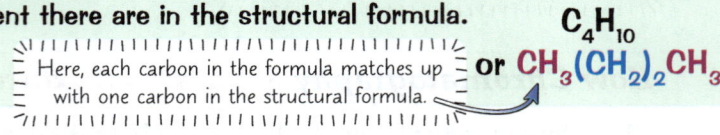

Here, each carbon in the formula matches up with one carbon in the structural formula.

C_4H_{10} or $CH_3(CH_2)_2CH_3$

It's Useful to Know the Formulae of Common Molecules

It's a good idea to learn the chemical formulae of these common molecules. They crop up all the time.

- Water — H_2O
- Ammonia — NH_3
- Carbon dioxide — CO_2
- Hydrogen — H_2
- Chlorine — Cl_2
- Oxygen — O_2

You Can Work Out the Formula of an Ionic Compound

1) Ionic compounds are made up of a positively charged part and a negatively charged part.
2) The overall charge of any compound is zero. So all the negative charges in the compound must balance all the positive charges.
3) You can use the charges on the individual ions present to work out the formula for the ionic compound.
4) You need to be able to write formulae using chemical symbols.

A table of formulae for common ions is given on page 118.

EXAMPLE: What is the chemical formula of calcium nitrate?
1) Write out the formulae for the calcium and nitrate ions. — Ca^{2+}, NO_3^-
2) The overall charge on the formula must be zero, so work out the ratio of Ca : NO_3 that gives an overall neutral charge. — To balance the 2+ charge on Ca^{2+}, you need two NO_3^- ions. So formula = $Ca(NO_3)_2$

The brackets show you need two of the whole nitrate ion.

$(+2) + (2 \times -1) = 0$

My phone is like an ionic compound — it has zero overall charge...

Make sure you can understand formulae, whether they're written as a molecular or a structural formula.

Q1 The formula of the compound pentanol can be written $CH_3(CH_2)_4OH$.
How many hydrogen atoms are there in one molecule of pentanol? [1 mark]

Unit 1a — The Nature of Substances and Chemical Reactions

Chemical Equations

If you thought maths equations were a drag then I'm here to tell you it gets much, much ~~worse~~ better...

Equations Show the Reactants and Products of a Reaction

A chemical reaction can be described as the process of going from reactants to products.
You can write word equations or symbol equations to show any chemical reaction.

> E.g. magnesium reacts with oxygen to produce magnesium oxide:
>
> Word equation: magnesium + oxygen → magnesium oxide
> Symbol equation: $2Mg + O_2 \rightarrow 2MgO$

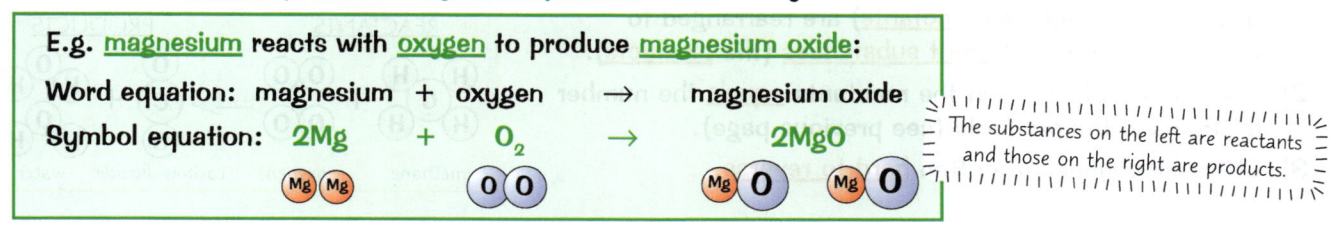

The substances on the left are reactants and those on the right are products.

Look out for state symbols in equations — they tell you the physical states of reactants and products:

(s) — Solid   (l) — Liquid   (g) — Gas   (aq) — Aqueous (dissolved in water)

Here's the example including state symbols: $2Mg(s) + O_2(g) \rightarrow 2MgO(s)$

Solid magnesium reacts with oxygen gas to make solid magnesium oxide.

Symbol Equations Need to be Balanced

1) There must always be the same number of atoms of each element on both sides of the equation — atoms can't just appear or disappear.
2) You balance the equation by putting numbers in front of the formulae where needed. Take this equation for reacting sulfuric acid with sodium hydroxide:

$$H_2SO_4 + NaOH \rightarrow Na_2SO_4 + H_2O$$

3) The formulae are all correct but the numbers of some atoms don't match up on both sides.
4) You can't change formulae like H_2SO_4 to H_2SO_5. You can only put numbers in front of them.
5) The more you practise, the quicker you get, but all you do is this:

- Find an element that doesn't balance and pencil in a number to try and sort it out.
- See where it gets you. It may create another imbalance, but if so, pencil in another number and see where that gets you.
- Carry on chasing unbalanced elements and it'll sort itself out pretty quickly.

EXAMPLE: In the equation above you'll notice you're short of H atoms on the RHS (Right-Hand Side).
1) The only thing you can do about that is make it $2H_2O$ instead of just H_2O:

$$H_2SO_4 + NaOH \rightarrow Na_2SO_4 + 2H_2O$$

2) But that now gives too many H atoms and O atoms on the RHS, so to balance that up you could try putting a 2 in front of the NaOH on the LHS (Left-Hand Side):

$$H_2SO_4 + 2NaOH \rightarrow Na_2SO_4 + 2H_2O$$

Putting a 2 in front of the NaOH has sorted out the Na atoms too.

3) And suddenly there it is — everything balances.

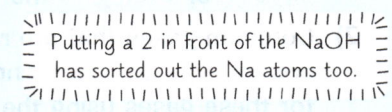

Balanced Equation — the hardest yoga pose...

There's not much to balancing equations — it's just trial and error, really. It'll get a lot easier with practice...

Q1 Balance the equation: $Fe + Cl_2 \rightarrow FeCl_3$ [1 mark]

Q2 Hydrogen and oxygen molecules are formed in a reaction where water splits apart.
For this reaction: a) State the word equation. b) Give a balanced symbol equation. [3 marks]

Unit 1a — The Nature of Substances and Chemical Reactions

Chemical Reactions

Chemical reactions often give a change in appearance, or some indication that a reaction is going on.

Atoms are Rearranged During Chemical Reactions

1) Chemical changes happen during chemical reactions, when bonds between atoms break and the atoms change places. The atoms from the substances you start off with (the reactants) are rearranged to form one or more different substances (the products).
2) The number of atoms in the reactants equals the number of atoms in the products (see previous page).
3) Chemical changes are often hard to reverse.

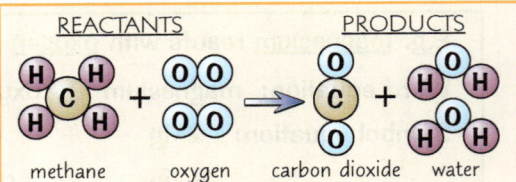

There are Observations that Show a Reaction is Happening

It's normally obvious that chemical reactions are happening — they are often seen by a change in colour or temperature, or by effervescence (bubbles).

Colour Changes

1) Colour changes in chemical reactions can show pH changes (p.109), displacement reactions (p.33), redox reactions (p.76) etc.
2) For example, if copper(II) carbonate is heated, it changes from green to black — this shows a reaction has taken place (a thermal decomposition reaction, see p.56).

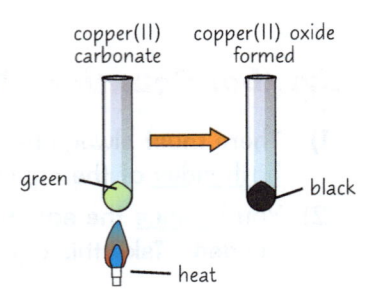

Temperature Changes

1) When a chemical reaction happens, energy is either taken in or given out — this is shown by a temperature change.
2) Energy is transferred from the reactants to the surroundings in an exothermic reaction.
3) Energy is transferred from the surroundings to the reactants in an endothermic reaction. (There's more on exothermic and endothermic reactions on page 84).
4) An example of this is the reaction between sodium and water. When sodium is added to water, the heat from the reaction is transferred to the surroundings, which get hot enough to melt the sodium. This shows that there has been a reaction because there is a temperature increase — it's an exothermic reaction.
5) This reaction also effervesces...

Effervescence

1) Sometimes gases are formed when a chemical reaction takes place. When these gases escape from the solution you'll see bubbles or fizzing — the fancy word for this is effervescence.
2) Common gases that are released during chemical reactions are hydrogen, oxygen and carbon dioxide — you can test for these gases using the tests on page 35 and page 48.
3) For example, when an acid reacts with a carbonate, carbon dioxide is formed and the solution effervesces (p.69).

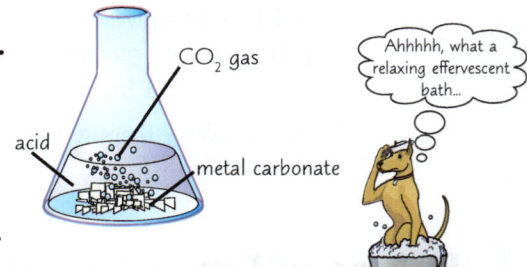

I can relate to chemical changes, I also find it hard to reverse...

Even if a solution turns colourless, that's still a colour change. Don't get mixed up between a 'clear' solution and a 'colourless' solution though. Clear solutions can still have a colour — the 'clear' just means they are see-through.

Q1   Give one observation that indicates a reaction is taking place.   [1 mark]

Unit 1a — The Nature of Substances and Chemical Reactions

Relative Formula Mass

Calculating <u>relative formula mass</u> is straightforward enough, but things can get a bit more confusing when you start working out the <u>percentage compositions</u> of compounds. Best get cracking, I suppose...

Compounds Have a Relative Formula Mass, M_r

1) You can use the <u>relative atomic mass</u>, A_r, to calculate the <u>masses of reactants</u> and <u>formulae of reactions</u> — see pages 21-22.
2) Don't mix up A_r and <u>mass number</u> — they're similar, but not the same. The A_r of an <u>element</u> is the average mass of all its atoms, taking into account its <u>isotopes</u> (see p.26). The mass number of an atom is the <u>total number</u> of <u>protons</u> and <u>neutrons</u> in its <u>nucleus</u> (see p.25).
3) If you have a compound like $MgCl_2$ then it has a <u>relative formula mass</u>, M_r, which is just the relative atomic masses of all the atoms in the molecular formula <u>added together</u>.

EXAMPLE: Find the relative formula mass of $MgCl_2$.
A_r of Mg = 24 and A_r of Cl = 35.5
<u>Add up</u> all the relative atomic masses of the atoms in the compound.
$Mg + (2 \times Cl) = 24 + (2 \times 35.5) = 95$ So M_r of $MgCl_2 = 95$
There are two chlorine atoms in $MgCl_2$, so the relative atomic mass of chlorine needs to be multiplied by 2.

You might also see the phrase 'relative molecular mass'. This is only used if the compound contains molecules, but you work it out in the same way.

You Can Calculate the % Mass of an Element in a Compound

This is actually <u>dead easy</u> — so long as you've learnt this <u>formula</u>:

$$\text{Percentage mass of an element in a compound} = \frac{A_r \times \text{number of atoms of that element}}{M_r \text{ of the compound}} \times 100$$

EXAMPLE: Find the percentage mass of sodium in sodium carbonate, Na_2CO_3.
A_r of sodium = 23, A_r of carbon = 12, A_r of oxygen = 16
M_r of $Na_2CO_3 = (2 \times 23) + 12 + (3 \times 16) = 106$
Percentage mass of sodium = $\frac{A_r \times \text{number of atoms of that element}}{M_r \text{ of the compound}} \times 100 = \frac{23 \times 2}{106} \times 100 = 43\%$ (2 s.f.)

You might also come across more <u>complicated</u> questions where you need to work out the <u>percentage mass</u>.

EXAMPLE: A mixture contains 20% iron ions by mass. What mass of iron(II) chloride ($FeCl_2$) would you need to provide the iron ions in 50 g of the mixture? A_r of Fe = 56, A_r of Cl = 35.5.

1) Find the <u>mass</u> of iron in the mixture.
The mixture contains 20% iron by mass, so in 50 g there will be $50 \times \frac{20}{100} = 10$ g of iron.

2) Calculate the <u>percentage mass</u> of iron in <u>iron(II) chloride</u>.
Percentage mass of iron = $\frac{A_r \times \text{number of atoms of that element}}{M_r \text{ of the compound}} \times 100 = \frac{56}{56 + (2 \times 35.5)} \times 100 = 44.09...\%$

3) Calculate the <u>mass</u> of <u>iron(II) chloride</u> that contains 10 g of iron.
Iron(II) chloride has 44.09% iron by mass, so there will be 10 g of iron in $10 \div \frac{44.09...}{100} = 23$ g (2 s.f.)
So you need 23 g of iron chloride to provide the iron in 50 g of the mixture.

Relative mass — when you go to church with your parents...

Get to grips with all this stuff by practising.
You'll need these for the questions below: $A_r(H) = 1$, $A_r(O) = 16$, $A_r(Li) = 7$, $A_r(S) = 32$, $A_r(K) = 39$.

Q1 Calculate the relative formula mass (M_r) of: a) H_2O b) LiOH   c) H_2SO_4 [3 marks]

Q2 Calculate the percentage composition by mass of potassium in potassium hydroxide (KOH).   [2 marks]

Unit 1a — The Nature of Substances and Chemical Reactions

The Mole

Moles can be pretty confusing. It's probably the word that puts people off. It's difficult to see the relevance of the word "mole" to anything but a small burrowing animal.

"The Mole" is Simply the Name Given to an Amount of a Substance

1) Just like "a million" is this many: 1 000 000; or "a billion" is this many: 1 000 000 000, so "the Avogadro constant" is this many: 600 000 000 000 000 000 000 000 or 6×10^{23}. And that's all it is. Just a number.

2) One mole of any substance is just an amount of that substance that contains an Avogadro number of particles — so 6×10^{23} particles. The particles could be atoms, molecules, ions or electrons.

3) The burning question, of course, is why is it such a silly long number like that, and with a 6 at the front?

4) The answer is that the mass of that number of atoms or molecules of any substance is exactly the same number of grams as the relative atomic mass (A_r) or relative formula mass (M_r) of the element or compound.

5) In other words, one mole of atoms or molecules of any substance will have a mass in grams equal to the relative formula mass (A_r or M_r) for that substance. Here are some examples:

> Carbon has an A_r of 12.   So one mole of carbon weighs exactly 12 g.
> Nitrogen gas, N_2, has an M_r of 28 (2×14).   So one mole of N_2 weighs exactly 28 g.
> Carbon dioxide, CO_2, has an M_r of 44 ($12 + [2 \times 16]$). So one mole of CO_2 weighs exactly 44 g.

6) This means that 12 g of carbon, or 28 g of N_2, or 44 g of CO_2, all contain the same number of particles, namely one mole or 6×10^{23} atoms or molecules.

Nice Formula to Find the Number of Moles in a Given Mass:

$$\text{number of moles} = \frac{\text{mass in g (of an element or compound)}}{M_r \text{ (of the element or compound)}}$$

EXAMPLE: How many moles are there in 66 g of carbon dioxide (CO_2)?
A_r of C = 12 and A_r of O = 16.

1) Calculate the M_r of carbon dioxide. M_r of $CO_2 = 12 + (16 \times 2) = 44$
2) Use the formula above to find out   No. of moles = Mass (g) ÷ M_r = 66 ÷ 44 = 1.5 mol
   how many moles there are.   Easy Peasy.

'mol' is the symbol for the unit 'moles'.

You can rearrange the equation above using this handy formula triangle. You could use it to find the mass of a known number of moles of a substance, or to find the M_r of a substance from a known mass and number of moles. Just cover up the thing you want to find with your finger and write down what's left showing.

EXAMPLE: What mass of carbon is there in 4 moles of carbon dioxide?
There are 4 moles of carbon in 4 moles of CO_2.
Cover up 'mass' in the formula triangle. That leaves you with 'no. of moles × M_r'.
So the mass of 4 moles of carbon = $4 \times 12 = 48$ g

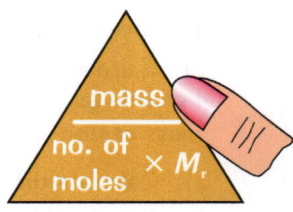

What do moles have for pudding? Jam moly-poly...

Calculations involving moles can send some people into a spin. Don't be one of those people — there's really no need to freak out about moles. Go back over this page until you've got your head round it all.

Q1   Calculate the number of moles in 90 g of water (H_2O). A_r(O) = 16, A_r(H) = 1.   [2 marks]

Q2   Calculate the mass of 0.20 mol of sodium sulfate (Na_2SO_4). A_r(Na) = 23, A_r(S) = 32, A_r(O) = 16.   [2 marks]

Unit 1a — The Nature of Substances and Chemical Reactions

Calculating Masses in Reactions

These can be kinda scary too, but no need to fear — just grab a brew, relax and enjoy.

You can Calculate the Amount of Product from a Mass of Reactant

You can use a balanced chemical equation to work out the mass of product formed from a given mass of a reactant (and vice versa). Here's how...

The total relative mass of the reactants must be equal to the total relative mass of the products.

1) Write out the balanced equation.
2) Work out relative formula masses (M_r) of the reactant and product you're interested in.
3) Find out how many moles there are of the substance you know the mass of.
4) Use the balanced equation to work out how many moles there'll be of the other substance (i.e. how many moles of product will be made by this many moles of reactant).
5) Use the number of moles to calculate the mass.

What mass of magnesium oxide (MgO) is produced when 60 g of magnesium is burnt in air?
$A_r(Mg) = 24$, $A_r(O) = 16$.

1) Write out the balanced equation: $2Mg + O_2 \rightarrow 2MgO$
2) Work out the relative formula masses of the reactants and products you're interested in:
   Mg: 24   MgO: 24 + 16 = 40

   In this reaction, O_2 is in excess. This means that there is more O_2 available to react than there is Mg. So, it's the amount of Mg that determines how much MgO is made.

3) Calculate the number of moles of magnesium in 60 g:
   moles = mass ÷ M_r = 60 ÷ 24 = 2.5
4) Look at the ratio of moles in the equation — 2 moles of Mg react to produce 2 moles of MgO. So 2.5 moles of Mg will react to produce 2.5 moles of MgO.
5) Calculate the mass of 2.5 moles of magnesium oxide:
   mass = moles × M_r = 2.5 × 40 = 100 g

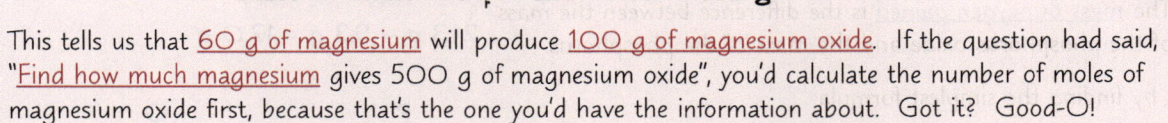

This tells us that 60 g of magnesium will produce 100 g of magnesium oxide. If the question had said, "Find how much magnesium gives 500 g of magnesium oxide", you'd calculate the number of moles of magnesium oxide first, because that's the one you'd have the information about. Got it? Good-O!

The mass of product (in this case magnesium oxide) is called the yield of a reaction. Masses you calculate in this way are called theoretical yields. In practice you never get 100% of the yield, so the amount of product you get will be less than you calculated.

Percentage Yield Compares Actual and Theoretical Yield

The more reactant you start with, the higher the yield will be — that's pretty obvious. But the percentage yield doesn't depend on the amount of reactants you started with — it's a percentage.

1) The theoretical yield of a reaction can be calculated from the balanced equation (see above).
2) Percentage yield is given by the formula:

$$\text{percentage yield} = \frac{\text{actual yield (grams)}}{\text{theoretical yield (grams)}} \times 100$$

3) Percentage yield is always somewhere between 0 and 100%.
4) A 100% yield means that you got all the product you expected to get.
5) A 0% yield means that no reactants were converted into product, i.e. no product at all was made.

These pages — masses and masses of fun...

A specially organically grown, hand-picked question for you, my dear. $A_r(Cl) = 35.5$, $A_r(K) = 39$, $A_r(Br) = 80$.

Q1   Chlorine (Cl_2) and potassium bromide (KBr) react according to this equation: $Cl_2 + 2KBr \rightarrow Br_2 + 2KCl$
   a) Calculate the mass of Br_2 formed when 23.8 g of KBr reacts with an excess of Cl_2.   [4 marks]
   b) When carried out, the reaction gives a yield of 12.4 g of Br_2. What is the percentage yield?   [2 marks]

Unit 1a — The Nature of Substances and Chemical Reactions

Calculating Formulae from Reacting Masses

This sounds a lot worse than it really is. Just follow the same method every time and you'll be laughing.

Finding the Formula of a Compound (from Masses or Percentages)

1) The smallest whole number ratio of atoms in a compound is used to find the molecular formula.
2) Try this for an easy peasy stepwise method for calculating a molecular formula:

   1) List all the elements in the compound (there are usually only two or three).
   2) Underneath them, write their experimental masses.
   3) Find the number of moles of each element by dividing each mass by the relative atomic mass (A_r) for that particular element.
   4) Turn the numbers you get into a nice simple ratio by dividing by the smallest number of moles.
   5) Get the ratio in its simplest whole number form. This is the simplest formula that tells you the ratio of atoms of different elements in the compound.
   6) This is different to the molecular formula of a compound, which tells you the actual number of atoms of each element in a single molecule.
   7) The molecular formula is found by comparing the relative molecular mass to the relative molecular mass of the simplest formula (empirical formula).

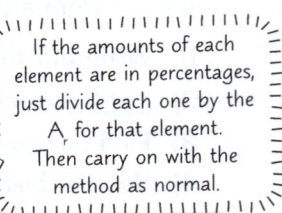

If the amounts of each element are in percentages, just divide each one by the A_r for that element. Then carry on with the method as normal.

The simplest formula is sometimes called the empirical formula.

EXAMPLE:

In an experiment, 9.3 g of phosphorus combined with oxygen to form 21.3 g of a phosphorus oxide. Find the molecular formula of the phosphorus oxide.
M_r of phosphorus oxide = 284, A_r(P) = 31, A_r(O) = 16.

1) The mass of oxygen gained is the difference between the mass of the phosphorus oxide and the mass of the phosphorus.

   21.3 g − 9.3 g = 12.0 g

Start by finding the simplest formula:

	P	O
2) Divide the experimental masses by the relative atomic masses, to find the number of moles of each element.	9.3 ÷ 31 = 0.3	12.0 ÷ 16 = 0.75
3) Divide by the smallest number of moles.	0.3 ÷ 0.3 = 1	0.75 ÷ 0.3 = 2.5
4) Multiply to get whole numbers.	1 × 2 = 2	2.5 × 2 = 5

So the simplest formula is 2 atoms of P to 5 atoms of O — P_2O_5.

You don't have to multiply if you get whole numbers in step 4.

Find the molecular formula from the relative molecular mass:

5) Find the mass of the simplest formula. (2 × 31) + (5 × 16) = 142 g
6) Divide the relative molecular mass by the mass of the simplest formula. 284 ÷ 142 = 2
7) Multiply the simplest formula by this value to work out the molecular formula. P_2O_5 × 2 = P_4O_{10}

My simplest ratio of work to rest is 0:1...

Make sure you read through the example thoroughly, until you're sure you can follow what's going on.

Q1 A sample of a sulfur oxide is made up of 40.0 % sulfur and 60.0% oxygen. Calculate the simplest formula of this sulfur oxide. A_r(S) = 32, A_r(O) = 16. [2 marks]

Q2 A 45.6 g sample of an oxide of nitrogen contains 13.9 g of nitrogen. A_r(N) = 14, A_r(O) = 16. What is the simplest formula of the nitrogen oxide? [3 marks]

Unit 1a — The Nature of Substances and Chemical Reactions

Calculating Formulae from Reacting Masses

Ever wanted to know how some experiments can determine the molecular formula of a compound? No? Can't say I have either. Unfortunately you need to know how anyway...

You can find Empirical Formulae using Combustion...

Combustion happens when a substance reacts with oxygen when it's burned in air. Here's how you could use combustion to calculate the simplest formula of a metal oxide, e.g. magnesium oxide:

1) Get a crucible and heat it until it's red hot. (This will make sure it's clean and there are no traces of oil or water lying around from a previous experiment.)
2) Leave the crucible to cool, then weigh it, along with its lid.
3) Add some clean magnesium ribbon to the crucible. Reweigh the crucible, lid and magnesium ribbon. The mass of magnesium you're using is this reading minus the initial reading for the mass of the crucible and lid.
4) Heat the crucible containing the magnesium. Put the lid on the crucible so as to stop any bits of solid from escaping, but leave a small gap to allow air to enter the crucible.
5) Heat the crucible strongly for around 10 minutes, or until all the magnesium ribbon has turned white.
6) Allow the crucible to cool and reweigh the crucible with the lid and its contents. The mass of magnesium oxide you have is this reading, minus the initial reading for the mass of the crucible and lid.

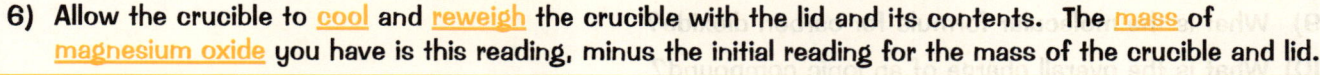

Once you've done the experiment, you should have all the data you need to work out the simplest formula of the magnesium oxide using the method on the previous page. If you know the relative molecular mass, you could use the simplest formula to work out the molecular formula (again, the method's on the previous page).

If the data collected gives a molecular formula that you know is wrong, there might have been an incomplete reaction.

... or using Reduction

Reduction is the loss of oxygen from a substance (see page 76 for more on reduction). When you reduce a metal oxide, you're left with the pure metal — e.g. the product from reducing copper(II) oxide is copper. You can reduce a metal oxide to find out its simplest formula. Here's how you'd do it for copper(II) oxide:

1) Place a rubber bung (with a hole through the middle) into a test tube with a small hole in the end, and weigh them.
2) Take the bung out of the test tube and spread out a small amount of copper(II) oxide in the middle of the tube.
3) Re-insert the bung and weigh the test tube again. Set up the equipment as shown in the diagram.
4) Expel the air from the test tube by gently turning on the gas. After about 5 seconds, light the gas by holding a burning splint next to the hole in the end of the test tube. You can control the size of the flame by changing the amount of gas that's flowing through the test tube.
5) Use a Bunsen burner to heat the copper(II) oxide for about 10 minutes (or until the solid changes colour from black to a brownish-pink colour). You should be left with copper as all the oxygen has now been lost.
6) Turn off the Bunsen burner and leave the test tube to cool.
7) Once the tube has cooled, turn off the gas and weigh the test tube with the bung and its contents.

As above, you can use the data to calculate the simplest formula of copper(II) oxide.

A red hot crucible — the scene of hotly contested snooker matches...

In both of these practicals, you weigh the container three times — before and after adding the solid, and after heating.

Q1 Describe how combustion could be used to find the information needed to calculate the empirical formula of a metal oxide. [4 marks]

Unit 1a — The Nature of Substances and Chemical Reactions

Revision Questions for Unit 1a

That's about it for Unit 1a — there's just these few revision questions to go and then you're all done.
- Try these questions and tick off each one when you get it right.
- When you've done all the questions for a topic and are completely happy with it, tick off the topic.

Elements, Compounds and Separating Mixtures (p.13-15)

1) How many different types of atom make up an element?
2) Explain the difference between a compound and a mixture.
3) What could you separate using evaporation?
4) Describe the process of filtration.
5) Explain how simple distillation can separate two liquids.
6) Explain why some solutes travel further than others in paper chromatography.
7) How do you calculate an R_f value in chromatography?

Chemical Formulae, Equations and Reactions (p.16-18)

8) How many atoms of hydrogen are in a molecule of $CH_3(CH_2)_2CH_3$?
9) What is the molecular formula for carbon dioxide?
10) What is the overall charge of an ionic compound?
11) State what is shown on the right-hand side of a chemical equation.
12) What observation indicates that copper carbonate has undergone a thermal decomposition reaction?
13) What type of observable change occurs in an endothermic reaction?
14) What is the name given to the release of bubbles during a chemical reaction?

Relative Mass and The Mole (p.19-20)

15) How do you calculate the relative formula mass, M_r, of a substance?
16) How can you calculate the percentage mass of an element in a compound?
17) How is the Avogadro constant related to the definition of a mole?
18) What is the formula that relates the number of moles of a substance to its mass and M_r?

Calculating Masses and Formulae (p.21-23)

19) What is the equation for calculating percentage yield?
20) What is the percentage yield of a reaction where no products are made?
21) How does the molecular formula of a compound relate to its simplest formula?

Unit 1a — The Nature of Substances and Chemical Reactions

The Atom

All substances are made of atoms. They're really tiny — too small to see, even with a microscope.

Atoms Contain Protons, Neutrons and Electrons

The atom is made up of three subatomic particles — protons, neutrons and electrons.

- Protons are heavy and positively charged.
- Neutrons are heavy and neutral.
- Electrons have hardly any mass and are negatively charged.

Particle	Relative mass	Relative charge
Proton	1	+1
Neutron	1	0
Electron	0.0005	−1

Relative mass (measured in atomic mass units) measures mass on a scale where the mass of a proton or neutron is 1.

Protons and neutrons are still teeny tiny — they're just heavy compared to electrons.

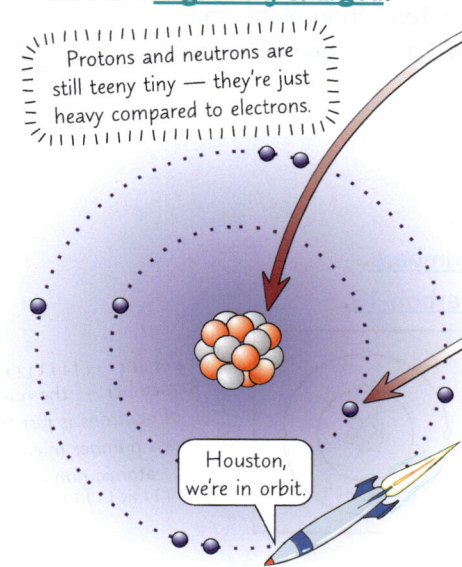

The Nucleus

1) It's in the middle of the atom.
2) It contains protons and neutrons.
3) It has a positive charge because of the protons.
4) Almost the whole mass of the atom is concentrated in the nucleus.
5) Compared to the overall size of the atom, the nucleus is tiny. Its radius is 10^{-14} m (around 1/10 000 of the radius of an atom).

The Electrons

1) Electrons orbit around the nucleus in electron shells.
2) They're negatively charged.
3) They're tiny, but they cover a lot of space.
4) The orbit of the outer electron(s) determines the size of the atom. Atoms have a radius (known as the atomic radius) of about 10^{-10} m.
5) Electrons have a tiny mass (so small that it's sometimes given as zero).

Houston, we're in orbit.

In an Atom the Number of Protons Equals the Number of Electrons

1) Atoms are neutral — they have no charge overall (unlike ions).
2) This is because they have the same number of protons as electrons.
3) The charge on the electrons is the same size as the charge on the protons, but opposite — so the charges cancel out.

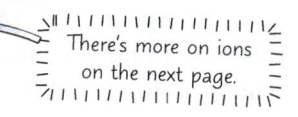

There's more on ions on the next page.

Atomic Number and Mass Number Describe an Atom

1) The nuclear symbol of an atom tells you its atomic number and mass number.
2) The atomic number tells you how many protons an atom has. Every atom of an element has the same number of protons.
3) For a neutral atom, the number of protons equals the number of electrons, so the number of electrons equals the atomic number.
4) The mass number tells you the total number of protons and neutrons in the atom.
5) To work out the number of neutrons in an atom, just subtract the atomic number from the mass number.

Nuclear symbol for sodium.
Mass number → 23
Atomic number → 11
Na
Element symbol

Think like a proton — stay positive...

You need to learn what's in that table with the relative masses and relative charges of the different parts of the atom.

Q1 A certain neutral atom of potassium has an atomic number of 19 and a mass number of 39. Give the number of electrons, protons and neutrons in the atom. [3 marks]

Unit 1b — Atomic Structure and the Periodic Table

Ions, Isotopes and Relative Atomic Mass

Atoms were reasonably straightforward weren't they? Think again. Here come isotopes to spice things up.

Ions have Different Numbers of Protons and Electrons

1) Ions form when atoms (or groups of atoms) gain or lose electrons.
2) Negative ions form when atoms gain electrons — they have more electrons than protons.
   Positive ions form when atoms lose electrons — they have more protons than electrons.

- F^- — there's a single negative charge, so there must be one more electron than protons.
  F has an atomic number of 9, so has 9 protons. So F^- must have 9 + 1 = 10 electrons.
- Fe^{2+} — there's a 2+ charge, so there must be two more protons than electrons.
  Fe has an atomic number of 26, so has 26 protons. So Fe^{2+} must have 26 − 2 = 24 electrons.

Isotopes are the Same Except for Extra Neutrons

1) Isotopes are different forms of the same element, which have the same number of protons but a different number of neutrons.
2) So isotopes have the same atomic number but different mass numbers.
3) A very popular example of a pair of isotopes is carbon-12 and carbon-13.

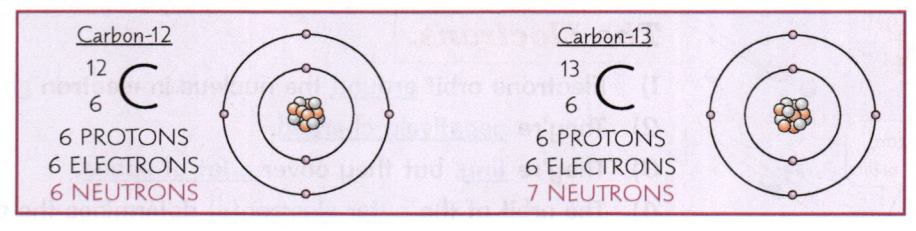

Carbon-12
$^{12}_{6}C$
6 PROTONS
6 ELECTRONS
6 NEUTRONS

Carbon-13
$^{13}_{6}C$
6 PROTONS
6 ELECTRONS
7 NEUTRONS

Remember — the number of neutrons is just the mass number minus the atomic number.

Relative Atomic Mass Takes Isotopes Into Account

1) In the periodic table, the elements all have two numbers next to them. The bigger one is the relative atomic mass (A_r) of the element.
2) Because many elements can exist as a number of different isotopes, relative atomic mass (A_r) is used instead of mass number when referring to an element as a whole.
3) If an element only has one isotope, its A_r will be the same as its mass number.
4) If an element has more than one isotope, its A_r is the average of the mass numbers of all the different isotopes, taking into account how much there is of each one. So, it might not be a whole number.
5) You can work out the A_r of an element with more than one isotope by using this formula:

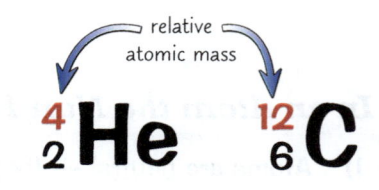

relative atomic mass (A_r) $= \dfrac{\text{sum of (isotope abundance} \times \text{isotope mass number)}}{\text{sum of abundances of all the isotopes}}$

$^{4}_{2}He$ $^{12}_{6}C$ — relative atomic mass

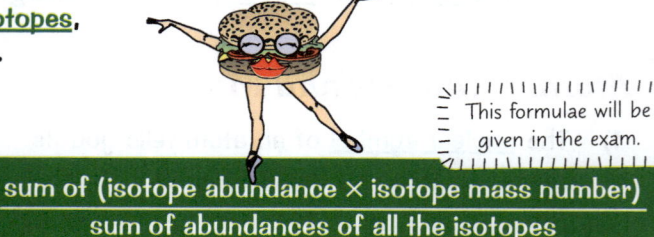

This formulae will be given in the exam.

EXAMPLE: Copper has two stable isotopes. Cu-63 has an abundance of 69.2% and Cu-65 has an abundance of 30.8%. Calculate the relative atomic mass of copper to 1 decimal place.

Relative atomic mass $= \dfrac{(69.2 \times 63) + (30.8 \times 65)}{69.2 + 30.8} = \dfrac{4359.6 + 2002}{100} = \dfrac{6361.6}{100} = 63.616 = 63.6$

It's elemental my dear Watson...

Atoms, ions and isotopes — make sure you know what they are and the differences between them.

Q1 a) Bromine has an atomic number of 35. It exists naturally with 2 isotopes, bromine-79 and bromine-81. Work out how many neutrons, protons and electrons are in each isotope. [2 marks]
    b) Bromine tends to react by forming Br^- ions. How many electrons are in a Br^- ion? [1 mark]

Unit 1b — Atomic Structure and the Periodic Table

The Periodic Table

The periodic table gives you information about all the elements. I present to you a chemist's best friend...

The Periodic Table Helps you to See Patterns in Properties

1) There are 100ish elements, which all materials are made of.
2) In the periodic table the elements are laid out in order of increasing atomic number. Arranging the elements like this means there are repeating patterns in the properties of the elements. (The properties are said to occur periodically, hence the name periodic table.)
3) If it wasn't for the periodic table organising everything, you'd have a heck of a job remembering all those properties. It's ace.

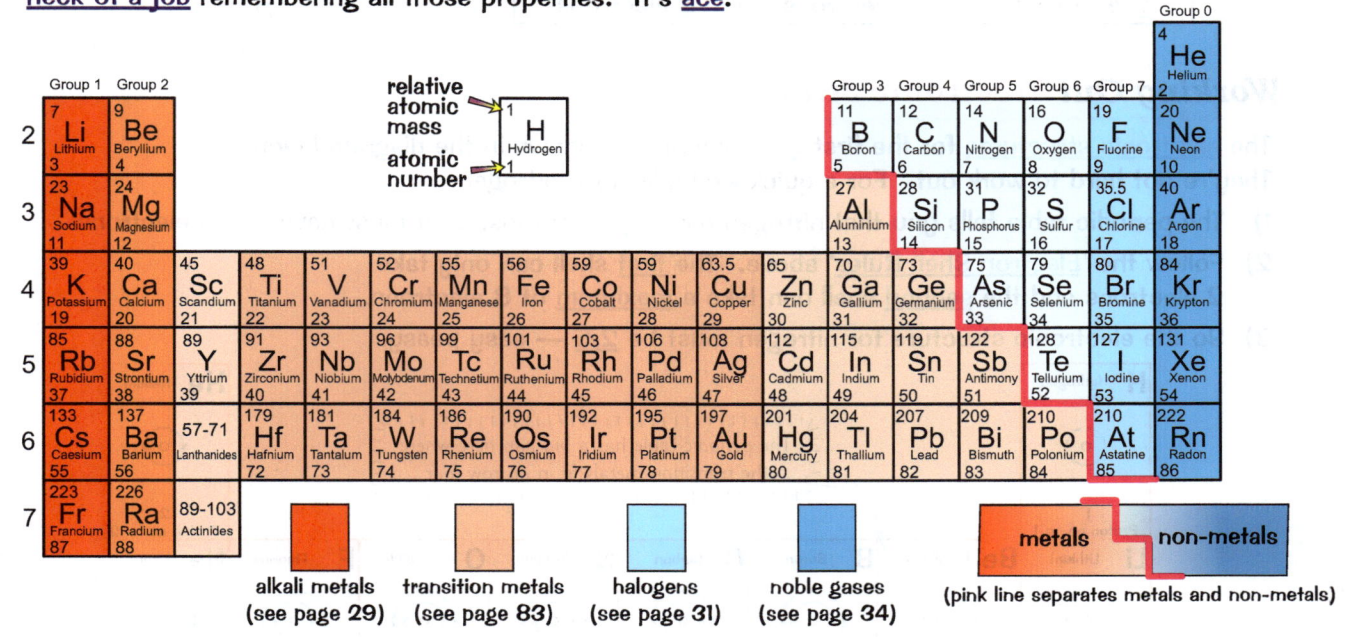

4) Elements with similar properties form columns.
5) These vertical columns are called groups.
6) The group number tells you how many electrons there are in the outer shell. For example, Group 1 elements all have one electron in their outer shell and Group 7 all have seven electrons in their outer shell. The exception to the rule is Group 0, for example helium has two electrons in its outer shell. This is useful as the way atoms react depends upon the number of electrons in their outer shell. So all elements in the same group are likely to react in a similar way.
7) If you know the properties of one element, you can predict properties of other elements in that group — and in the exam, you might be asked to do this. For example the Group 1 elements are Li, Na, K, Rb, Cs and Fr. They're all alkali metals and they react in a similar way (see pages 29-30).
8) You can also make predictions using trends in reactivity. E.g. in Group 1, the elements react more vigorously as you go down the group. And in Group 7, reactivity decreases as you go down the group.
9) The rows are called periods. Each new period represents another full shell of electrons.
10) The properties of elements change as you move across a period. Elements on the left and in the centre of a period have metallic properties, whilst elements on the right are non-metals. Many elements between the metals and non-metals (in Groups 3, 4 and 5) show both metallic and non-metallic properties.

I'm in a chemistry band — I play the symbols...

Because the periodic table is organised into groups and periods, it allows us to see trends in both reactivity and physical properties. And this means we can make predictions about how reactions will occur. Isn't that neat?

Q1 Using a periodic table, state how many electrons beryllium has in its outer shell. [1 mark]

Q2 Chlorine reacts in a similar way to bromine. Suggest a reason why. [1 mark]

Q3 Sodium readily forms 1+ ions. Suggest what ions potassium forms and explain your answer. [1 mark]

Unit 1b — Atomic Structure and the Periodic Table

Electron Shells

Like snails, electrons live in shells. Unlike snails, electrons won't nibble on your petunias...

Electron Shell Rules:

1) Electrons occupy shells (sometimes called energy levels).
2) The lowest energy levels are always filled first.
3) Only a certain number of electrons are allowed in each shell:

1st shell	2nd shell	3rd shell
2 electrons	8 electrons	8 electrons

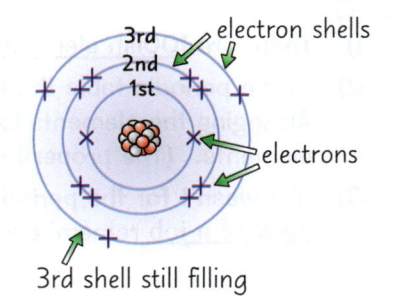

Working Out Electronic Structures

The electronic structures for the first 20 elements are shown in the diagram below. They're not hard to work out. For a quick example, take nitrogen:

1) The periodic table tells you that nitrogen has seven protons, so it must have seven electrons.
2) Follow the 'Electron Shell Rules' above. The first shell can only take 2 electrons and the second shell can take a maximum of 8 electrons.
3) So the electronic structure for nitrogen must be 2.5 — easy peasy.

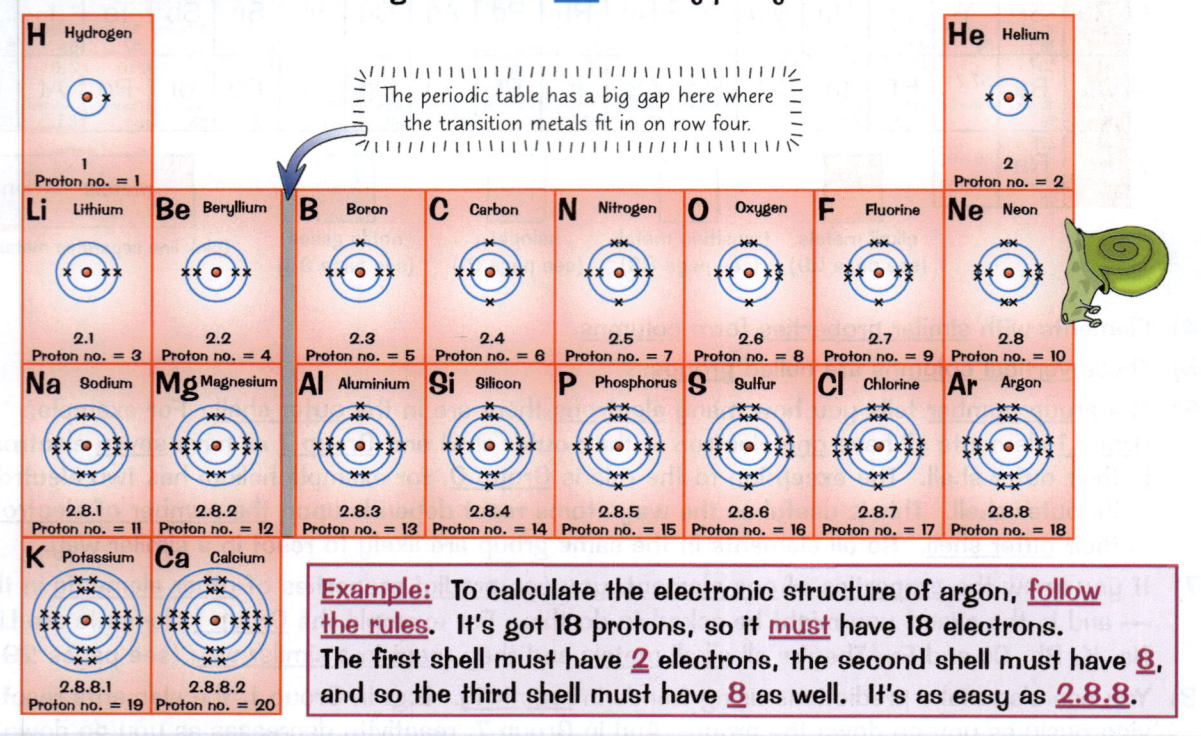

The periodic table has a big gap here where the transition metals fit in on row four.

Example: To calculate the electronic structure of argon, follow the rules. It's got 18 protons, so it must have 18 electrons. The first shell must have 2 electrons, the second shell must have 8, and so the third shell must have 8 as well. It's as easy as 2.8.8.

You can also work out the electronic structure of an element from its period and group.
- The number of shells which contain electrons is the same as the period of the element.
- The group number tells you how many electrons occupy the outer shell of the element.

Example: Sodium is in period 3, so it has 3 shells occupied — so the first two shells must be full (2.8). It's in Group 1, so it has 1 electron in its outer shell. So its electronic structure is 2.8.1.

The electronic structure of the fifth element — it's a bit boron...

Electronic structures may seem a bit complicated at first but once you learn the rules, they're a piece of cake.

Q1   Give the electronic structure of aluminium (atomic number = 13). [1 mark]

Q2   In which group and period of the periodic table would you expect to find the element with electronic structure 2.8.8.2? [2 marks]

Unit 1b — Atomic Structure and the Periodic Table

Group 1 — The Alkali Metals

Group 1 elements are known as the alkali metals — these are silvery solids that have to be stored in oil (and handled with forceps) as they react vigorously with water. As elements go, they're pretty demanding...

The Group 1 Elements are Reactive, Soft Metals

1) The alkali metals are lithium, sodium, potassium, rubidium, caesium and francium.
2) They all have one electron in their outer shell which makes them very reactive and gives them similar properties.
3) The alkali metals are all soft and have low density. The first three in the group are less dense than water.

Melting and Boiling Points Decrease Down Group 1

1) Group 1 metals form regular structures held together with metallic bonds (see page 59). In these bonds, the outer electron of each atom is free to move around (delocalised). There are strong attractions between these electrons and the positively charged nuclei.
2) As you go down Group 1, the atoms get bigger — the nucleus is further away from the free electrons, so the attractions get weaker.
3) This means that less energy is needed to break the metallic bonds and turn the solid metal into a liquid and then to a gas — so melting and boiling points decrease down the group.

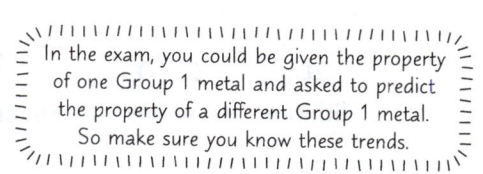

In the exam, you could be given the property of one Group 1 metal and asked to predict the property of a different Group 1 metal. So make sure you know these trends.

Group 1 Metals are Very Reactive

1) The Group 1 metals want to have a full outer shell so that they have a stable electronic structure. The easiest way to achieve this is by losing their single outer electron to form a 1+ ion.
2) The more readily a metal loses its outer electrons, the more reactive it is — so the Group 1 metals are very reactive.
3) As you go down Group 1, the alkali metals get more reactive. The negatively charged outer electron is less strongly attracted to the positively charged nucleus. This is because it's further away (there are more electron shells) — so it's more easily lost, as less energy is needed to remove it.
4) Group 2 elements are less reactive than Group 1 elements because they have to lose 2 electrons to get a full outer shell — this is harder than losing just 1 electron.

Group 1 Elements React in Similar Ways

1) Group 1 elements can take part in different reactions, e.g. with water and chlorine gas.
2) Because Group 1 elements all have a single outer electron, they will react with a particular reactant to produce the same type of product. E.g. the reactions of Group 1 metals with chlorine gas produce metal chlorides. This means that the balanced symbol equations will follow the same pattern — make sure you know how to write them.
3) Although the reactions are similar, the reactions become more vigorous as atomic number increases. This is because the elements become more reactive down the group.
4) So, if you know how one Group 1 metal reacts, you can use the pattern of reactivity to predict how other Group 1 metals will react and the products that will form.

Wanna know more about Group 1 metals? K. Really? Na...

Well, I'm afraid we still have another page to go about Group 1. It's a good one though — I'm not even Li-ing...

Q1 State and explain the trend in reactivity as you go down Group 1. [3 marks]

Unit 1b — Atomic Structure and the Periodic Table

Reactions of the Alkali Metals

Now you've learnt the basics about the Group 1 elements it's time to learn some cool reactions.

Group 1 Metals React with Oxygen in the Air

1) The Group 1 metals are shiny when freshly cut, but quickly react with oxygen and water in air and tarnish as a metal oxide is formed. Different oxides will form depending on the Group 1 metal.
2) As you go down Group 1, the elements tarnish much more quickly.
3) Lithium, sodium and potassium are stored in oil to prevent the reaction with air.
4) Rubidium and caesium are much more reactive, so are sealed in glass tubes under special conditions.
5) Group 1 metals will also burn in air to produce white metal oxides. You can identify the metal from the colour of the flame — see page 35 for more.

Reaction with Cold Water Produces a Hydroxide and Hydrogen Gas

1) When the alkali metals are put in water, they react to produce hydrogen gas and a metal hydroxide (an alkali). For example, here are the overall equations for the reactions of the first three alkali metals with water:

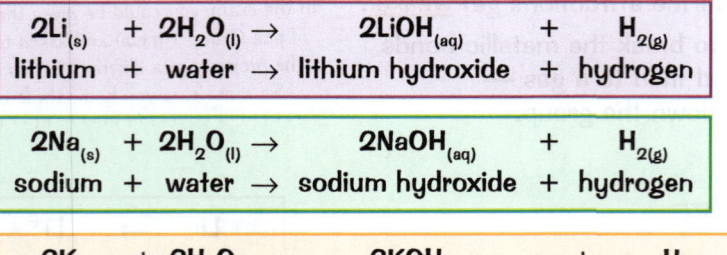

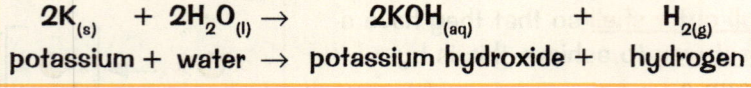

$$2Li_{(s)} + 2H_2O_{(l)} \rightarrow 2LiOH_{(aq)} + H_{2(g)}$$
lithium + water → lithium hydroxide + hydrogen

$$2Na_{(s)} + 2H_2O_{(l)} \rightarrow 2NaOH_{(aq)} + H_{2(g)}$$
sodium + water → sodium hydroxide + hydrogen

$$2K_{(s)} + 2H_2O_{(l)} \rightarrow 2KOH_{(aq)} + H_{2(g)}$$
potassium + water → potassium hydroxide + hydrogen

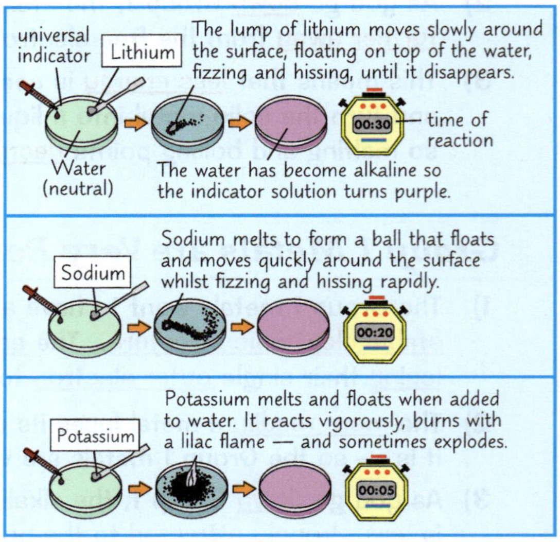

2) As you go down Group 1, the elements become more reactive (in fact, rubidium and caesium actually explode).
3) You can see this in the rate of reaction with water (i.e. the time taken for a lump of the same size of each element to react completely with the water and disappear).
4) Lithium takes longer than sodium or potassium to react, so it's the least reactive. Potassium takes the shortest time to react of these three elements, so it's the most reactive.
5) The reaction between water and potassium produces enough heat to melt the metal. Similarly, the reaction between sodium and water produces enough heat to melt the sodium until it forms a ball. Lithium reacts more slowly, and has a higher melting point, so it doesn't melt during the reaction.

Reactions with Group 7 Elements Produce a Salt

1) The Group 1 metals react vigorously when heated in a Group 7 gas (see next page) to form white crystalline salts called 'metal halides'. The colour of the flame produced depends on the metal used.
2) As you go down Group 1, reactivity increases so the reaction with Group 7 elements gets more vigorous.

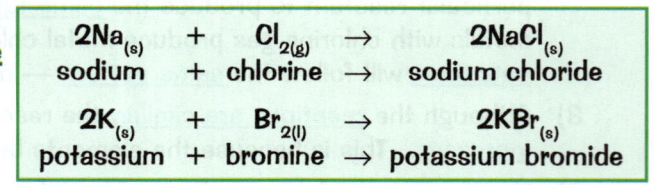

$$2Na_{(s)} + Cl_{2(g)} \rightarrow 2NaCl_{(s)}$$
sodium + chlorine → sodium chloride

$$2K_{(s)} + Br_{2(l)} \rightarrow 2KBr_{(s)}$$
potassium + bromine → potassium bromide

Back to the drawing board with my lithium swim shorts design...

The reactions of alkali metals with water need safety precautions because they fizz and might explode. Cool stuff.

Q1 Which Group 1 element has the least vigorous reaction with chlorine gas? [1 mark]

Q2 Give the balanced symbol equation for the reaction between sodium and water. [2 marks]

Unit 1b — Atomic Structure and the Periodic Table

Group 7 — The Halogens

Here's a page on another periodic table group that you need to be familiar with — the halogens.

Group 7 Elements are Known as the Halogens

Group 7 is made up of the elements fluorine, chlorine, bromine, iodine and astatine.

1) All Group 7 elements have 7 electrons in their outer shell — so they all have similar chemical properties.
2) The halogens exist as diatomic molecules (e.g. Cl_2, Br_2, I_2). Sharing one pair of electrons in a covalent bond (see page 62) gives both atoms a full outer shell.
3) As you go down Group 7, the melting points and boiling points of the halogens increase.
4) This means that at room temperature:
   - Chlorine (Cl_2) is a poisonous (toxic), green gas (it has a low boiling point).
   - Bromine (Br_2) is a poisonous, red-brown liquid, which gives off an orange vapour at room temperature.
   - Iodine (I_2) is a dark grey crystalline solid which gives off a purple vapour when heated.

Reactivity Decreases Going Down Group 7

1) A halogen atom only needs to gain one electron to form a 1− ion with a stable electronic structure.
2) The easier it is for a halogen atom to attract an electron, the more reactive the halogen will be.
3) As you go DOWN Group 7, the halogens become less reactive — it gets harder to attract the extra electron to fill the outer shell when it's further away from the nucleus (the atomic radius is larger).
4) Group 6 elements are less reactive than Group 7 elements because they have to gain two electrons to get a full outer shell — this is harder than gaining just one electron.

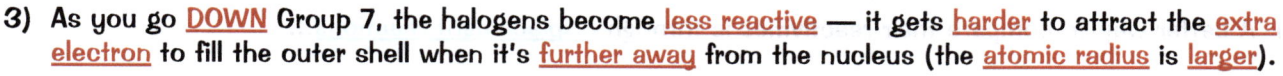

Chlorine and Iodine have Lots of Uses

1) Chlorine is toxic — it kills disease-causing microorganisms, such as bacteria.
2) It's an important part of water treatment. Adding chlorine to water sterilises it, making it safe to drink or swim in. The amount of chlorine used is carefully monitored so it is sufficient to kill harmful bacteria without making the water toxic to people.
3) If we didn't treat our drinking water with chlorine in this way, we'd be at risk of getting all sorts of nasty and potentially dangerous infections.
4) Chlorine is also used to make cleaning products.

1) Iodine is also toxic — it is used as an antiseptic in hospitals to sterilise skin before operations, because it kills bacteria.
2) Radioactive forms of iodine are used in nuclear medicine.

Halogens — one electron short of a full shell...

Another page, another periodic table group to learn the properties and the trends of. When you're pretty confident that you've got all the stuff from this page in your head, have a go at the question below, just to check.

Q1   The melting point of chlorine (Cl_2) is −101.5 °C. Predict whether bromine (Br_2) would be a solid, a liquid or a gas at −101.5 °C. Explain your answer. [2 marks]

Unit 1b — Atomic Structure and the Periodic Table

Reactions of the Halogens

There are a few reactions that the Group 7 elements take part in that you need to learn about.

The Halogens React With Alkali Metals to Form Salts

1) The halogens will react vigorously with alkali metals (Group 1 elements) to form white salts called 'metal halides'.
2) On the right is an example of this reaction. There are some more on page 30.

$$2K_{(s)} + I_{2(s)} \rightarrow 2KI_{(s)}$$
potassium + iodine → potassium iodide

The Halogens React With Iron to Form Iron Halides

1) When iron reacts with a Group 7 element an exothermic reaction occurs (page 84) and an iron halide (iron salt) is produced.
2) The salts formed are iron(III) salts. They are coloured solids.
3) Chlorine reacts the most vigorously with iron. Bromine and iodine react less vigorously — they have to be heated for a reaction to happen.

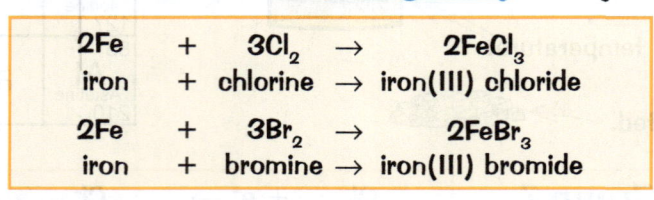

Iron(III) salts are ionic compounds that contain Fe^{3+} ions.

$$2Fe + 3Cl_2 \rightarrow 2FeCl_3$$
iron + chlorine → iron(III) chloride

$$2Fe + 3Br_2 \rightarrow 2FeBr_3$$
iron + bromine → iron(III) bromide

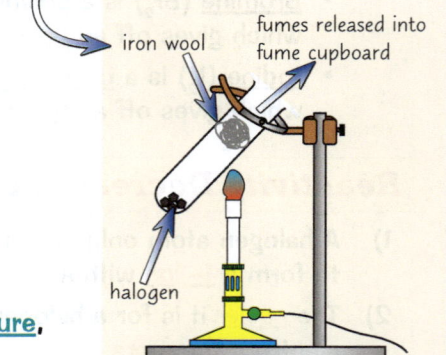

4) The reaction with iron becomes less vigorous down Group 7. Although this follows the general trend in Group 7 reactivity, it isn't actually a very fair comparison of the reactivities of the halogens.
5) This is because the halogens are in different states at room temperature, which affects how reactive they are.
6) A better way to compare their reactivities is through displacement reactions...

A More Reactive Halogen Will Displace a Less Reactive One

1) A displacement reaction is a good way to compare the reactivities of two halogens as they compete directly against each other.
2) A displacement reaction is where a more reactive element 'pushes out' (displaces) a less reactive element from a compound.
3) For example, chlorine is more reactive than bromine (it's higher up Group 7). If you add chlorine water (an aqueous solution of Cl_2) to potassium bromide solution, the chlorine will displace the bromine from the salt solution.
4) The chlorine is reduced to chloride ions, so the salt solution becomes potassium chloride. The bromide ions are oxidised to bromine, which turns the solution orange.

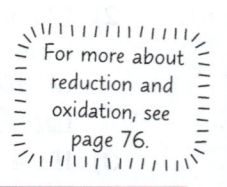

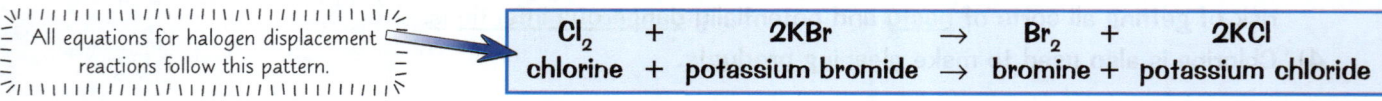

For more about reduction and oxidation, see page 76.

All equations for halogen displacement reactions follow this pattern.

$$Cl_2 + 2KBr \rightarrow Br_2 + 2KCl$$
chlorine + potassium bromide → bromine + potassium chloride

5) The halogens always gain electrons whilst the halide ions lose electrons.

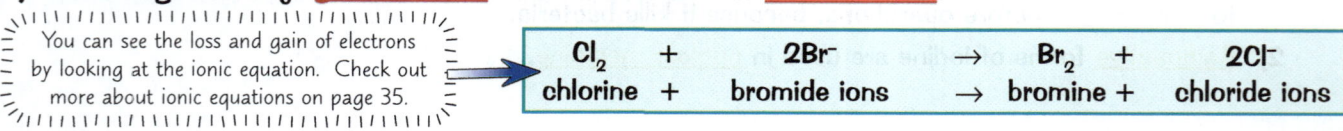

You can see the loss and gain of electrons by looking at the ionic equation. Check out more about ionic equations on page 35.

$$Cl_2 + 2Br^- \rightarrow Br_2 + 2Cl^-$$
chlorine + bromide ions → bromine + chloride ions

Bro-mine — the coolest element...

Don't forget that iron(III) salts are formed in those halogen reactions, you can't just say 'iron salts' in the exam.

Q1 Write a balanced symbol equation for the reaction between sodium metal (Na) and iodine (I_2). [2 marks]

Q2 Write a balanced symbol equation for the reaction between iron (Fe) and chlorine (Cl_2). [2 marks]

Unit 1b — Atomic Structure and the Periodic Table

Halogen Displacement Reactions

The halogens are a pretty competitive lot really. The more reactive ones are always pushing the less reactive ones out of compounds. How uncivilised — has nobody ever taught them that it's bad manners to push?

Displacement Reactions Show Reactivity Trends

Displacement reactions can be used to provide evidence for the reactivity trend of the halogens. Here's how they're done:

1) First, a small amount of a halide salt solution is measured out and added to a test tube. All halide salt solutions are colourless.
2) A few drops of a halogen solution are added to the test tube, and the tube is shaken gently.
3) If there is a colour change, then a reaction has happened — the halogen has displaced the halide ions from the salt.
4) If no reaction happens, there won't be a colour change — the halogen is less reactive than the halide and so can't displace it.
5) The process can be repeated using different combinations of halide salt and halogen.
6) The table below shows what should happen when different combinations of chlorine, bromine and iodine water are mixed with solutions of the salts potassium chloride, potassium bromide and potassium iodide.

Start with:	Potassium chloride solution $KCl_{(aq)}$ — colourless	Potassium bromide solution $KBr_{(aq)}$ — colourless	Potassium iodide solution $KI_{(aq)}$ — colourless
Add chlorine water $Cl_{2\,(aq)}$ — colourless	no reaction	orange solution ($Br_{2\,(aq)}$) formed	brown solution ($I_{2\,(aq)}$) formed
Add bromine water $Br_{2\,(aq)}$ — orange	no reaction	no reaction	brown solution ($I_{2\,(aq)}$) formed
Add iodine water $I_{2\,(aq)}$ — brown	no reaction	no reaction	no reaction

7) Chlorine displaces both bromine and iodine from salt solutions. E.g.:

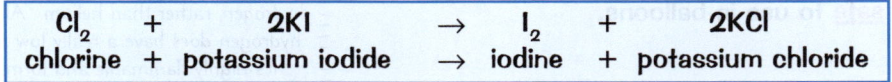

$$Cl_2 + 2KI \rightarrow I_2 + 2KCl$$
chlorine + potassium iodide → iodine + potassium chloride

8) Bromine can't displace chlorine, but it does displace iodine.

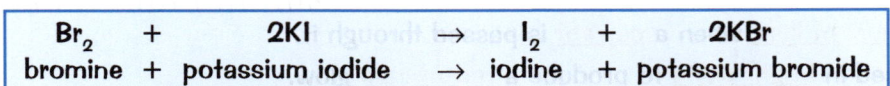

$$Br_2 + 2KI \rightarrow I_2 + 2KBr$$
bromine + potassium iodide → iodine + potassium bromide

9) Iodine can't displace chlorine or bromine.
10) This provides evidence for the reactivity trend — the halogens can only displace halide ions of halogens that are below them in Group 7. So they get less reactive as you go down the group.

You can use the Results to make Predictions

1) For example, you can use the trend you've identified to predict how astatine might react.
2) Since astatine is even lower in Group 7 than iodine, you'd predict it to be the least reactive halogen. Therefore you'd predict it wouldn't displace any other halogens from their salt solutions.

New information displaces old information from my brain...

If you remember that the halogens get less reactive as you go down the group, you can work out what will happen when you mix any halogen with any halide salt. You need to know the colour changes that go with the reactions too.

Q1   A student added a few drops of a halogen solution to some potassium iodide solution. The solution turned brown. She added a few drops of the same halogen solution to some potassium bromide solution. No reaction occurred. Name the halogen solution that the student used.   [1 mark]

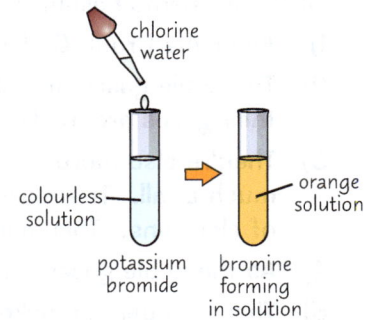

Unit 1b — Atomic Structure and the Periodic Table

Group 0 — The Noble Gases

The elements in Group 0 of the periodic table are known as the noble gases. 'Noble' here is just being used in the old chemistry sense of being unreactive — nothing to do with them being particularly honourable or good.

Group 0 Elements are All Inert, Colourless Gases

Group 0 elements are called the noble gases. Group 0 is made up of the elements helium, neon, argon, krypton, xenon and radon.

1) All of the Group 0 elements are colourless gases at room temperature.
2) The noble gases are all monatomic — that just means that their gases are made up of single atoms (not molecules).
3) They're also more or less inert — this means they don't react with much at all. The reason for this is that they have a full outer shell of electrons. This means they don't easily give up or gain electrons.
4) As the noble gases are inert, they're non-flammable — they won't set on fire.
5) These properties make the gases pretty hard to observe — it took a long time for them to be discovered.

Group 7	Group 0
	4 He Helium 2
F	20 Ne Neon 10
Cl	40 Ar Argon 18
Br	84 Kr Krypton 36
I	131 Xe Xenon 54
At	222 Rn Radon 86

The Noble Gases have Many Everyday Uses...

The properties of the noble gases make them suitable for a few different uses:

Helium

1) Helium has a very low density — lower than air.
2) Helium is used in airships, weather balloons and party balloons — its low density makes balloons float in air.
3) Helium is very unreactive and also non-flammable. This makes it safe to use in balloons.

The first gas balloons used in weather balloons and airships were filled with hydrogen, rather than helium. Although hydrogen does have a really low density, it's highly flammable and forms an explosive mixture with air, which was sometimes a recipe for disaster.

Neon

1) Neon emits a bright light when a current is passed through it.
2) It's mostly used in bright signs to produce a red-orange glow.
3) Neon is also used in cryogenics and lasers.

Argon

1) Argon is inert which basically means it's very unreactive.
2) It's used in filament lamps (light bulbs). If air was used inside filament lamps, the oxygen in the air would react with the hot filament in the lamp and damage it. Argon won't react with the filament and so is used instead of air.
3) Argon can also be used to protect metals that are being welded. The inert atmosphere stops the hot metal reacting with oxygen.

Noble gas jokes are rubbish — I never get a reaction from them...

The noble gases might seem a bit dull, given how unreactive they are, but they're not so bad. They'd be pretty good at hide and seek for a start. And what would helium balloon sellers be without them? Deflated — that's what.

Q1   Explain why Group 0 elements are unreactive.   [1 mark]

Unit 1b — Atomic Structure and the Periodic Table

Tests for Ions and Hydrogen **PRACTICAL**

Have you ever wondered how you could identify mystery ions and gases? Well you're in for a treat...

Ionic Equations Show Just the Useful Bits of Reactions

In an ionic equation only the particles that react and the products they form are shown. For example...

1) This ionic equation just shows the displacement of zinc ions by magnesium metal. ⟹ $Mg_{(s)} + Zn^{2+}_{(aq)} \rightarrow Mg^{2+}_{(aq)} + Zn_{(s)}$
2) Here's what the full equation would be if you'd started off with zinc chloride: ⟹ $Mg_{(s)} + ZnCl_{2(aq)} \rightarrow MgCl_{2(aq)} + Zn_{(s)}$
3) If you write out the equations showing all the ions, you'll see that the chloride ions don't change — they're spectator ions. They're of no interest here, so can be crossed out.
   $Mg_{(s)} + Zn^{2+}_{(aq)} + 2Cl^{-}_{(aq)} \rightarrow Mg^{2+}_{(aq)} + 2Cl^{-}_{(aq)} + Zn_{(s)}$
4) Instead, the ionic equation for this displacement reaction just concentrates on the substances which are actually reacting (p.32).

Ionic equations should always include state symbols. You'll be told if there's a mark for doing this in the exam.

Ionic equations are handy for showing what happens in a test for an ion...

Test for Halide Ions Using Silver Nitrate Solution

To test for chloride ions (Cl⁻), bromide ions (Br⁻) or iodide ions (I⁻), add some dilute nitric acid (HNO_3), followed by a few drops of silver nitrate solution ($AgNO_3$).

A chloride gives a **white** precipitate of silver chloride.
$Ag^{+}_{(aq)} + Cl^{-}_{(aq)} \rightarrow AgCl_{(s)}$

A bromide gives a **cream** precipitate of silver bromide.
$Ag^{+}_{(aq)} + Br^{-}_{(aq)} \rightarrow AgBr_{(s)}$

An iodide gives a **yellow** precipitate of silver iodide.
$Ag^{+}_{(aq)} + I^{-}_{(aq)} \rightarrow AgI_{(s)}$

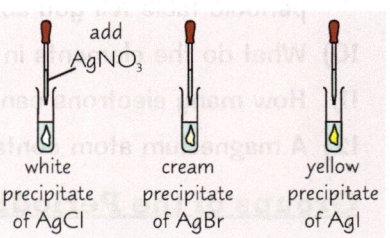

The nitric acid is added first to get rid of any carbonate ions — they produce a white precipitate with silver nitrate solution too, which would confuse the results. You can't use hydrochloric acid, because you'd be adding chloride ions.

There are also spectator ions in these reactions. E.g. if NaCl is tested, Na⁺ and NO₃⁻ are spectator ions. They are unchanged in the reaction: $Na^{+}_{(aq)} + Cl^{-}_{(aq)} + Ag^{+}_{(aq)} + NO_{3}^{-}_{(aq)} \rightarrow AgCl_{(s)} + Na^{+}_{(aq)} + NO_{3}^{-}_{(aq)}$

There's a test for carbonate ions (CO_3^{2-}) too — it's on page 69.

You Can Use Flame Tests to Identify Metal Ions

Compounds of some metals produce a characteristic colour when heated in a flame.

1) You can test for metal ions by putting the substance in a flame and seeing what colour the flame goes.
   - **Lithium**, Li⁺, gives a red flame.
   - **Sodium**, Na⁺, gives a yellow-orange flame.
   - **Potassium**, K⁺, gives a lilac flame.
   - **Calcium**, Ca²⁺, gives a brick red flame.
   - **Barium**, Ba²⁺, gives an apple green flame.

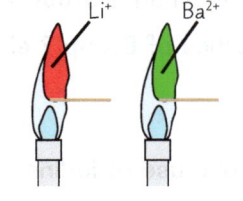

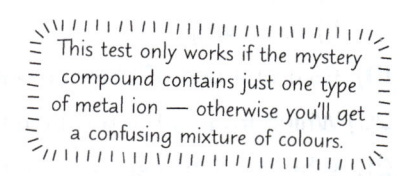

Remember — metals always form positive ions.

This test only works if the mystery compound contains just one type of metal ion — otherwise you'll get a confusing mixture of colours.

2) To carry out a flame test in the lab, first dip a damp wooden splint into the metal compound being tested.
3) Then hold the splint in the blue part of a Bunsen flame (the hottest bit). Record what colour the flame goes.

Test for Hydrogen Using a Lit Splint

If you hold a lit splint at the open end of a test tube containing hydrogen, you'll get a "squeaky pop". (The noise comes from the hydrogen burning quickly with the oxygen in the air to form H_2O.)

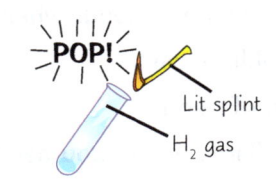

Squeaky pop is all I hear on the radio nowadays...

Try to find an easy way to remember the flame test colours that works for you e.g. purple potassium.

Q1   In a flame test, which element does an apple green flame indicate the presence of?   [1 mark]

Unit 1b — Atomic Structure and the Periodic Table

Revision Questions for Unit 1b

Well that's Unit 1b nearly finished — just this page and then it's time for a nice cup of tea and a biscuit.
- Try these questions and tick off each one when you get it right.
- When you've done all the questions for a topic and are completely happy with it, tick off the topic.

Atoms, Ions and Isotopes (p.25-26) ☐

1) Which subatomic particle is negatively charged?
2) Which subatomic particle has a relative mass of 1 and a relative charge of 0?
3) What two subatomic particles make up the nucleus of an atom?
4) What does the mass number tell you about an atom?
5) How can you calculate the number of neutrons in an atom?
6) How many electrons does a Mg^{2+} ion have?
7) What are isotopes?
8) True or false? The relative atomic mass of an element is the sum of the mass numbers of all its different isotopes.

The Periodic Table and Electronic Structure (p.27-28) ☐

9) What does the group number of an element in the periodic table tell you about its electronic structure?
10) What do the elements in each period have in common?
11) How many electrons can the first electron shell of an atom contain?
12) A magnesium atom contains 12 electrons. What is the electronic structure of magnesium?

Groups of the Periodic Table (p.29-35) ☐

13) What happens to the melting/boiling point of Group 1 elements as you move down a group?
14) Do Group 1 elements gain or lose electrons during reactions? How many?
15) What happens to a Group 1 element if it is left in air? What type of substance is formed?
16) Which Group 1 metal has the least vigorous reaction with water?
17) What type of product is formed when a Group 1 metal reacts with chlorine gas?
18) What happens to these properties of Group 7 elements as you move down a group:
    a) melting / boiling point?
    b) reactivity?
19) Give one use of chlorine and one use of iodine.
20) Which iron salt is produced when iron reacts with bromine?
21) Why do displacement reactions give stronger evidence for the Group 7 reactivity series than their reactions with iron?
22) What would you observe if chlorine water was added to potassium iodide solution?
23) Why does no reaction occur when iodine water is added to potassium bromide?
24) Name two noble gases.
25) Give one use of neon.
26) What colour flame would you see if testing for calcium?
27) Describe the test used to identify hydrogen gas.

Unit 1b — Atomic Structure and the Periodic Table

Unit 1c — Water and the Earth

Water Treatment

Water treatment is essential for a healthy life — untreated water can make you very poorly.

There are a Variety of Water Resources

There are a number of sources of water, which can be treated to provide drinking water. These include:

1) **GROUNDWATER**: from rocks that trap water underground (aquifers). This contains ions such as Mg^{2+}, Ca^{2+}, Na^+ and K^+ — these ions come from minerals in the rocks.
2) **RAINWATER**: from rain — this contains dissolved gases such as CO_2 and O_2. When CO_2 dissolves in water it lowers the pH of the water.

Water sources contain man-made pollutants like pesticides, fertilisers, and household and industrial waste. As well as man-made pollutants, water can also contain natural pollutants like bacteria and viruses.

There is a Demand for Sustainable Water

1) Fresh water is crucial to humans — not just for drinking, but also for farming and industry.
2) The global population is increasing, so there is an even greater need for water.
3) Because of this, water is expected to become more scarce with water shortages being possible. Climate change also increases the risk of droughts, which makes water shortages more likely.
4) As the demand for water goes up so will the price, so to make our water supply sustainable and affordable we need to reduce our water consumption.
5) We also need to collect and treat our water in ways that don't damage the environment.

Water is Purified in Water Treatment Plants

The water that comes out of your taps doesn't come straight from the source — first it has to be purified. How much purification it needs depends on the source. But, wherever it comes from, most of our water is purified using the following processes:

1) **Sedimentation** — large solid particles in the water settle at the bottom of the water tank because of gravity.
2) **Filtration** — small insoluble particles are removed by filtering through layers of sand and gravel.
3) **Chlorination** — chlorine gas is bubbled through to kill harmful bacteria and other microbes.

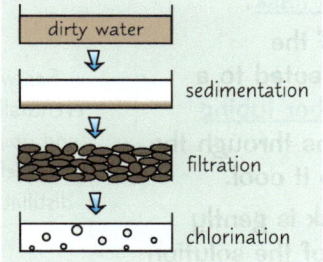

Some soluble impurities that are dissolved in the water are not removed as they can't be filtered out — these include the minerals which cause water hardness (p.41).

Adding Fluoride to Water Has Pros and Cons

Fluoride ions are found naturally in a lot of water sources. Adding more fluoride ions to water supplies is a controversial issue in the UK. There are some advantages and disadvantages that you should know:

1) There is strong evidence that fluoride ions prevent tooth decay in children — reliable surveys of school children support this claim.
2) Some studies however have linked high doses of fluoride to bone and stomach cancer and infertility in humans, so some people believe that fluoride shouldn't be added to drinking water. There is also concern about whether it's right to 'mass medicate' — people can choose whether to use a fluoride toothpaste or mouthwash, but they can't choose whether their tap water has added fluoride.
3) Levels of chemicals added to drinking water need to be carefully monitored. For example, in some areas the water may already contain a lot of fluoride, so adding more could be harmful.

There's more about ethics in science in the 'Working Scientifically' section on page 3.

If water from the ground is ground water, why isn't rain sky water?

Ahhh... Every glass of tap water I drink tastes all the sweeter for knowing what it had to go through to get to me...

Q1   Outline how water is purified in a water treatment plant.   [3 marks]

Distillation and Desalination

Distillation means <u>separating</u> a pure liquid from a solution by <u>evaporation</u> and <u>condensation</u>.
You can <u>distil sea water</u> to get <u>fresh water</u> — this is called '<u>desalination</u>' (removing all of the salt).

You Can Get Safe Water by Distilling Sea Water

1) In some <u>dry</u> countries, sea water is <u>distilled</u> to produce drinking water — this is the <u>simplest</u> way of removing the salt.
2) On a small scale, sea water can be distilled using a <u>solar still</u>.
3) On a larger scale, traditional <u>distillation apparatus</u> is used, which usually involves <u>burning fossil fuels</u> to heat the water.
4) This needs <u>loads of energy</u> (and therefore loads of money) to heat such a large amount of water. This makes it <u>expensive</u> and <u>impractical</u> — it's not always a viable process in poorer countries.
5) Distillation is also only possible in countries that are <u>near the sea</u>.
6) There are other ways of removing salt from sea water. For example, the salt water can be forced through <u>membranes</u> which only allow the water molecules through, and not the salt.

Simple Distillation Separates Out Solutions

All <u>pure liquids</u> boil at a <u>specific temperature</u> (known as the boiling point) — water boils at <u>100 °C</u>. If you have a <u>mixture</u> of two or more liquids with <u>different boiling points</u>, you can <u>separate</u> them out using <u>distillation</u>. Distillation can also be used to <u>desalinate</u> sea water. It works like this:

Distillation can be difficult when the boiling points of the two liquids are fairly close. For example ethanol boils at 78 °C — if you tried to distil ethanol from a solution of ethanol in water, some of the water would also evaporate during the process.

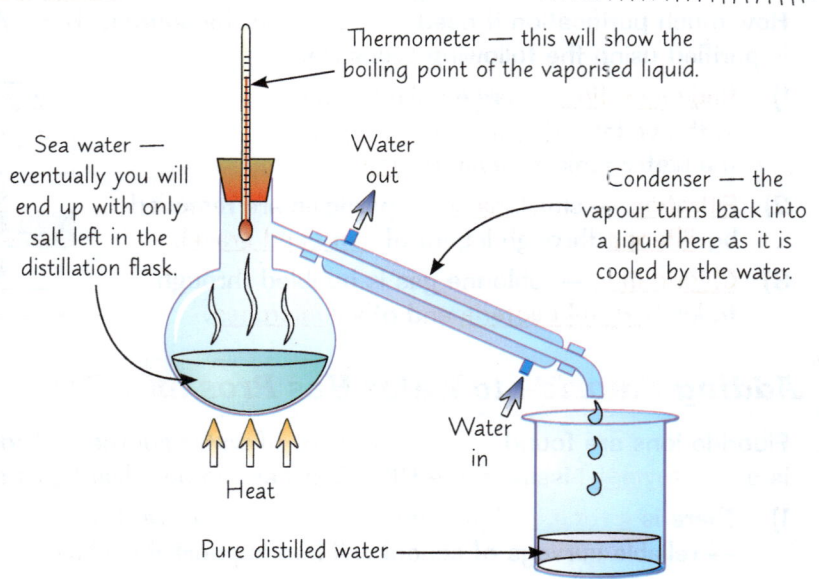

1) The sample of sea water is poured into the <u>distillation flask</u>.
2) The bottom end of the <u>condenser</u> is connected to a cold tap using <u>rubber tubing</u> and <u>cold water</u> runs through the condenser to keep it cool.
3) The distillation flask is gently heated. The part of the solution that has the lowest boiling point will <u>evaporate</u> — in this case, that's the water.
4) The water <u>vapour</u> passes into the condenser where it <u>cools</u> and <u>condenses</u> (turns back into a liquid). It then flows into the beaker where it is <u>collected</u>.
5) Eventually you'll end up with just the <u>salt</u> left in the flask, and <u>pure water</u> in the beaker.

Thermometer — this will show the boiling point of the vaporised liquid.

Sea water — eventually you will end up with only salt left in the distillation flask.

Water out

Condenser — the vapour turns back into a liquid here as it is cooled by the water.

Water in

Heat

Pure distilled water

If you're not part of the solution you're part of the... pure liquid?

Distillation might be the easiest method of desalinating sea water, but that doesn't mean it's easy to remember — read over the method of distillation and then try scribbling it down until you know it off by heart.

Q1   Why is distillation an expensive method of desalinating sea water?   [1 mark]

Unit 1c — Water and the Earth

Solubility Curves

This page is all about solutions. Study it carefully and you might even get some solutions to exam questions...

Solubility is a Measure of How Much Solute will Dissolve in a Solvent

1) A solute is a substance that dissolves in a liquid to make a solution. The solvent is the liquid that the solute dissolves in.
2) The ability of a solute to dissolve in a solvent is known as its solubility.
3) When no more of the solute can dissolve in the solvent, the solution is saturated.
4) Solubility is often measured in grams of solute per 100 grams of solvent.

> For example: If 23 grams of a substance can dissolve in 100 grams of water before the solution becomes saturated, that substance has a solubility of 23 g per 100 g of water.

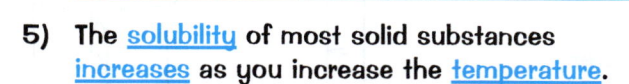

5) The solubility of most solid substances increases as you increase the temperature.
6) A graph of solubility versus temperature is known as a solubility curve:
7) The temperature scale on a solubility curve usually ranges from 0 °C – 100 °C because water freezes at 0 °C and boils at 100 °C.
8) You can use solubility curves to find the solubility of a substance at a specific temperature.
9) To do this, draw a line from the temperature that you're interested in (on the x-axis) up to the curve. Then, read across from the curve to the y-axis to find the solubility of the substance at that particular temperature. For example, on the graph on the right, the solubility at 25 °C is 32 g per 100 g of solvent.

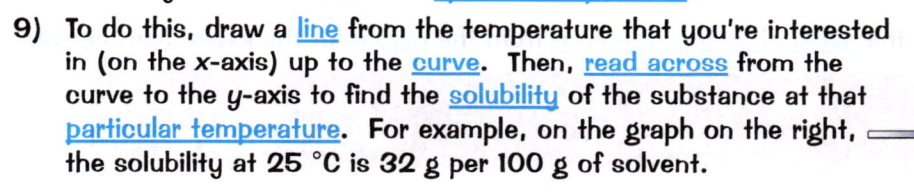

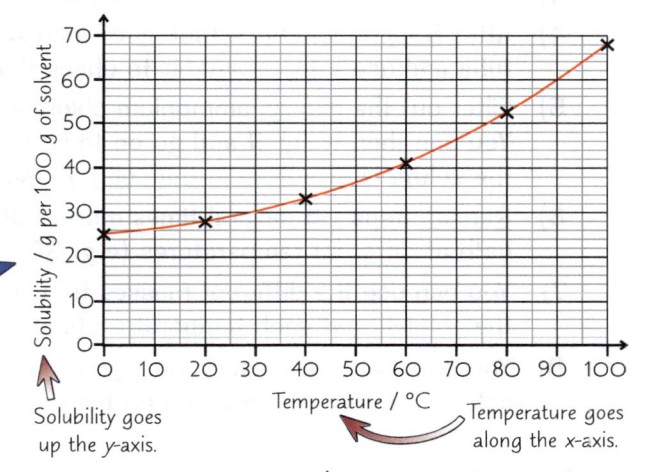

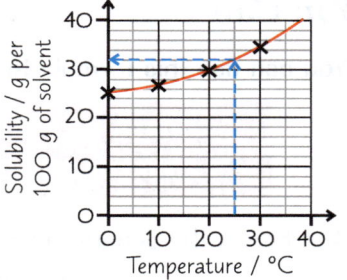

You Can Plot a Solubility Curve — Here's how you do it:

1) Measure out a set volume of water. Let it stand for a while until it reaches room temperature.
2) Weigh out a set mass of the solute. It must be a bit greater than the mass that will dissolve in that volume of water at room temperature.
   If you're not sure what mass to use, do a trial run, where you add the solute a bit at a time, to work it out.
3) Add the solute to the water and stir until most of the solute has dissolved.
4) Now heat the solution gently until all of the solute has dissolved.
5) Leave the solution to cool. Record the temperature at which crystals start to appear.
   You might need to use an ice bath to cool the solution.
6) Divide the mass of the solute by the mass of the water then multiply by 100 to find the solubility (in g per 100 g of solvent) at this temperature.
   (This is the formula for calculating solubility that's shown on the next page.)
7) Repeat the experiment several times. Use a slightly greater volume of water each time, but always add the same mass of solute that you used in the first experiment.
8) Find the solubility at each temperature. Plot these values on a graph to make a solubility curve.

How do dissolved soldiers greet their General? They give a solute...

Learning all the definitions in chemistry can be a right pain, but it's worth it for those juicy marks in the exam.

Q1 What is meant by the 'solubility' of a substance? [1 mark]

Q2 Look at the first graph on this page. What is the solubility when the temperature is 70 °C? [1 mark]

Unit 1c — Water and the Earth

Investigating Solubility

You can measure solubility by making saturated solutions at different temperatures.

You Can Investigate how Temperature Affects Solubility

Here's how you could investigate how the solubility of solid ammonium chloride is affected by temperature:

1) Measure out a set volume of water and put it in a boiling tube.
2) Weigh out a mass of ammonium chloride that's greater than the amount that will dissolve in this much water. Add it to the water.

   Adding an excess of the solid means you can be sure that the solution you've made is saturated.

3) Give the solution a good stir and place the boiling tube in a water bath set to 25 °C.
4) After 5 minutes, check that all of the excess solid has sunk to the bottom of the tube and use a thermometer to check that the solution has reached 25 °C.
5) Filter out the excess ammonium chloride and allow it to dry. You can then weigh it and go on to work out how much of the solute is dissolved in the solution (see below).
6) Repeat steps 1-5 several times more, but with the water bath at different temperatures (e.g. 35 °C, 45 °C, etc.).
7) You can use the different masses to work out the solubility at each temperature (see below).
8) You could plot the results on a graph to give a solubility curve, like the one on the previous page.

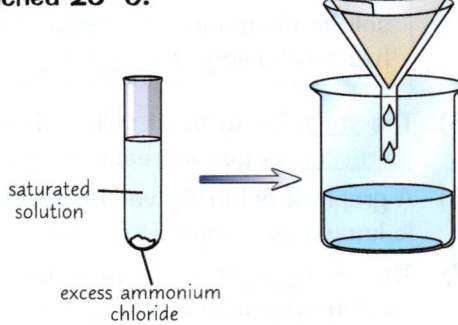

You Can Calculate the Solubility from the Masses of the Solid and Water

You can use this formula to find the mass of solute dissolved from the results of the experiment above:

$$\text{Mass of solute dissolved (g)} = \text{mass of solid added to solvent (g)} - \text{mass of dried excess solid (g)}$$

And here's the general formula for calculating the solubility of a solid:

$$\text{solubility (g per 100 g of solvent)} = \frac{\text{mass of solute dissolved (g)}}{\text{mass of water (g)}} \times 100$$

Example: Use the following experimental data to find the solubility of ammonium chloride at 35 °C.

Mass of ammonium chloride added	65.0 g
Mass of excess dried ammonium chloride	13.3 g
Mass of water	120.0 g

Method:
1) Find the mass of the solute dissolved in the solution:
   mass of solute dissolved = mass of solid added − mass of dried excess solid
   = 65.0 g − 13.3 g = 51.7 g
2) Use the equation above to calculate the solubility:
   solubility = (mass of solute dissolved ÷ mass of water) × 100
   = (51.7 ÷ 120.0) × 100 = 43.0833... = 43.1 g per 100 g of water (to 3 s.f.)

Adding some sugar to your morning beverage — solubilitea...

Who knows, you might be lucky enough to get to do this experiment in class. Wouldn't that be exciting...

Q1 Describe an experiment that could be used to determine the solubility of a solid at 40 °C. [5 marks]

Unit 1c — Water and the Earth

Water Hardness

Water where you live might be hard or soft. It depends on the rocks your water meets on its way to you.

Hard Water Makes Scum and Scale

1) If you live in an area with soft water, you'll get a nice lather when you use soap. But with hard water you get a nasty scum instead. The problem is dissolved ions in the water (see below) reacting with the soap to make scum which is insoluble. So to get a decent lather you need to use more soap.
2) When heated, hard water also forms furring or scale (mostly calcium carbonate) on the insides of pipes, boilers and kettles. This makes them less efficient and can even completely block pipes.

Hardness is Caused by Ca^{2+} and Mg^{2+} Ions

1) Most hard water is hard because it contains lots of calcium ions (Ca^{2+}) and magnesium ions (Mg^{2+}).
2) Rain falling on some types of rocks (e.g. limestone, chalk and gypsum) can dissolve compounds like magnesium sulfate (which is soluble), and calcium sulfate (which is also soluble, though only a bit).
3) Ca^{2+} ions are good for healthy teeth and bones.
4) Studies found that people who live in hard water areas are at less risk of developing heart disease than people who live in soft water areas. This could be to do with the minerals in hard water.

Remove the Dissolved Ca^{2+} and Mg^{2+} Ions to Make Hard Water Soft

There are two kinds of hardness — temporary and permanent.
- Temporary hardness is caused by dissolved calcium hydrogencarbonate or magnesium hydrogencarbonate.
- Permanent hardness is caused by dissolved calcium sulfate or magnesium sulfate (amongst other things).

1) Temporary hardness can be removed cheaply — by boiling water in an ordinary kettle. But this won't get rid of permanent hardness, and you can only use it to treat small amounts of water.

   The metal hydrogencarbonate decomposes on heating to form an insoluble metal carbonate. This solid is the 'limescale' in your kettle.

   e.g. | calcium hydrogencarbonate → calcium carbonate + water + carbon dioxide |

2) Both types of hardness can be softened by adding sodium carbonate, Na_2CO_3 (washing soda). This causes limescale to form, which can block washing machine pipes.

   The carbonate ions react with the Ca^{2+} and Mg^{2+} ions to make an insoluble precipitate (limescale) that is either calcium carbonate or magnesium carbonate. Removing the Ca^{2+} and Mg^{2+} ions from the water makes it soft.

   e.g. $Ca^{2+}_{(aq)} + CO_3^{2-}_{(aq)} \rightarrow CaCO_{3(s)}$

3) Both types of hardness can be removed by running water through 'ion exchange columns' which are sold in shops. This is a continuous process that uses concentrated sodium chloride, which is low cost and widely available. However, ion exchange columns are quite expensive to buy.

   These columns have big resin molecules with lots of sodium ions (or hydrogen ions) attached to them. They 'exchange' these for calcium or magnesium ions in the water that runs through them.

   e.g. $Na_2Resin_{(s)} + Ca^{2+}_{(aq)} \rightarrow CaResin_{(s)} + 2Na^+_{(aq)}$

   ('Resin' is a huge insoluble resin molecule.)

   For every Ca^{2+} ion removed from the water, two Na^+ ions are released from the resin.

   All of the sodium ions will eventually be used up so no more calcium ions can be removed. The columns can be regenerated by being rinsed in a cheap sodium chloride solution so that they can be used again.

And if the water's really hard, you can chip your teeth...

Hard water provides minerals that are good for health, but it creates an awful lot of unnecessary expense.

Q1 Explain how ion exchange columns remove hardness from water. [2 marks]

Unit 1c — Water and the Earth

PRACTICAL: Measuring Water Hardness

If you live in an area of hard water you might already know about it because you sometimes get a grimy layer of scale floating on the top of your tea... Plus you get through more shampoo than you can shake a stick at...

Use Titration to Compare the Hardness of Water Samples

Method

1) Fill a burette with 50 cm³ of soap solution.
2) Add 50 cm³ of the first water sample to a flask.
3) Use the burette to add 1 cm³ of soap solution to the flask.
4) Put a bung in the flask and shake for 5 seconds.
5) Repeat steps 3 and 4 until a good lasting lather is formed. (A lasting lather is one where the bubbles cover the surface for at least 30 seconds.)
6) Record how much soap solution was needed to create a lasting lather.
7) Repeat steps 1-6 with the other water samples.
8) Next, boil fresh samples of each type of water for ten minutes, and repeat the experiment.

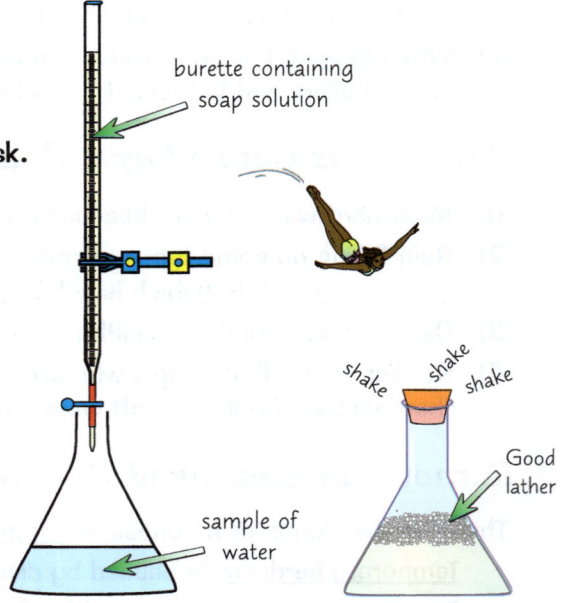

You could also determine the hardness in different samples of water by mixing the samples with a given volume of soap solution and measuring the amount of lather produced. The more lather produced, the softer the water sample.

Results

This method was carried out on 3 types of water — distilled water, local tap water and imported tap water. Here's the table of results:

Sample	Volume of soap solution needed to give a good lather	
	using unboiled water (cm³)	using boiled water (cm³)
Distilled	1	1
Local water	7	1
Imported water	14	8

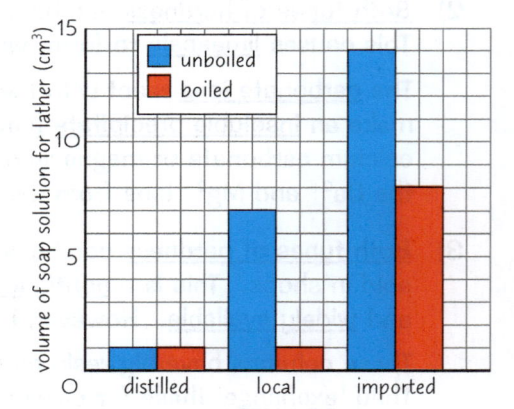

1) You can represent these results with a bar chart. The results tell you the following things about the water:
2) Distilled water contains little or no hardness — only the minimum volume of soap solution was needed.
3) The sample of imported water contains more hardness than local water — more soap solution was needed to produce a lather.
4) The local water contains temporary hardness — all the hardness is removed by boiling. You can tell because the same volume of soap solution was needed for boiled local water and distilled water.
5) The imported water contains both temporary and permanent hardness. 8 cm³ of soap solution is still needed to produce a lather after boiling.
6) If your brain's really switched on, you'll see that the local water and the imported water contain the same amount of temporary hardness. In both cases, the amount of soap solution needed in the boiled sample is 6 cm³ less than in the unboiled sample.

My water's harder than yours...

Read this page carefully to make sure you really understand this method. Once you're confident, try this question.

Q1   Describe an investigation that could be used to test which of three water solutions was temporary hard water, which was permanent hard water and which was soft water.   [6 marks]

Unit 1c — Water and the Earth

The Earth's Structure

This page is all about the structure of the Earth — what the planet's like inside, and how scientists study it...

The Earth has a Crust, a Mantle and a Core

1) The crust is Earth's thin outer layer of solid rock (its average depth is 20 km).
2) The lithosphere includes the crust and upper part of the mantle, and is made up of a jigsaw of 'tectonic plates'. The lithosphere is relatively cold and rigid, and is over 100 km thick in places.
3) The mantle is the semi-solid section between the crust and the core. Near the crust it's fairly rigid. As you go deeper into the mantle the temperature increases — here it becomes less rigid and can flow slowly.
4) At the centre of the Earth is the core, which is made mainly of iron.
5) The core is just over half the Earth's radius. The inner core is solid, while the outer core is molten liquid.
6) Radioactive decay is responsible for a lot of the heat inside the Earth. This heat creates convection currents in the mantle, which causes the plates of the lithosphere to move.

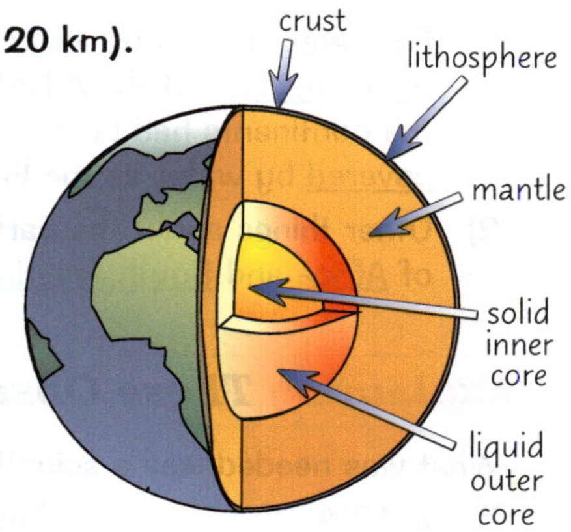

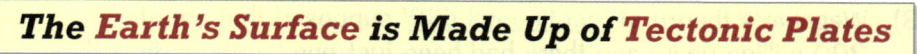

The Earth's Surface is Made Up of Tectonic Plates

1) The crust and the upper part of the mantle are cracked into about seven major pieces and lots of minor pieces called tectonic plates. These plates are a bit like big rafts that 'float' on the mantle.
2) The plates don't stay in one place though. That's because the convection currents in the mantle cause the plates to drift.
3) This map shows the edges of the plates as they are now, and the directions they're moving in (red arrows).
4) Most of the plates are moving at speeds of a few cm per year relative to each other.
5) Occasionally, the plates move very suddenly, causing an earthquake.
6) Volcanoes and earthquakes often occur at the boundary between two tectonic plates.

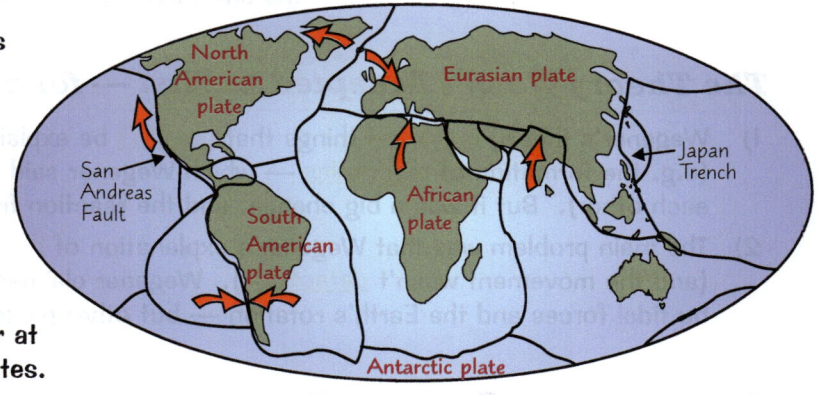

Earthquakes and Volcanoes Show Tectonic Plates

If you plot active volcanoes and earthquakes on a map of the world, you can see that the markers tend to sit along the same lines as the plate boundaries (see page 45).

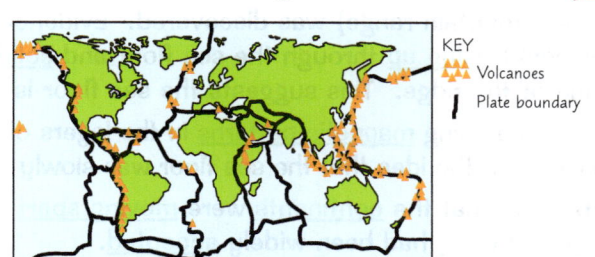

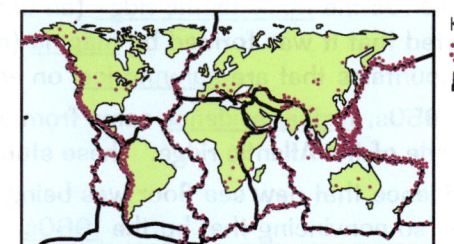

Wash tectonic plates by hand — they won't fit in the dishwasher...

So everyone standing on the surface of our little blue-green planet is actually floating round very slowly on a sea of semi-liquid rock. Make sure you understand the stuff about tectonic plates — there's more coming up...

Q1 Which metal mostly makes up the Earth's core? [1 mark]

Unit 1c — Water and the Earth

Plate Tectonics

The idea that the Earth's surface is made up of moving plates of rock took a while to catch on.

Observations About the Earth Hadn't Been Explained

1) For years, fossils of very similar plants and animals had been found on opposite sides of the Atlantic Ocean. Most people thought this was because the continents had been linked by 'land bridges', which had sunk or been covered by water as the Earth cooled. But not everyone was convinced.

2) Other things about the Earth puzzled people too — like why the coastlines of Africa and South America look like they could fit together.

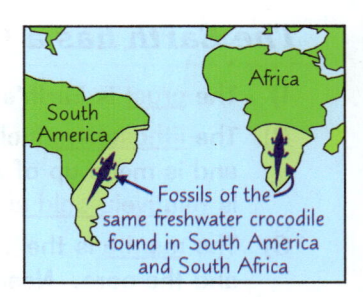

Fossils of the same freshwater crocodile found in South America and South Africa

Explaining These Observations Needed a Leap of Imagination

What was needed was a scientist with a bit of insight... a smidgeon of creativity... a touch of genius...

1) In 1914 Alfred Wegener hypothesised that Africa and South America had previously been one continent which had then split. He started to look for more evidence to back up his hypothesis. He found it...

2) For example there were matching layers of the same age and type of rocks on different continents, and fossils of similar plants and animals found on opposite sides of huge oceans.

3) Wegener's theory of 'continental drift' supposed that about 300 million years ago there had been just one 'supercontinent' — which he called Pangaea. According to Wegener, Pangaea broke into smaller chunks, and these chunks (our modern-day continents) are still slowly 'drifting' apart. This idea is the basis behind the modern theory of plate tectonics.

The Theory Wasn't Accepted at First — for a Variety of Reasons

1) Wegener's theory explained things that couldn't be explained by the 'land bridge' theory (e.g. the formation of mountains — which Wegener said happened as continents smashed into each other). But it was a big change, and the reaction from other scientists was hostile.

2) The main problem was that Wegener's explanation of how the 'drifting' happened wasn't convincing (and the movement wasn't detectable). Wegener claimed the continents' movement could be caused by tidal forces and the Earth's rotation — but other geologists showed that this was impossible.

Eventually, the Evidence Became Overwhelming

1) As far back as the 1930s, scientists began to suggest that it could be convection currents in the mantle that caused the plates to move. But at that time many people still weren't convinced by the theory of continental drift, because there wasn't much evidence to show that the plates actually were moving.

2) In the 1940s the Mid-Atlantic ridge (an underwater mountain range) was discovered. Evidence suggested that it was formed by magma (molten rock) rising up through the sea floor and solidifying, to form mountains that are symmetrical on each side of the ridge. This suggests the sea floor is spreading.

3) In the 1950s, further evidence came from studies of matching magnetic patterns in the layers of rocks on either side of the Atlantic ridge. These studies backed up the idea that the sea floor was slowly spreading.

4) The evidence that new sea floor was being created and that the continents were moving apart became so convincing that by the 1960s, Wegener's theory had been widely accepted.

I told you so — but no one ever believes me...

Wegener wasn't right about everything, but his main idea was correct. The scientific community was a bit slow to accept it, but once there was more evidence to support it, they got on board. That's science for you...

Q1   Give one piece of evidence that Wegener gave for his theory of continental drift.   [1 mark]

Unit 1c — Water and the Earth

Plate Boundaries

The Earth's surface is made of huge floating plates that are constantly moving... Rock on.

There are Three Types of Plate Boundary

1) The outer layer of the Earth is the crust (page 43) — the crust is divided into slabs called tectonic plates that float on the mantle.
2) Plates are made of two types of crust — continental (thick crust beneath the land) and oceanic (thinner crust beneath the sea).
3) The plates move slowly because of convection currents in the mantle underneath the crust.
4) The places where plates meet are called plate boundaries.

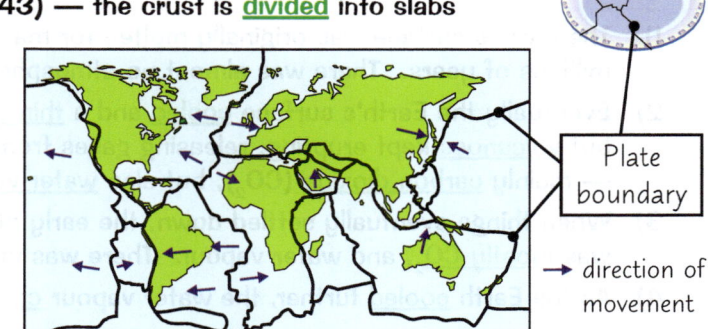

Constructive Boundaries

1) Constructive boundaries are where two plates are moving away from each other. This usually happens at a mid-ocean ridge, e.g. at the mid-Atlantic ridge.
2) Magma (molten rock) rises from the mantle to fill the gap and cools, creating new crust made from igneous rock.
3) You get lots of volcanic activity and earthquakes at constructive boundaries.

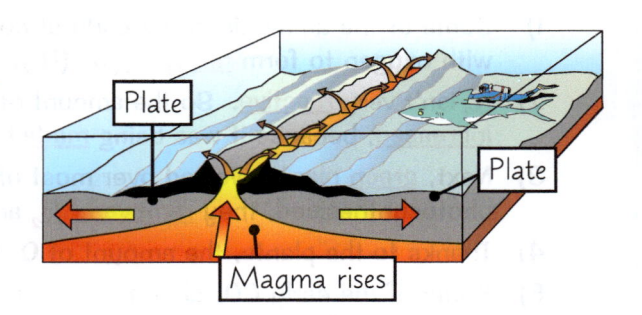

Destructive Boundaries

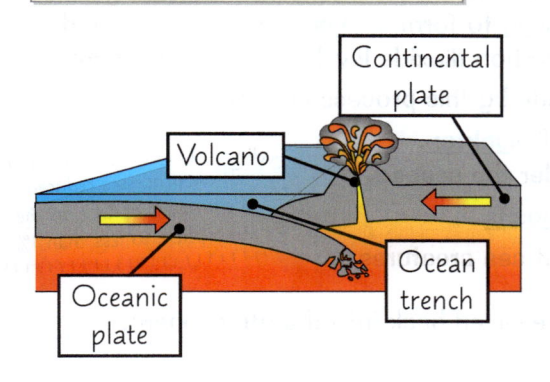

1) Destructive boundaries are where two plates are moving towards each other, e.g. along the west coast of South America.
2) Where an oceanic plate meets a continental plate, the denser oceanic plate is forced down into the mantle and melted to give magma. This creates volcanoes and ocean trenches (very deep sections of the ocean floor where the oceanic plate goes down).
3) Earthquakes also often occur at destructive boundaries.

Where two continental plates collide, the ground folds and creates mountain ranges.

Conservative Boundaries

1) Conservative boundaries are where two plates are moving sideways past each other, or are moving in the same direction but at different speeds, e.g. along the west coast of the USA.
2) Crust isn't created or destroyed.
3) This type of movement creates powerful earthquakes.
4) No volcanoes are created since neither plate is melted.

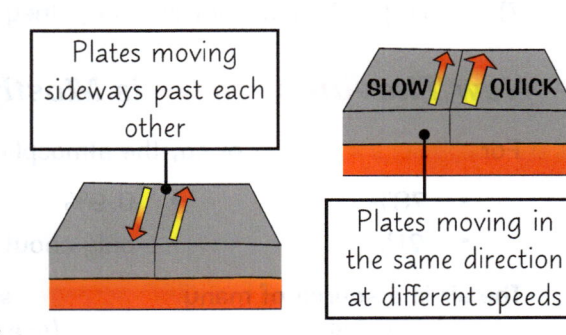

Giant plates whacking into each other — smashing stuff...

That's it for all this Earth structure and plate tectonics stuff. Make sure you understand the Earth's structure and what tectonic plates are — try writing out a quick description of each type of plate boundary to see what you know.

Q1   Describe how constructive boundaries create new crust.   [2 marks]

Unit 1c — Water and the Earth

The Atmosphere

Scientists have looked at evidence from rocks, air bubbles in ice and fossils to see how our atmosphere has changed over millions of years. Here's the most widely accepted theory about how our atmosphere evolved...

Volcanoes Gave Out Carbon Dioxide and Water Vapour

1) The Earth's surface was originally molten for many millions of years. There was almost no atmosphere.
2) Eventually the Earth's surface cooled and a thin crust formed, but volcanoes kept erupting, releasing gases from inside the Earth — mainly carbon dioxide (CO_2), but also water vapour and ammonia.
3) When things eventually settled down, the early atmosphere was mostly CO_2, and water vapour. There was very little oxygen.
4) As the Earth cooled further, the water vapour condensed to form the oceans.

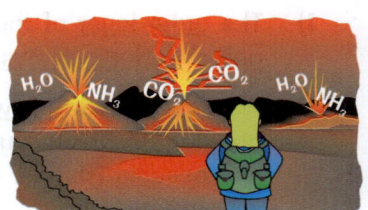

This change happened fairly quickly compared to the changes below, which took billions of years.

Green Plants Evolved and Produced Oxygen

1) Some of the ammonia in the early atmosphere reacted with oxygen to form nitrogen gas (N_2).
2) N_2 isn't very reactive. So the amount of N_2 in the atmosphere increased, because it was being made but not broken down.
3) Next, green plants evolved over most of the Earth. As they photosynthesised, they removed CO_2 and produced O_2.
4) Thanks to the plants, the amount of O_2 in the air gradually built up and the level of CO_2 fell.
5) Some of the early CO_2 also dissolved into the oceans. And much of the remaining CO_2 eventually got locked up in fossil fuels and sedimentary rocks:

- When ancient marine plants and animals died, they fell to the seabed and were buried by sediment. Over millions of years, they were compressed to form sedimentary rocks, oil and gas — locking the carbon within them and reducing carbon dioxide levels in the atmosphere.
- Things like coal, crude oil and natural gas that are made by this process are called 'fossil fuels'.
- Crude oil and natural gas are formed from deposits of plankton. Pockets of these fossil fuels get trapped in rocks under the seabed.
- Coal is a sedimentary rock made from thick plant deposits.
- Limestone and chalk formed from the shells of ancient sea creatures.

These processes reduced the amount of CO_2 in the atmosphere to less than 1%.

6) As we burn fossil fuels, more of this 'locked up' CO_2 gets released back into the atmosphere. O_2 is used up too.
7) When plants and animals respire they also release CO_2 into the atmosphere (and take in O_2).

Now The Atmosphere is Mostly Nitrogen and Oxygen

For 200 million years or so, the atmosphere has been about how it is now:

- 78% nitrogen
- 21% oxygen
- 0.9% argon (and other noble gases)
- only about 0.04% carbon dioxide

Air also contains a variable amount of water vapour.

The air is a source of many useful gases such as nitrogen, oxygen, neon and argon. These gases can be separated using fractional distillation (see page 87) because they all have different boiling points.

I went to a restaurant on the moon — nice view, no atmosphere...

We can breathe easy knowing that our atmosphere has developed into a lovely oxygen-rich one. Aaaahh.

Q1 The atmosphere of Earth was originally composed mostly of carbon dioxide. Explain how the proportion of carbon dioxide in the atmosphere decreased over time. [3 marks]

Unit 1c — Water and the Earth

Greenhouse Gases and Climate Change

Greenhouse gases are important but can also cause problems — it's all about keeping a delicate balance.

Carbon Dioxide is a Greenhouse Gas

1) Greenhouse gases like carbon dioxide, methane and water vapour act like an insulating layer in the Earth's atmosphere — this helps the Earth to stay warm enough to support life.
2) All particles absorb certain frequencies of radiation. Greenhouse gases don't absorb the incoming short wavelength radiation from the Sun — but they do absorb the long wavelength radiation that gets radiated back from the Earth. Then they re-radiate it in all directions — including back towards the Earth. The long wavelength radiation is thermal radiation, so it results in warming of the surface of the Earth. This is the greenhouse effect.
3) Some forms of human activity affect the amount of greenhouse gases in the atmosphere. For example carbon that is 'locked up' in fossil fuels is released as carbon dioxide when fossil fuels are burned.

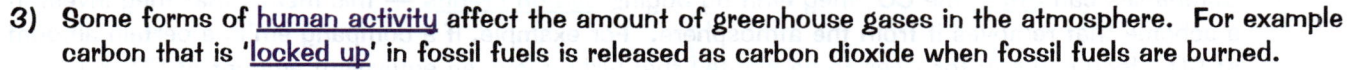

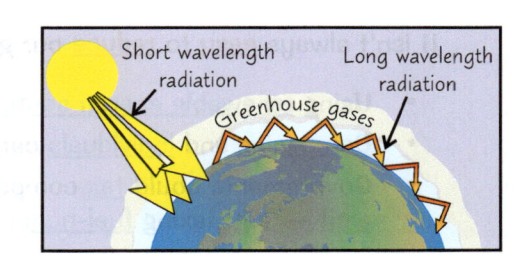

Increasing Carbon Dioxide is Linked to Climate Change

1) Over the last 200 years, the percentage of carbon dioxide in the atmosphere has increased — this correlates with an increased use of fossil fuels by people as well as an increase in global temperature (global warming).
2) The Earth's temperature varies naturally, but recently the average temperature of the Earth's surface has been increasing. Most scientists agree that extra CO_2 and other greenhouse gases from human activity are causing this increase and this will lead to further climate change.
3) Many studies looking at rising CO_2 levels and climate change have produced similar findings — increasing our confidence in the evidence.

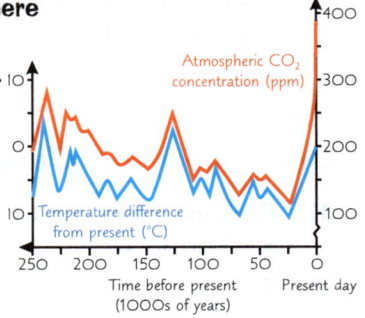

Historical Data is Much Less Accurate Than Current Records

1) Current global temperature and carbon dioxide levels can be worked out pretty accurately as they're based on measurements taken all over the world.
2) Historical data is less accurate — less data was taken over fewer locations and the methods used to collect the data were less accurate. If you go back far enough, there are no records of global temperature and carbon dioxide levels at all...
3) But there are ways to estimate past data. For example, you can analyse fossils, tree rings or gas bubbles trapped in ice sheets to estimate past levels of atmospheric carbon dioxide.
4) The problem with using these kinds of measurements is that they're less precise than current measurements made using instrumental sampling. They're also less representative of global levels.

Climate Change Could Have Dangerous Consequences

The Earth's climate is complex, but it's still important to make predictions about the possible consequences of climate change so that policy-makers can make decisions now. For example:

> 1) An increase in global temperature could lead to increased melting of polar ice caps, sea ice and glaciers — causing a further rise in sea levels.
> 2) Changes in climate and rainfall patterns could cause some areas to get hotter and drier, leading to droughts, while others get more rain, leading to flooding.

Give the climate some privacy — it's changing...

It's not all depressing news. There are steps we can take to cut our carbon dioxide emissions coming up, so chin up.

Q1 Give an example of an environmental problem that could be caused by global warming. [1 mark]

Unit 1c — Water and the Earth

Reducing Pollution and Tests for Gases

When you burn fossil fuels you release lots of carbon dioxide — and some other nasties like sulfur dioxide too.

There are Ways of Reducing Greenhouse Gas Emissions

It isn't always easy to reduce our greenhouse gas emissions — here are a few ways that it can be done:

- Using renewable energy sources (like solar or wind energy) or nuclear energy instead of fossil fuels.
- Companies and individuals can reduce their energy use whenever possible.
- Governments could tax companies or individuals based on the amount of greenhouse gases they emit — e.g. taxing fuel-hungry cars could mean that people choose to buy more fuel-efficient ones.

Large-scale greenhouse gas producers can also take steps to deal with the gases they do produce:

- Companies can offset the CO_2 they emit by buying carbon credits — this means that they invest in a scheme that removes it from the atmosphere. For example, if a company emits a certain amount of CO_2, they can pay for trees to be planted that will remove an equivalent amount of CO_2 by photosynthesis. If a business offsets all its greenhouse gas emissions, it's said to be carbon neutral.
- There's also technology that captures the CO_2 produced by burning fossil fuels before it's released into the atmosphere. The CO_2 can then be stored deep underground in gaps in the rocks. This is called carbon capture and storage.

Sulfur Dioxide Causes Acid Rain

1) Carbon dioxide isn't the only gas produced when fossil fuels are burned — sulfur dioxide (SO_2) is a problem too.
2) The sulfur dioxide comes from compounds containing sulfur in the fossil fuels.
3) When sulfur dioxide mixes with water in clouds, it forms dilute sulfuric acid. This falls as acid rain — normal rain has a pH of about 5.5 but acid rain has a lower pH of 2-4.
4) Acid rain causes lakes to become acidic and many plants and animals die as a result.
5) Acid rain kills trees and other plants, damages limestone buildings and stone statues and can also make metal statues and buildings (like bridges) corrode faster.
6) Soil and lakes that have been affected by acid rain can be treated with a weak alkali to neutralise them.
7) A technique called sulfur scrubbing is used in power stations to remove the sulfur dioxide before gases escape.

You Can Test for Carbon Dioxide and Oxygen Gas

Carbon Dioxide:
Bubbling carbon dioxide through an aqueous solution of calcium hydroxide (also known as limewater) makes the solution turn milky.

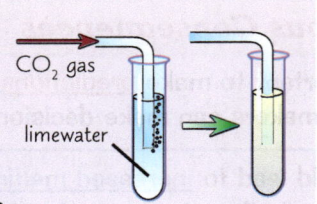

Oxygen:
If you put a glowing splint inside a test tube containing oxygen, the oxygen will relight the glowing splint.

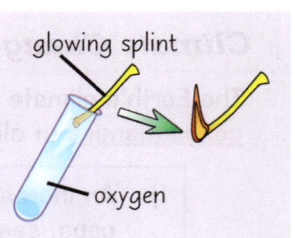

Cutting greenhouse gas production — emission possible...?

If you're wondering why the gas tests are on this page, it's not just 'cause I had to fit them in *somewhere*. Honest...

Q1   Suggest one thing a company could do to reduce the harmful effect of the carbon dioxide it emits.   [1 mark]

Q2   Give two examples of problems caused by acid rain.   [2 marks]

Unit 1c — Water and the Earth

Revision Questions for Unit 1c

Unit 1c is finally finished — time to see what you've actually remembered with some lovely questions.
- Try these questions and tick off each one when you get it right.
- When you've done all the questions for a topic and are completely happy with it, tick off the topic.

Water Treatment (p.37-38)
1) Name two man-made pollutants that may be present in water sources.
2) Give one advantage and one disadvantage of adding fluoride ions to drinking water.
3) Give one reason why distilling sea water isn't always a viable option for producing drinking water.
4) Draw the apparatus you would use to carry out simple distillation.

Solubility (p.39-40)
5) Define the term 'saturated solution'.
6) What variables go on the x-axis and y-axis of a solubility curve?
7) Write down the formula that you would use to calculate the solubility of a substance in units of g/100 g of solvent.

Hard Water (p.41-42)
8) What are the two main ions that cause water hardness?
9) Give two possible health benefits of drinking hard water.
10) Give two methods of removing permanent hardness from water.

The Earth's Structure and Tectonics (p.43-45)
11) Describe the inner structure of the Earth.
12) Give the name of Wegener's 'supercontinent'.
13) Briefly explain why some scientists didn't accept Wegener's theory of continental drift at first.
14) Describe what happens to the plates at each of these types of plate boundary:
    a) Constructive
    b) Destructive
    c) Conservative

The Atmosphere (p.46-48)
15) Name two of the gases given out by volcanoes millions of years ago that formed the Earth's early atmosphere.
16) How was nitrogen gas originally put into the atmosphere?
17) What are the current % proportions of oxygen, nitrogen, argon and carbon dioxide in the atmosphere?
18) Explain how the greenhouse effect works to keep the Earth warm.
19) How is human activity leading to an increase in carbon dioxide in the atmosphere?
20) Explain how acid rain is formed.
21) What is the chemical test for oxygen?

Unit 1c — Water and the Earth

Unit 1d — Rate of Chemical Change and Thermal Decomposition

Reaction Rates

Reactions can be fast or slow — you've probably already realised that. It's exciting stuff. Honest.

The Rate of Reaction is a Measure of How Fast the Reaction Happens

The rate of a reaction is how quickly a reaction happens. It can be observed either by measuring how quickly the reactants are used up or how quickly the products are formed. The rate of a reaction can be calculated using the following formula:

$$\text{Rate of Reaction} = \frac{\text{amount of reactant used or amount of product formed}}{\text{time}}$$

It's usually a lot easier to measure products forming.

You Can Do Experiments to Follow Reaction Rates

There are different ways that the rate of a reaction can be measured. Here are three examples:

Precipitation

1) This method works for any reaction where mixing two see-through solutions produces a precipitate, which clouds the solution.
2) You mix the two reactant solutions and put the flask on a piece of paper that has a mark on it.
3) Observe the mark through the mixture and measure how long it takes for the mark to be obscured. The faster it disappears, the faster the reaction.
4) The result is subjective — different people might not agree on exactly when the mark 'disappears'.
5) Using data-logging apparatus (e.g. a light sensor connected to a computer) can help you decide more accurately when the mixture reaches a certain level of cloudiness.

You can use this method to investigate how temperature affects the rate of the reaction between sodium thiosulfate and dilute hydrochloric acid. See page 52.

Change in Mass (Usually Gas Given Off)

1) You can measure the rate of a reaction that produces a gas (e.g. the reaction of an acid with a metal or a carbonate) using a mass balance.
2) As the gas is released, the lost mass is easily measured on the balance. The quicker the reading on the balance drops, the faster the reaction.
3) You know the reaction has finished when the reading on the balance stops changing.
4) You can use your results to plot a graph of change in mass against time.
5) This method does release the gas produced straight into the room — so if the gas is harmful, you must take safety precautions, e.g. do the experiment in a fume cupboard.

The cotton wool lets gases through but stops any solid, liquid or aqueous reactants flying out during the reaction.

The Volume of Gas Given Off

1) You can use a gas syringe to measure the volume of gas given off.
2) The more gas given off during a set time interval, the faster the reaction.
3) You can tell the reaction has finished when no more gas is produced.
4) You can use your results to plot a graph of gas volume against time elapsed.
5) You need to be careful that you're using the right size gas syringe for your experiment though — if the reaction is too vigorous, you can blow the plunger out of the end of the syringe.

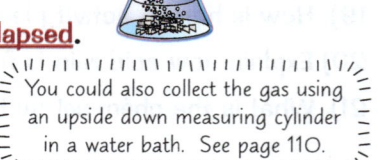

You could also collect the gas using an upside down measuring cylinder in a water bath. See page 110.

Retraction rate — how fast my mates disappear when I tell a joke...

Lots of different ways to follow reaction rates here — well... three. Precipitation, mass loss and gas formation.

Q1 Outline how you could use a mass balance to measure the rate of a reaction where a gas is formed. [3 marks]

Q2 Give one advantage of using data-logging apparatus in reaction rate investigations. [1 mark]

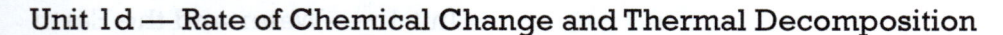

Unit 1d — Rate of Chemical Change and Thermal Decomposition

Rate Experiments Involving Gases — PRACTICAL

You'll probably have to measure the rate of a reaction in class at some point. Time to learn how to do it...

You can Measure how Surface Area Affects Rate

Here's how you can carry out an experiment to measure the effect of surface area on rate, using marble chips and hydrochloric acid.

1) Set the apparatus up as shown in the diagram on the right.
2) Measure the volume of gas produced using a gas syringe (or a measuring cylinder in a water bath — see page 110). Take readings at regular time intervals and record the results in a table.
3) You can plot a graph of your results — time goes on the x-axis and volume goes on the y-axis.
4) Repeat the experiment with exactly the same volume and concentration of acid, and exactly the same mass of marble chips, but with the marble more crunched up.
5) Then repeat with the same mass of powdered chalk.

It's important your system is airtight so no gas escapes.

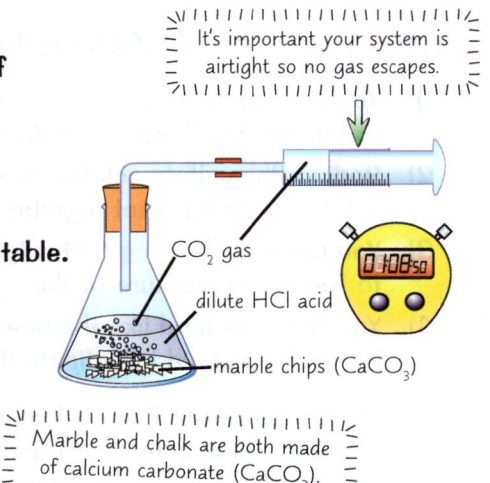

CO_2 gas
dilute HCl acid
marble chips ($CaCO_3$)

Marble and chalk are both made of calcium carbonate ($CaCO_3$).

Finer Particles of Solid Mean a Higher Rate

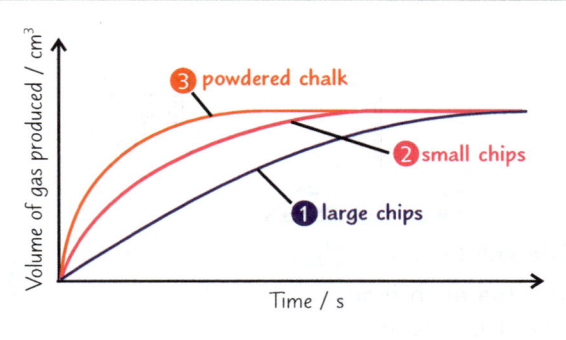

1) The sooner a reaction finishes, the faster the reaction.
2) The steeper the gradient of the graph, the faster the rate of reaction. When the line becomes flat, no more gas is being produced and the reaction has finished.
3) Using finer particles means that the marble has a larger surface area.
4) Lines 1 to 3 on the graph on the left show that the finer the particles are (and the greater the surface area of the solid reactants), the faster the reaction and the sooner the reaction finishes.

Graph: Volume of gas produced / cm^3 vs Time / s — ❸ powdered chalk, ❷ small chips, ❶ large chips.

Changing the Concentration of Acid Affects the Rate too

The reaction between marble chips and hydrochloric acid is good for measuring how changing the reactant concentration affects reaction rate. This experiment can also be carried out with a strip of magnesium instead of marble chips.

You could also measure the rates of these reactions by measuring the loss of mass as the gas is produced.

More Concentrated Solutions Mean a Higher Rate

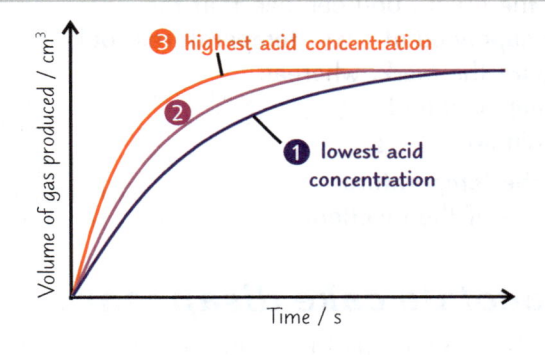

1) You can measure the effect of concentration on rate by following the same method described above. However, this time you repeat the experiment with exactly the same mass and surface area of marble chips and exactly the same volume of acid, but using different concentrations of acid.
2) Lines 1 to 3 on the graph show that a higher concentration gives a faster reaction, with the reaction finishing sooner.

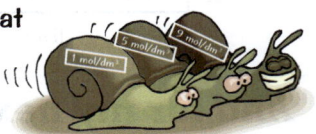

Graph: Volume of gas produced / cm^3 vs Time / s — ❸ highest acid concentration, ❷, ❶ lowest acid concentration.

I prefer chalk to marble chips — I like the finer things in life...

Doing rate experiments lets you collect data. Collecting data lets you plot graphs, and you can use graphs to find reaction rates. But that's all still to come. I bet you're just itching to read on...

Q1 Describe how you could investigate how the surface area of calcium carbonate affects the rate of reaction between calcium carbonate and hydrochloric acid. [3 marks]

Unit 1d — Rate of Chemical Change and Thermal Decomposition

Rate Experiments Involving Precipitation

That's right — another page, another reaction rate experiment to learn. But this one involves a pretty precipitation reaction. Beautiful stuff, don't say I don't spoil you...

Reaction Rate is Also Affected by Temperature

PRACTICAL

1) You can see how temperature or concentration affects reaction rate by looking at the reaction between sodium thiosulfate and hydrochloric acid.
2) Sodium thiosulfate solution and hydrochloric acid are both clear, colourless solutions. They react together to form a yellow precipitate of sulfur.
3) You can use the time that it takes for the coloured precipitate to form as a measure of the rate of this reaction.
4) You use a method like the one on page 50 to carry out this experiment. Here's how you'd investigate the effect of temperature on the rate of reaction:

How temperature, concentration and pressure affect the rate of a reaction can be explained using particle theory (pages 54-55).

- Measure out fixed volumes of sodium thiosulfate solution (warmed to 60°C in a water bath) and hydrochloric acid, using a measuring cylinder.
- Mix the solutions in a conical flask. Place the flask over a black mark on a piece of paper which can be seen through the solution. Watch the black mark disappear through the cloudy, yellow sulfur and time how long it takes to go.

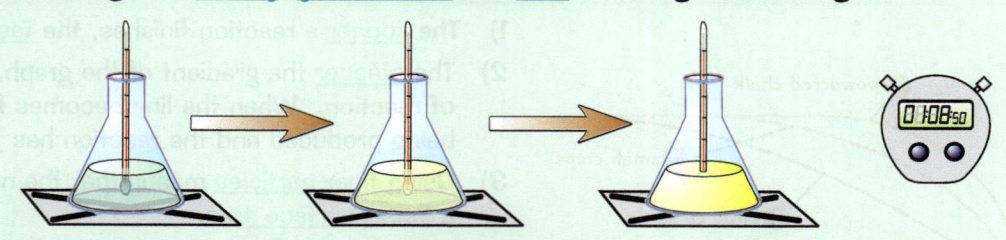

- The reaction can be repeated for sodium thiosulfate solutions at different temperatures.
- The depth and volumes of liquid must be kept the same each time. The concentrations of the solutions must also be kept the same.
- You can use your results to measure what effect changing the temperature has on the rate of the reaction. The shorter the length of time taken for the mark to be obscured, the faster the rate.

You'll need one lot of sodium thiosulfate solution that's been cooled to 5 °C and another lot that's been heated to 60 °C in a water bath. Then you just mix different proportions of these together to produce sodium thiosulfate solutions at a whole range of temperatures.

Higher Temperatures Mean a Higher Rate

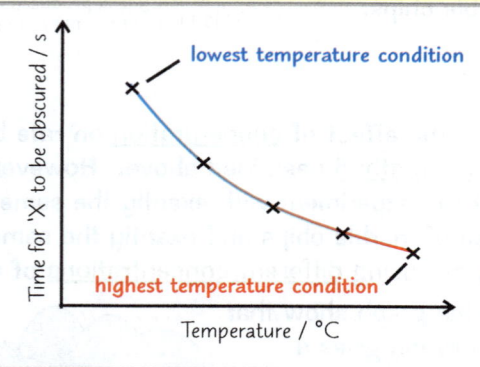

1) You can plot the time taken for the mark to disappear against the temperature of the reacting solutions.
2) If you look at the graph, you can see that the reactions that happened at lower temperatures took longer to obscure the mark, whereas the reactions happening at higher temperatures did so sooner.
3) So increasing the temperature increases the rate of the reaction.

You can calculate the rate of the reaction using $\frac{1}{time}$, and plot a graph of that too.

And for my next trick, I'll make this chocolate cake disappear...

When repeating this experiment, you need to keep everything exactly the same apart from the temperature — then you can sleep easy knowing that it was the temperature change that affected the reaction rate and not anything else.

Q1 Azim carries out an experiment to measure how temperature affects the rate of reaction between sodium thiosulfate and hydrochloric acid. He uses the time taken for a mark underneath the reaction vessel to be obscured as a measure of rate. How would you expect the time taken for the mark to disappear to change as the temperature of the reacting sodium thiosulfate was increased?

[1 mark]

Unit 1d — Rate of Chemical Change and Thermal Decomposition

Calculating Rates

You can work out rates of reaction using graphs. I bet you can't wait to find out how...

Faster Rates of Reaction are Shown by Steeper Gradients

1) If you have a graph of amount of product formed (or reactant used up) against time, then the gradient (slope) of the graph will be equal to the rate of the reaction.
2) The steeper the slope, the more product that is being formed (or reactant used up) per second, and so the faster the rate.

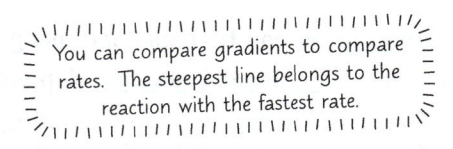

You can compare gradients to compare rates. The steepest line belongs to the reaction with the fastest rate.

Draw a Tangent to Find the Gradient of a Curve

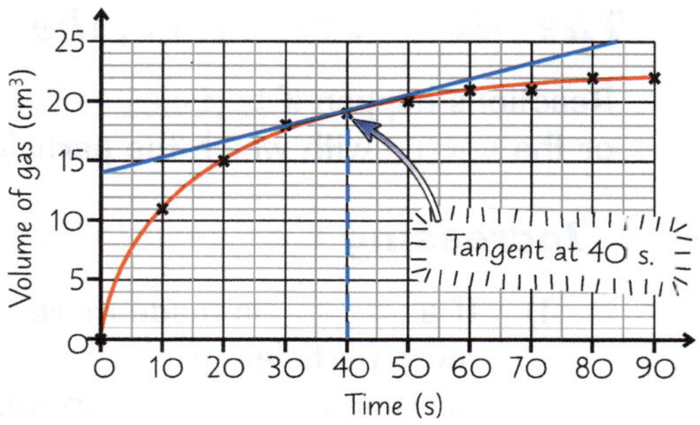

1) If your graph (or part of it) is a curve, the gradient, and therefore rate, is different at different points along the curve.
2) To find the gradient of the graph at a certain point, you'll have to draw a tangent at that point.
3) A tangent is just a line that touches the curve and has the same gradient as the line at that point.
4) To draw a tangent, place a ruler on the line of best fit at the point you're interested in, so you can see the whole curve. Adjust the ruler so the space between the ruler and the curve is the same on both sides of the point. Draw a line along the ruler to make the tangent.
5) The rate at that point is then just the gradient of the tangent.
6) The gradient of a straight line is given by the equation:

$$\text{gradient} = \text{change in } y \div \text{change in } x$$

EXAMPLE:
The graph below shows the concentration of product formed, measured at regular intervals during a chemical reaction. What is the rate of reaction at 3 minutes?

1) Position a ruler on the graph at the point where you want to know the rate — here it's 3 minutes.
2) Adjust the ruler until the space between the ruler and the curve is equal on both sides of the point.
3) Draw a line along the ruler to make the tangent. Extend the line right across the graph. 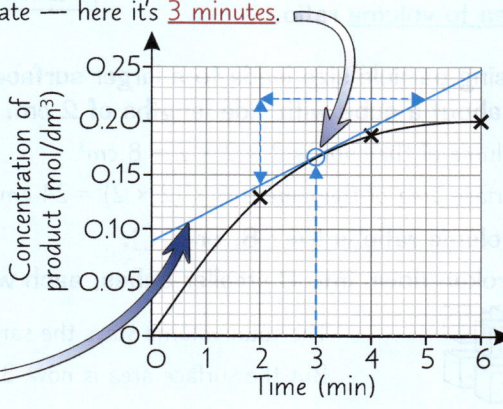
4) Pick two points on the line that are easy to read. Use them to calculate the gradient of the tangent in order to find the rate:

gradient = change in y ÷ change in x
= (0.22 − 0.14) ÷ (5.0 − 2.0)
= 0.08 ÷ 3.0
= 0.027

So, the rate of reaction at 3 minutes was 0.027 mol/dm³/min.

...and that's why I love cows — oh sorry, I went off on a tangent...

Lots of nifty graph skills here. Gradients aren't too hard, but make sure those tangents don't trip you up.
Use the graph at the top of the page to answer the following question:

Q1   Work out the rate of reaction at 20 seconds.   [2 marks]

Unit 1d — Rate of Chemical Change and Thermal Decomposition

Factors Affecting Rate of Reaction

The rate of a reaction depends on these things — temperature, concentration (or pressure for gases) and the size of the particles (for solids). The next couple of pages explain why these things affect the reaction rate.

Particles Must Collide with Enough Energy in Order to React

Reaction rates can be explained using particle theory. It's simple really.
The rate of a chemical reaction depends on:

- The collision frequency of reacting particles (how often they collide). The more successful collisions there are, the faster the reaction is.
- The energy transferred during a collision. There is a minimum amount of energy that particles need in order to react when they collide. Particles must collide with at least this minimum energy for the collision to be successful.

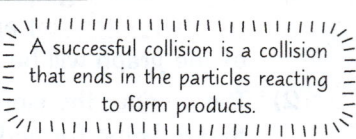

A successful collision is a collision that ends in the particles reacting to form products.

The More Collisions, the Higher the Rate of Reaction

Reactions happen if particles collide with enough energy to react. So, if you increase the number of collisions or the energy with which the particles collide, the reaction happens more quickly (i.e. the rate increases).

Increasing Concentration (or Pressure) Increases Rate

1) If a solution is made more concentrated it means there are more particles of reactant in the same volume. This makes collisions more likely, so the reaction rate increases.
2) In a gas, increasing the pressure means that the particles are more crowded. This means that the frequency of collisions between particles will increase — so the rate of reaction will also increase.

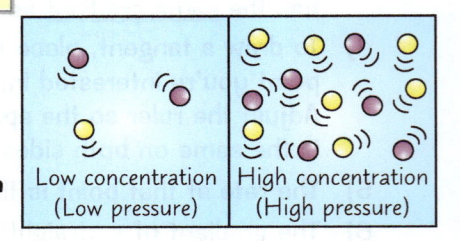

Low concentration (Low pressure) | High concentration (High pressure)

Smaller Solid Particles (or More Surface Area) Means a Higher Rate

1) If one reactant is a solid, breaking it into smaller pieces will increase its surface area to volume ratio (i.e. more of the solid will be exposed, compared to its overall volume).
2) The particles around it will have more area to work on, so the frequency of collisions will increase.
3) This means that the rate of reaction is faster for solids with a larger surface area to volume ratio.

Small surface area to volume ratio | Large surface area to volume ratio

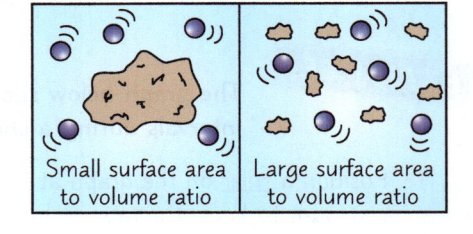

- You can see how decreasing particle size leads to a larger surface area to volume ratio by thinking about a cube with side lengths of 2 cm.

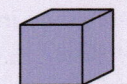

  The volume of the cube is $2 \times 2 \times 2 = 8$ cm^3.
  The surface area of the cube is $6 \times (2 \times 2) = 24$ cm^2.

  So the surface area to volume ratio is 24 : 8, or 3 : 1.

- The 2 cm cube can be broken down into 8 smaller cubes, each with side lengths of 1 cm.

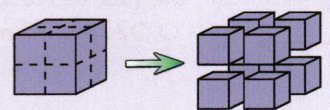

  The total volume stays the same: $8 \times (1 \times 1 \times 1) = 8$ cm^3.
  But the surface area is now: $8 \times (6 \times (1 \times 1)) = 48$ cm^2.

  So the surface area to volume ratio is 48 : 8, or 6 : 1.

Collision theory — it's always the other driver...

Remember — more collisions mean a faster reaction. But don't be fooled, as not every collision results in a reaction.

Q1 Describe the two factors, in terms of collisions, that affect the rate of reaction. [2 marks]

Q2 Explain why breaking a solid reactant into smaller pieces increases the rate of a reaction. [3 marks]

Unit 1d — Rate of Chemical Change and Thermal Decomposition

More Factors Affecting Rate of Reaction

As well as the effects of temperature, you also need to know about catalysts. Catalysts increase reaction rate and reduce energy costs in industrial reactions, so they're very important for commercial reasons.

Temperature Also Affects the Number of Collisions

1) When the temperature is increased the particles move faster. If they move faster, they're going to have more collisions.
2) Higher temperatures also increase the energy of the collisions, since the particles are moving faster. Reactions only happen if the particles collide with enough energy.
3) So at higher temperatures there will be more successful collisions (more particles will collide with enough energy to react). So increasing the temperature increases the rate of reaction.

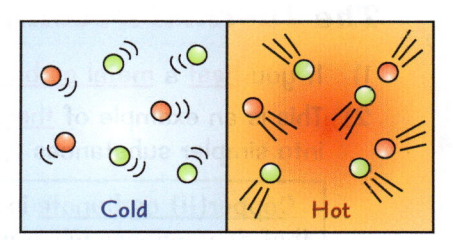

A Catalyst Increases the Rate of a Reaction

1) A catalyst is a substance which increases the rate of a reaction, without being chemically changed or used up in the reaction.
2) Using a catalyst won't change the products of the reaction — so the reaction equation will stay the same.
3) Because it isn't used up, you only need a tiny bit to catalyse large amounts of reactants.
4) Catalysts tend to be very fussy about which reactions they catalyse though — you can't just stick any old catalyst in a reaction and expect it to work.

A Catalyst Lowers the Energy Required for Successful Collisions

1) Catalysts work by decreasing the energy the particles need to have for a reaction to occur.
2) They do this by providing an alternative reaction pathway.
3) As a result, more of the particles have at least the minimum amount of energy needed for a reaction to occur when the particles collide.
4) This means there are more successful collisions, and so the rate of reaction increases.

Catalysts Need to be Replaced Regularly

1) Even though catalysts are not chemically changed or used up by the reactions they catalyse, they must be replaced regularly when they're used in industrial processes.
2) In industrial processes, there may be impurities present which do chemically change the catalyst.
3) These changes mean that over time the catalyst will lose its activity — it won't be able to increase the rate of reaction any more.
4) The reaction will slow back down to its uncatalysed rate until the catalyst is replaced.

Enzymes Control Cell Reactions

1) Enzymes are biological catalysts. This means that they catalyse the chemical reactions in cells.
2) Enzymes work best under specific conditions, known as their optimum conditions.
3) All enzymes have an optimum temperature. If the temperature is too low, the enzyme's activity will be limited. If it's too high (usually above 60° C) the enzyme can be denatured (damaged) and stop working.
4) Reactions catalysed by enzymes include respiration, photosynthesis and fermentation (see p.98).

The pH also affects enzymes. The optimum pH for many enzymes is 7. If it's too acidic or too alkaline, the enzyme could be denatured.

I wish there was a catalyst for making my takeaway arrive...

Catalysts are really handy. Some reactions take a very long time to happen by themselves, which isn't good for industrial reactions. Catalysts help to produce an acceptable amount of product in an acceptable length of time.

Q1   Explain why catalysts used in industrial processes need to be replaced regularly.   [2 marks]

Unit 1d — Rate of Chemical Change and Thermal Decomposition

Thermal Decomposition

Take care when the exam heat is on — stay composed by getting plenty of sleep. Don't be a metal carbonate...

The Thermal Decomposition of Metal Carbonates Produces CO_2

1) If you heat a metal carbonate, you get carbon dioxide and a metal oxide.
2) This is an example of thermal decomposition, which is when a substance breaks down into simpler substances when heated. Here are two examples you need to know:

> Copper(II) carbonate is a green powder that decomposes when it's gently heated. A black powder, copper(II) oxide, forms.
> $$CuCO_{3(s)} \rightarrow CuO_{(s)} + CO_{2(g)}$$
> copper(II) carbonate — copper(II) oxide — carbon dioxide

> Calcium carbonate needs to be heated vigorously for several minutes in order to decompose. When it's heated to a very high temperature, it glows.
> $$CaCO_{3(s)} \rightarrow CaO_{(s)} + CO_{2(g)}$$
> calcium carbonate — calcium oxide — carbon dioxide

Reactive Metals Form More Stable Carbonates

1) Copper(II) carbonate only needs gentle heating to decompose. This is because copper is quite an unreactive metal.
2) More reactive metals form more stable carbonates which need to be heated to a higher temperature to make them decompose.
3) Group 1 metals are very reactive. This means that they form very stable carbonates.
4) For example, sodium carbonate will not decompose even when heated at the highest temperature a Bunsen burner can reach. Since the reactivity of the metals in Group 1 increases down the group, metals below sodium form even more stable carbonates. None of these decompose when heated with a Bunsen burner.

You Can Compare The Stability of Metal Carbonates

PRACTICAL

1) Carbon dioxide is formed in thermal decomposition reactions, so the mass of solid being heated decreases as gas is lost.
2) You can measure the change in mass in a given time to compare the stability of metal carbonates.
3) First, measure the mass of the empty boiling tube. Then add about 2 g of metal carbonate and re-weigh it.
4) Heat the carbonate with a Bunsen burner, using a blue flame for around five minutes.
5) Turn off the flame and let the boiling tube cool down. Once it's cooled, re-weigh the boiling tube with the solid inside. Work out the change in mass from the start of the experiment.
6) Repeat the process using different metal carbonates. Compare the change in mass between the different carbonates. The more mass lost, the less stable the carbonate.
7) Very stable carbonates, such as sodium carbonate will not lose mass when they're heated because they do not decompose at the temperatures produced by Bunsen burners.

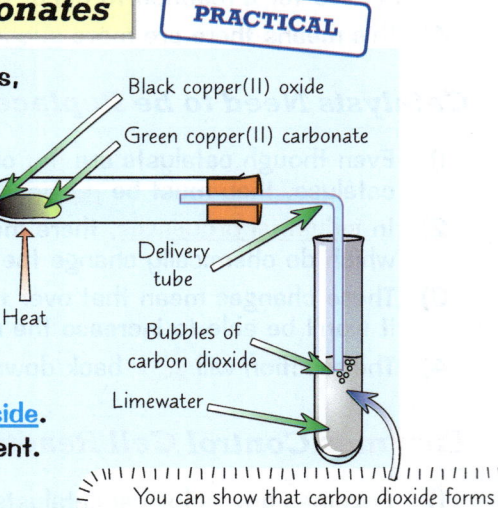

You can show that carbon dioxide forms when metal carbonates decompose by bubbling the gas through limewater. Limewater turns milky when carbon dioxide is bubbled through it (see page 48). Make sure you remove this test tube before you turn off the Bunsen flame, or the limewater might get sucked back into the tube.

I don't have a favourite song. I just love all decompositions...

More reactive metals form more stable metal carbonates which are harder to decompose. You'll need to know how to investigate the stability of metal carbonates, so make sure you've learned every little detail of how you do that.

Q1 Harshil uses a Bunsen burner to heat sodium carbonate in a boiling tube. He bubbles any gases produced through limewater. The limewater does not turn milky. Explain this observation. [3 marks]

Unit 1d — Rate of Chemical Change and Thermal Decomposition

Limestone

Limestone is a really important rock. It's got loads of important uses and makes some pretty handy chemicals.

Limestone is Used to Make Quicklime and Slaked Lime

1) Limestone is a rock formed from the shells of dead sea animals. It's mostly made from calcium carbonate. It's quarried from the ground for many uses, including as a building material and to make other products.

2) Quicklime (calcium oxide) and slaked lime (calcium hydroxide) are made in the limestone cycle:

   1) Quicklime is made by heating calcium carbonate (limestone) so that it decomposes (see previous page).
   $$CaCO_{3(s)} \rightarrow CaO_{(s)} + CO_{2(g)}$$

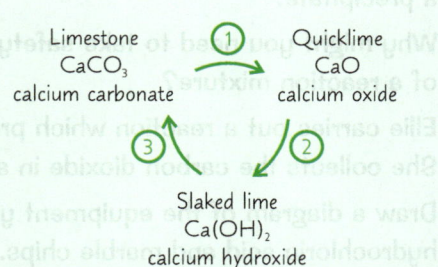

   2) Slaked lime can then be made by reacting quicklime with a small amount of water in a highly exothermic reaction. The quicklime crumbles and hisses as it reacts.
   $$CaO_{(s)} + H_2O_{(l)} \rightarrow Ca(OH)_{2(s)}$$

   3) Limewater is an aqueous solution of slaked lime. If CO_2 is bubbled through the solution, calcium carbonate precipitates out, turning the solution cloudy. And we're back to where we started...
   $$Ca(OH)_{2(aq)} + CO_{2(g)} \rightarrow CaCO_{3(s)} + H_2O_{(l)}$$

   This reaction is used to test for carbon dioxide (see p.48)

   Limestone $CaCO_3$ calcium carbonate → Quicklime CaO calcium oxide → Slaked lime $Ca(OH)_2$ calcium hydroxide

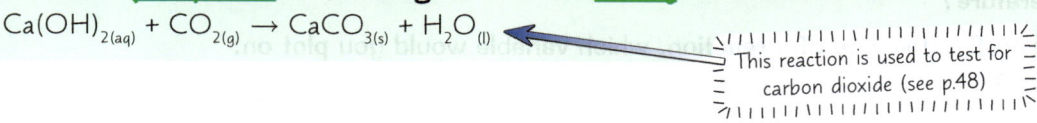

Limestone Products Are Really Useful

1) Limestone is used to make building materials like cement and glass, and to build roads. It's also added to the blast furnace when making iron and steel — see page 75.

2) Limestone blocks are used as a building material because limestone is hard-wearing, but still looks attractive. It's also widely available and cheaper than marble or granite.

3) Quicklime and slaked lime make alkaline solutions of calcium hydroxide when mixed with water. These (and powdered limestone) can be spread on farm land to neutralise acidic soils and improve crop yields. They can also be added to lakes and rivers to neutralise acidity caused by acid rain.

Quarrying Limestone Isn't Everyone's Cup of Tea...

Using limestone isn't all hunky-dory — tearing it out of the ground causes problems...

1) Quarrying processes, like blasting rocks apart with explosives, make lots of noise and dust in quiet, scenic areas. Lorries which transport rocks also add to the noise and dust.

2) Quarrying also harms wildlife by destroying the habitats of animals and plants.

3) Quarries can be unpleasant for people living near them. They make the landscape less attractive and they can also lower house prices.

However, quarries and associated businesses provide jobs for people and can bring more money into the local economy. This can bring local improvements in transport, roads, recreation facilities and health too.

It's got absolutely nothing to do with citrus...

Limestone quarrying has its downsides, but it's also a useful resource so it's important to find a balance. In the exam, you might need to discuss the benefits and disadvantages of quarrying in a certain area. Think about how it can affect the environment, landscape and the local economy.

Q1 Laura measures the temperature and pH of some water. When she adds calcium oxide, both the pH and temperature increase. Explain these observations. [2 marks]

Unit 1d — Rate of Chemical Change and Thermal Decomposition

Revision Questions for Unit 1d

Nice short section that, so you should rattle through this page in no time.
- Try these questions and tick off each one when you get it right.
- When you've done all the questions for a topic and are completely happy with it, tick off the topic.

Measuring Rates of Reaction (p.50-53)

1) Give the formula for calculating the rate of a reaction.
2) Explain how you could follow the rate of a reaction where two colourless solutions react to form a precipitate.
3) Why might you need to take safety precautions when measuring the change in mass of a reaction mixture?
4) Ellie carries out a reaction which produces carbon dioxide gas. She collects the carbon dioxide in a gas syringe. How will Ellie know when the reaction has finished?
5) Draw a diagram of the equipment you could use to measure the rate of reaction between hydrochloric acid and marble chips.
6) How does the rate of the reaction between sodium thiosulfate and hydrochloric acid change with temperature?
7) On a graph to find the rate of a reaction, which variable would you plot on:
   a) the x-axis?
   b) the y-axis?
8) The results from two experiments carried out under different conditions are plotted on the same graph. How could you tell from the graph which conditions produced the faster rate of reaction?
9) Graphs to find the rate of a reaction are usually curved. What does this tell you about the rate of a reaction over time?
10) Explain how you would find the gradient of a curved graph at a certain point on the graph.

Factors Affecting Rate of Reaction (p.54-55)

11) Explain what a 'successful collision' between two particles is.
12) How does concentration affect the rate of a reaction?
13) In a gaseous reaction, why would a decrease in pressure result in a slower rate of reaction?
14) Explain why powdered chalk reacts with hydrochloric acid more quickly than marble chips, when both are made of calcium carbonate ($CaCO_3$).
15) What effect will raising the temperature have on the rate of a reaction?

Catalysts and Enzymes (p.55)

16) True or false? All catalysts work equally well for all reactions.
17) What effect does a catalyst have on the energy needed for a reaction to take place?
18) True or false? Catalysts are not used up, so never need replacing in industrial reactions.
19) Describe how temperature affects an enzyme's activity.

Thermal Decomposition and Limestone (p. 56-57)

20) What is the balanced symbol equation for the thermal decomposition of calcium carbonate?
21) How can you show that carbon dioxide is produced when metal carbonates thermally decompose?
22) What is the chemical name for quicklime?
23) Describe how slaked lime is made from limestone.
24) Give two uses of limestone.

Unit 1d — Rate of Chemical Change and Thermal Decomposition

Unit 2a — Bonding, Structure and Properties

Metallic Bonding

Right, time to take a look at the bonding in different substances. First up — metals.

Metallic Bonding Involves Delocalised Electrons

1) Metals consist of a giant structure.
2) The electrons in the outer shell of the metal atoms are delocalised (free to move around). There are strong forces of electrostatic attraction between the lattice of positive metal ions and the shared sea of negative electrons.
3) These forces of attraction hold the atoms together in a regular structure and are known as metallic bonding. Metallic bonding is very strong.

I don't think he's from round here.

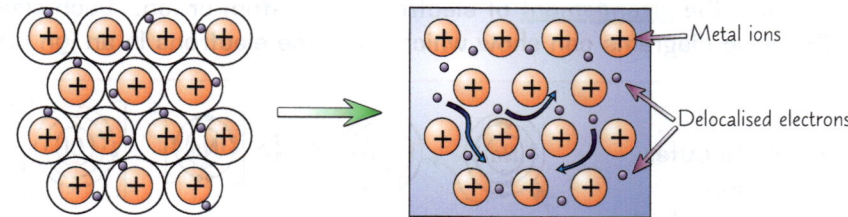

4) Substances that are held together by metallic bonding include metallic elements and alloys (see p.82).
5) It's the delocalised electrons in the metallic bonds which produce many of the properties of metals.

Most Metals are Solid at Room Temperature

1) The electrostatic forces between the metal atoms and the delocalised sea of electrons are very strong, so need lots of energy to be broken.
2) This means that most compounds with metallic bonds have very high melting and boiling points, so they're generally solid at room temperature.
3) Ions with higher charges have more delocalised electrons. This means they have stronger electrostatic forces of attraction. So metals that contain ions with higher charges generally have higher melting and boiling points than those that contain ions with lower charges.
4) E.g. aluminium contains Al^{3+} ions, so has a higher melting point than magnesium, which contains Mg^{2+} ions. Both aluminium and magnesium have higher melting points than sodium, which contains Na^+ ions.

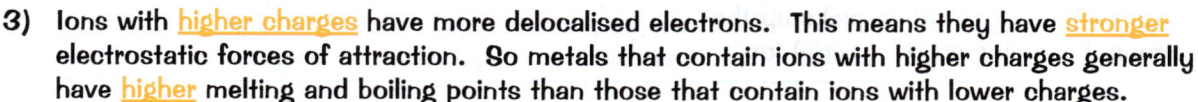

Metals aren't soluble — they don't dissolve in water.

Metals are Good Conductors of Electricity and Heat

The delocalised electrons carry electrical current and thermal (heat) energy through the whole structure, so metals are good conductors of electricity and heat.

Most Metals are Malleable and Ductile

1) The layers of atoms in a metal can slide over each other, making metals malleable — this means that they can be bent or hammered or rolled into flat sheets.
2) The layers of atoms within metals also make them ductile. This means that metals can be drawn out into thin wires without breaking.

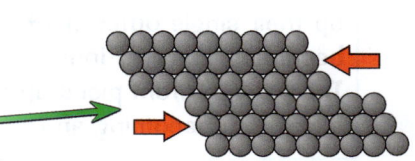

I saw a metal on the train once — he was the conductor...

If your knowledge of metals is still feeling a bit delocalised, the questions below will help...

Q1 Copper is a metallic element. Describe and explain what property of copper makes it suitable for use in electrical circuits. [2 marks]

Q2 Explain why magnesium has a higher melting point than sodium. [3 marks]

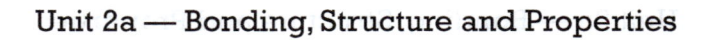

Ionic Bonding

Now you've cracked metallic bonding, you must be dying to know what happens when a metal and non-metal react.

Ionic Bonding — Transfer of Electrons

When a metal and a non-metal react together, the metal atom loses electrons to form a positively charged ion and the non-metal gains these electrons to form a negatively charged ion. These oppositely charged ions are strongly attracted to one another by electrostatic forces. This attraction is called an ionic bond.

Dot and Cross Diagrams Show How Ionic Compounds are Formed

Dot and cross diagrams show the arrangement of electrons in an atom or ion. Each electron is represented by a dot or a cross. So these diagrams can show which atom the electrons in an ion originally came from.

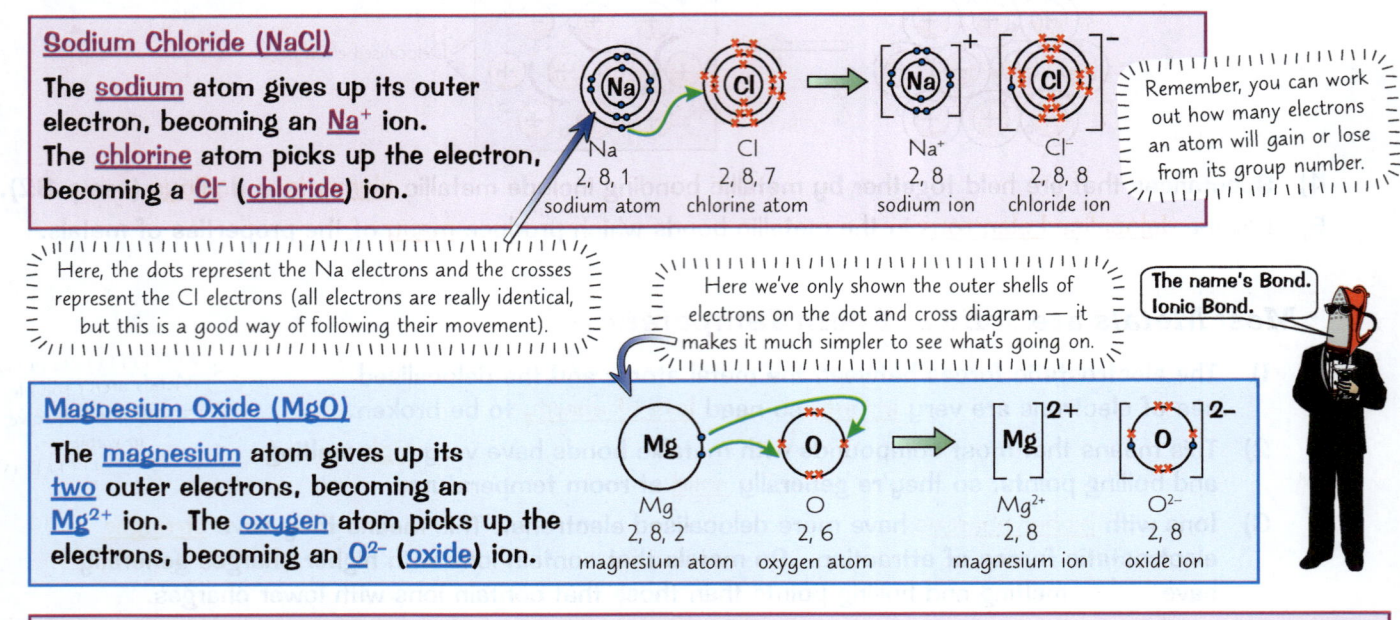

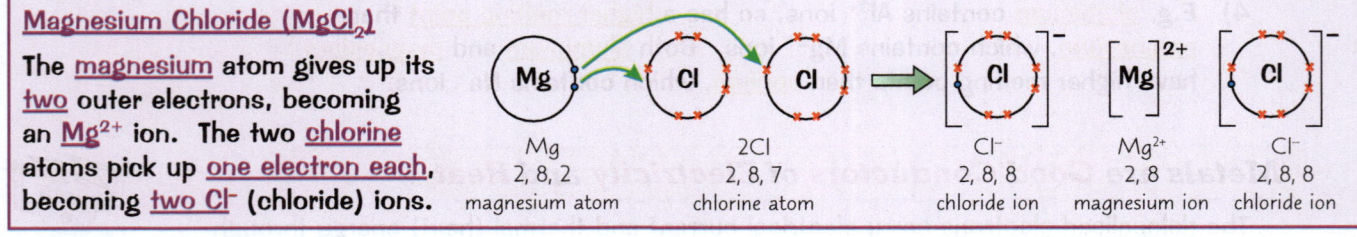

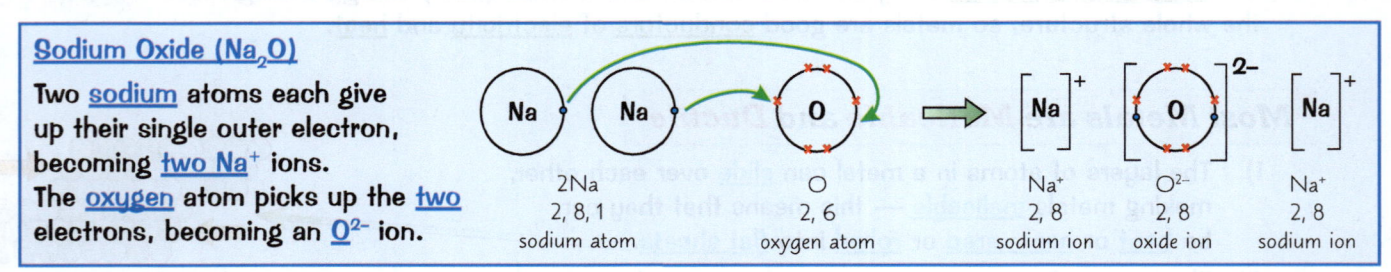

Sodium Chloride (NaCl)
The sodium atom gives up its outer electron, becoming an Na$^+$ ion. The chlorine atom picks up the electron, becoming a Cl$^-$ (chloride) ion.

Remember, you can work out how many electrons an atom will gain or lose from its group number.

Here, the dots represent the Na electrons and the crosses represent the Cl electrons (all electrons are really identical, but this is a good way of following their movement).

Here we've only shown the outer shells of electrons on the dot and cross diagram — it makes it much simpler to see what's going on.

The name's Bond. Ionic Bond.

Magnesium Oxide (MgO)
The magnesium atom gives up its two outer electrons, becoming an Mg^{2+} ion. The oxygen atom picks up the electrons, becoming an O^{2-} (oxide) ion.

Magnesium Chloride (MgCl$_2$)
The magnesium atom gives up its two outer electrons, becoming an Mg^{2+} ion. The two chlorine atoms pick up one electron each, becoming two Cl$^-$ (chloride) ions.

Sodium Oxide (Na$_2$O)
Two sodium atoms each give up their single outer electron, becoming two Na$^+$ ions. The oxygen atom picks up the two electrons, becoming an O^{2-} ion.

Stop slacking — I've got my ion you...

You need to be able to describe how ionic compounds are formed using both words and dot and cross diagrams. It gets easier with practice, so here are some questions to get you started.

Q1 Describe, in terms of electron transfer, how calcium and fluorine react to form calcium fluoride (CaF$_2$). [3 marks]

Q2 Draw a dot and cross diagram to show how potassium (a Group 1 metal) and bromine (a Group 7 non-metal) form potassium bromide (KBr). [3 marks]

Unit 2a — Bonding, Structure and Properties

Ionic Compounds

I'd take everything on this page with a pinch of salt if I were you... Ho ho ho — I jest, it's important really.

Ionic Compounds Have a Regular Lattice Structure

1) Ionic compounds have a structure called a giant ionic lattice.
2) The ions form a closely packed regular lattice arrangement and there are very strong electrostatic forces of attraction between oppositely charged ions, in all directions in the lattice.

A single crystal of sodium chloride (table salt) is one giant ionic lattice. The Na^+ and Cl^- ions are held together in a regular lattice. The lattice can be represented in different ways...

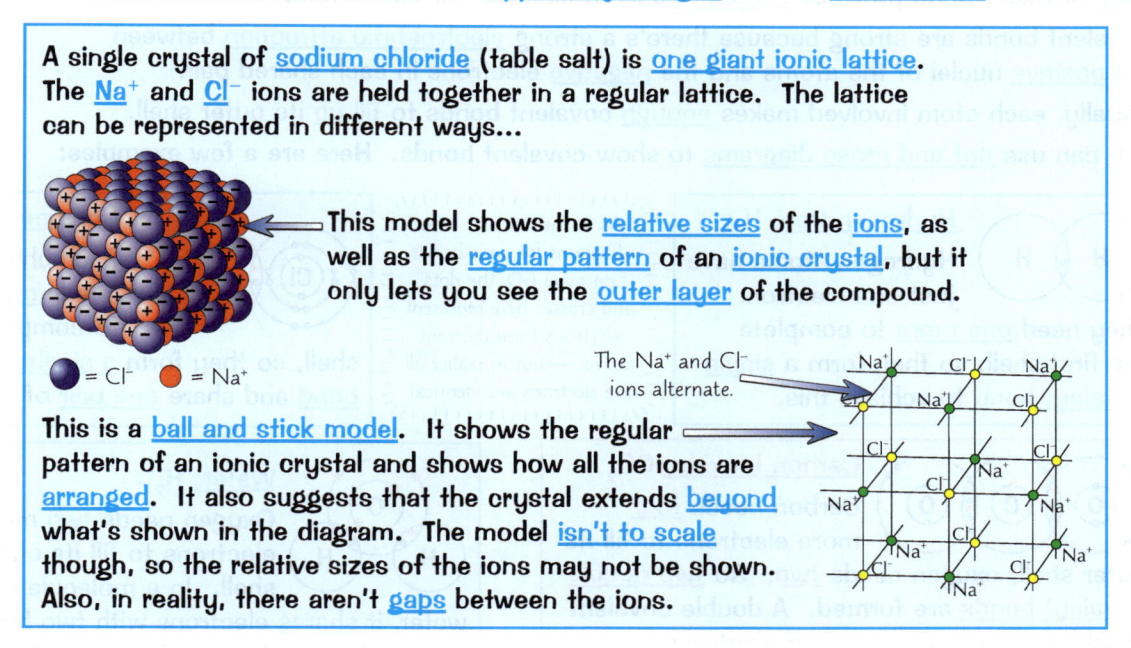

This model shows the relative sizes of the ions, as well as the regular pattern of an ionic crystal, but it only lets you see the outer layer of the compound.

● = Cl^- ● = Na^+

This is a ball and stick model. It shows the regular pattern of an ionic crystal and shows how all the ions are arranged. It also suggests that the crystal extends beyond what's shown in the diagram. The model isn't to scale though, so the relative sizes of the ions may not be shown. Also, in reality, there aren't gaps between the ions.

The Na^+ and Cl^- ions alternate.

Ionic Compounds All Have Similar Properties...

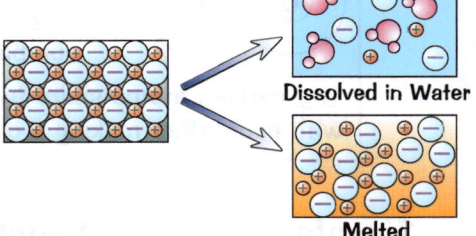

1) They all have high melting points and high boiling points due to the many strong bonds between the ions. It takes lots of energy to overcome this attraction.
2) When they're solid, the ions are held in place, so the compounds can't conduct electricity. When ionic compounds melt, the ions are free to move and they'll carry electric charge.
3) Some ionic compounds also dissolve in water. The ions separate and are all free to move in the solution, so they'll carry electric charge.

Dissolved in Water

Melted

... But Some Have Higher Melting Points and Boiling Points Than Others

1) Magnesium oxide and sodium chloride are both ionic compounds. However magnesium oxide has a higher melting point (and also a higher boiling point) than sodium chloride.
2) This is because the charges on the ions in magnesium oxide (Mg^{2+} and O^{2-}) are greater than the charges on the ions in sodium chloride (Na^+ and Cl^-). This makes the electrostatic forces of attraction stronger.
3) This means the ionic bonding in magnesium oxide is stronger than the bonding in sodium chloride. The ions are therefore harder to break apart and the melting and boiling points are higher.

Giant ionic lattices — all over your chips...

Okay, that's the final salt joke — I promise. Here's some more practice questions for you to have a crack at.

Q1   Caesium chloride is an ionic compound. Explain why it has a high melting point.   [1 mark]

Unit 2a — Bonding, Structure and Properties

Simple Molecules

These molecules might be simple, but you've still gotta know about them. I know, the world is a cruel place.

Covalent Bonds — Sharing Electrons

1) When non-metal atoms combine together, they form covalent bonds by sharing pairs of electrons.
2) This way, both atoms feel that they have a full outer shell, and that makes them happy.
3) Each covalent bond provides one extra shared electron for each atom.
4) Covalent bonds are strong because there's a strong electrostatic attraction between the positive nuclei of the atoms and the negative electrons in each shared pair.
5) Usually, each atom involved makes enough covalent bonds to fill up its outer shell.
6) You can use dot and cross diagrams to show covalent bonds. Here are a few examples:

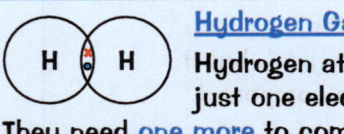

Hydrogen Gas: H_2
Hydrogen atoms have just one electron. They need one more to complete the first shell, so they form a single covalent bond to achieve this.

As in the dot and cross diagrams for ionic bonds on page 60, the dots and crosses here represent electrons from different atoms — but in reality all the electrons are identical.

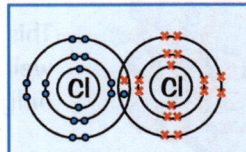

Chlorine Gas: Cl_2
Each chlorine atom needs one electron to complete its outer shell, so they form a single covalent bond and share one pair of electrons.

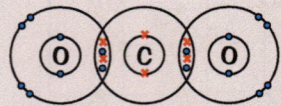

Carbon Dioxide: CO_2
Carbon needs four more electrons to fill its outer shell, oxygen needs two. So two double covalent bonds are formed. A double covalent bond has two shared pairs of electrons.

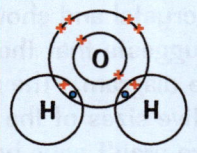

Water: H_2O
Oxygen needs two more electrons to fill its outer shell. In a molecule of water, it shares electrons with two hydrogen atoms, forming two single covalent bonds.

Oxygen Gas: O_2
Each oxygen atom needs two more electrons to complete its outer shell. Two oxygen atoms share two pairs of electrons with each other making a double covalent bond.

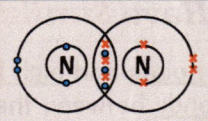

Nitrogen: N_2
Nitrogen atoms need three more electrons to fill their outer shells, so two nitrogen atoms share three pairs of electrons. This creates a triple bond.

Simple Molecular Substances Have Low Melting and Boiling Points

1) Substances formed with covalent bonds usually have simple molecular structures, like CO_2 and H_2O.
2) The atoms within the molecules are held together by very strong covalent bonds.
3) By contrast, the forces of attraction between these molecules are very weak. It's these feeble intermolecular forces that you have to overcome to melt or boil a simple covalent compound.
4) So the melting and boiling points are very low, because the molecules are easily parted from each other. 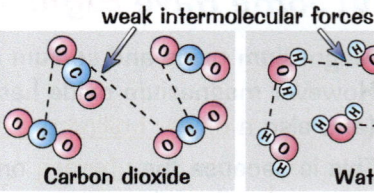 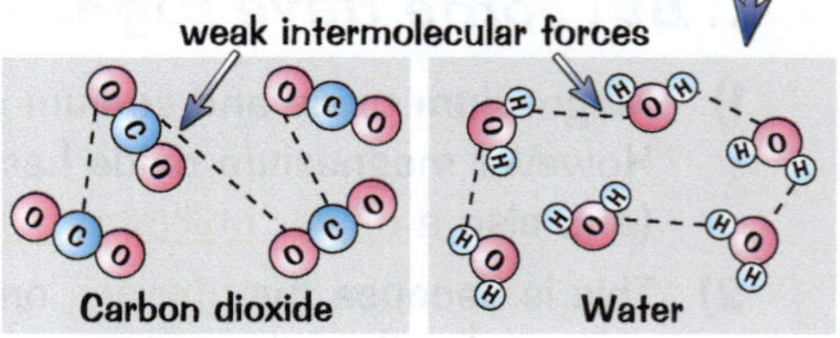
5) Most simple molecular substances are gases or liquids at room temperature.
6) Simple molecular substances don't conduct electricity, because they don't have free electrons or ions.
7) Simple molecular substances are usually quite insoluble in water.

May the intermolecular force be with you...

Remember — a covalent bond is just a shared pair of electrons. Easy-peasy.

Q1   In a molecule of ammonia, NH_3, a nitrogen atom is covalently bonded to three hydrogen atoms.
Draw a dot and cross diagram to show the bonding in an ammonia molecule.   [1 mark]

Unit 2a — Bonding, Structure and Properties

Giant Covalent Structures and Fullerenes

I hope you didn't think simple molecules would be the end of covalent bonding. Time to think giant.

Most Giant Covalent Structures Have Certain Properties

1) In giant covalent structures, all the atoms are bonded to each other by strong covalent bonds.
2) They have very high melting and boiling points as lots of energy is needed to break the covalent bonds.
3) They generally don't contain charged particles, so they don't conduct electricity. *Apart from graphite and graphene.*
4) They aren't soluble in water.
5) The following examples are all carbon-based giant covalent structures.

DIAMOND
- Diamond is made up of a network of carbon atoms that each form four covalent bonds.
- The strong covalent bonds take lots of energy to break, so diamond has a high melting point.
- The strong covalent bonds also hold the atoms in a rigid lattice structure, making diamond really hard — it's used to strengthen cutting tools (e.g. saw teeth and drill bits).
- It doesn't conduct electricity because it has no free electrons or ions.

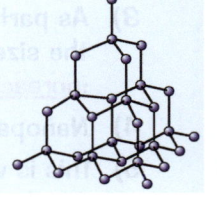

GRAPHITE
- In graphite, each carbon atom has three covalent bonds, creating sheets of carbon atoms arranged in hexagons.
- There aren't any covalent bonds between the layers — they're only held together weakly, so they're free to move over each other.
- This makes graphite soft and slippery, so it's ideal as a lubricating material.
- Graphite's got a high melting point — the covalent bonds in the layers need loads of energy to break.
- Only three out of each carbon's four outer electrons are used in bonds, so each carbon atom has one electron that's delocalised (free) and can move. So graphite conducts electricity.

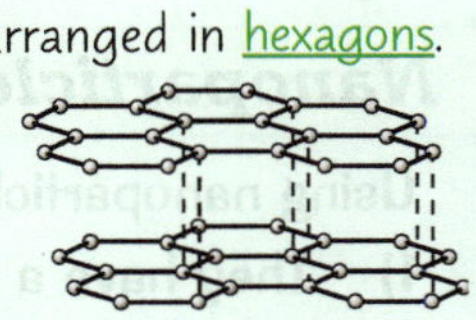

GRAPHENE
- Graphene is one layer of graphite.
- It's a sheet of carbon atoms joined together in hexagons.
- The sheet is just one atom thick, making it a two-dimensional compound.
- Graphene is one of the strongest materials ever tested. Like graphite, it has delocalised electrons which make it an excellent electrical conductor. However, it's not yet available in any products.

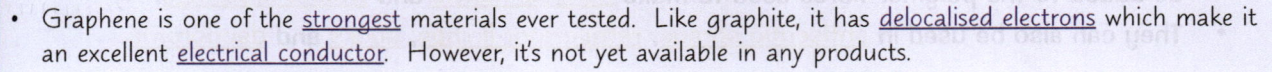

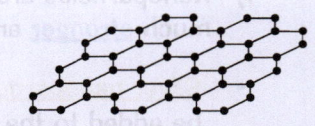

Fullerenes Form Spheres and Tubes

1) Fullerenes are molecules of carbon that form cage structures, like closed tubes or hollow balls.
2) They're made up of carbon atoms arranged in rings.
3) Fullerenes can be used to 'cage' other molecules. The fullerene structure forms around another atom or molecule, which is then trapped inside. This could be used to deliver a drug directly to cells in the body.
4) Fullerenes have a huge surface area, so they could help make great industrial catalysts — individual catalyst molecules could be attached to the fullerenes.
5) As well as drug delivery and catalyst uses, scientists are investigating fullerenes for use in lubricants.

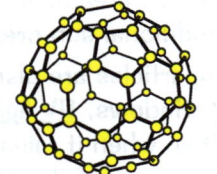

Buckminsterfullerene has the molecular formula C_{60} and forms a hollow sphere made up of 20 hexagons and 12 pentagons. It's a stable molecule that forms soft brownish-black crystals.

Catalysts speed up the rates of reactions without being used up (see page 55).

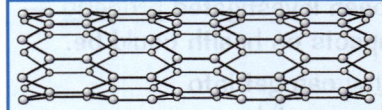

Nanotubes are also fullerenes. They are tiny tubes of graphene — so they have delocalised electrons meaning they conduct electricity. Their strong covalent bonds mean they have a high tensile strength (they don't break when stretched). They also have a very low density, so they can be used to strengthen materials without adding much weight.

Fullerenes are forever — doesn't quite have the same ring to it...

Did you know that buckminsterfullerene is the state molecule of Texas? True story...

Q1   Explain why graphite conducts electricity but diamond does not.   [2 marks]

Unit 2a — Bonding, Structure and Properties

Nanoparticles

There are loads of really useful properties of nanoparticles for you to learn.

Nanoparticles are Really Really Really Really Tiny

1) Really tiny particles, 1–100 nanometres across, are called 'nanoparticles' (1 nm = 0.000 000 001 m). Nanoparticles contain roughly a few hundred atoms — so they're bigger than atoms (atoms are around 0.1–0.5 nm) and simple molecules, but smaller than pretty much anything else.
2) A nanoparticle has very different properties from the 'bulk' chemical that it's made from — e.g. fullerenes, carbon nanotubes, diamond, graphite and graphene all have different properties even though they all just contain carbon atoms.

Fullerenes are nanoparticles — see previous page.

3) As particles decrease in size, the size of their surface area increases in relation to their volume — so their surface area to volume ratio increases.

surface area to volume ratio = surface area ÷ volume

4) Nanoparticles have a really high surface area to volume ratio compared to larger particles.
5) This is what causes the properties of a material to be different depending on whether it's a nanoparticle or whether it's in bulk.

Nanoparticles Can Modify the Properties of Materials

Using nanoparticles is known as nanoscience. Many new uses of nanoparticles are being developed:

1) They have a huge surface area to volume ratio, so they can make good catalysts (see p.55).
2) Nanomedicine is a hot topic. The idea is that tiny fullerenes are absorbed more easily by the body than most particles. This means they could deliver drugs right into the cells where they're needed.
3) New lubricant coatings using fullerenes could be used in, e.g. artificial joints and gears.
4) Nanoparticles are added to plastics in sports equipment. They make the plastic much stronger and more durable, without adding much mass.

As with carbon nanoparticles, silver nanoparticles have different properties to those in 'bulk' silver.

- Silver nanoparticles have antibacterial, antiviral and antifungal properties. They can be added to the polymer fibres used to make surgical masks and wound dressings.
- They can also be used in antiseptic sprays, refrigerator linings, socks and deodorants.

- Titanium dioxide nanoparticles are being used in sun creams. They are better than the materials in traditional sun creams at protecting skin from harmful UV rays. They also give better skin coverage than traditional sun creams, and are transparent (which lots of people prefer).
- Titanium dioxide nanoparticles are also used as a coating for self-cleaning glass. E.g. for self-cleaning windows, UV light from the sun causes the nanoparticles to catalyse the breakdown of dirt. Then when it rains, the nanoparticles spread out the water (which would otherwise form droplets on the surface of the glass) — this washes away the dirt without leaving streaks.

The Effects of Nanoparticles on Health Aren't Fully Understood

1) Although nanoparticles are useful, the way they affect the body isn't fully understood, so it's important that any new products are tested thoroughly to minimise the risks.
2) Some people are worried that products containing nanoparticles have been made available before any possible harmful effects on human health have been investigated properly — in other words, we don't know what the side effects or long-term impacts on health could be.
3) For example, it's not yet clear whether the nanoparticles in sun creams can get into your body, and, if they do, whether they might damage cells. It's also possible that when they are washed away they might damage the environment.

The large surface area to volume ratio could be making them more toxic.

Nanoparticles — when ants get into that old tin of baked beans...

It seems like small particles are big business — but as with any new tech there are pros and cons.

Q1   State one use of titanium dioxide nanoparticles.   [1 mark]

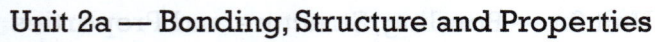

Unit 2a — Bonding, Structure and Properties

Smart Materials

Scientists are constantly developing new materials, such as smart materials, to fit new uses.

Smart Materials Change When Their Environment Changes

1) Smart materials react to changes in their environment.
2) This means that one or more of their properties can be changed by an external condition such as temperature, light, pH, etc.
3) The change that a smart material makes is reversible — the material will go back to how it was.
4) These properties make smart materials very useful.

Thermochromic Pigments

1) Thermochromic pigments change colour or become transparent when heated or cooled.
2) Baby products, like bath toys and baby spoons, often have them added as a safety feature — you can tell at a glance if the baby's bath water or food is too hot.

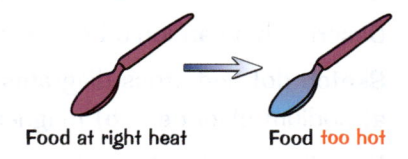

Food at right heat   Food too hot

Photochromic Pigments

1) Photochromic pigments change colour when light intensity changes.
2) Photochromic materials can be used in sunglasses — exposure to sunlight makes the lenses of the glasses darken to protect the eyes.

Polymer Gels

1) Polymer gels (also known as hydrogels) can expand or shrink by up to 1000 times in volume by absorbing or giving out water.
2) This volume change happens as a result of a change in pH or temperature.
3) Polymer gels have uses in medicine.

Shape Memory Alloys

1) An alloy is a mixture of two elements, one of which is a metal (p.82).
2) Some smart alloys have a shape memory property — they "remember" their original shape.
3) If you bend a wire made of a smart alloy, it'll go back to its original shape when it's heated.
4) Shape memory alloys are handy for things like glasses frames — if they get bent (or sat on) they can easily be reshaped.

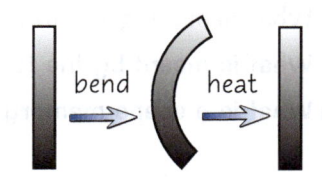

bend   heat

Shape Memory Polymers

1) These work the same as shape memory alloys, but are made out of polymers instead.
2) A polymer is a very large molecule made of a chain of smaller repeated molecules (p.95).
3) Shape memory polymers return to their original shape when heated.

Not smart enough to do the exam for you though...

Hmm, so scientists can faff about with materials until they can make them do exactly what they want. Well, I'd like a gold ring that can cook meals, do the washing up and tidy rooms.

Q1   A student was given samples of two different metals. Both had been bent. Describe what the student could do to find out which metal is a shape memory alloy and state what would be observed.   [2 marks]

Unit 2a — Bonding, Structure and Properties

Revision Questions for Unit 2a

Well, that's the end of Unit 2a — well, nearly the end. You know what's coming next...
- Try these questions and tick off each one when you get it right.
- When you've done all the questions for a topic and are completely happy with it, tick off the topic.

Metallic Bonding (p.59)
1) What is metallic bonding?
2) Explain why most metals are solid at room temperature.
3) Why are metals good conductors of heat?
4) Why are metals malleable?

Ionic Bonding and Ionic Compounds (p.60-61)
5) Describe how an ionic bond forms.
6) Sketch dot and cross diagrams to show the formation of:
   a) sodium chloride   b) magnesium oxide   c) magnesium chloride   d) sodium oxide
7) Describe the structure of a crystal of sodium chloride.
8) List the main properties of ionic compounds.
9) Explain why magnesium oxide has a higher melting point than sodium chloride.

Covalent Bonding and Nanoparticles (p.62-64)
10) Describe how a covalent bond forms.
11) Why do simple molecular substances have low melting and boiling points?
12) List three typical properties of giant covalent structures.
13) Name three substances that have a giant covalent structure.
14) What are nanoparticles?
15) Give a use of silver nanoparticles.

Smart Materials (p.65)
16) True or false? When a change occurs in a smart material, the change is reversible.
17) What happens to a thermochromic material when it is heated or cooled?
18) What name is given to a pigment that changes colour depending on light intensity?
19) What is meant by the term 'alloy'?
20) What is a shape memory alloy?

Unit 2a — Bonding, Structure and Properties

Acids and Bases

Testing the pH of a solution means using an indicator — and that means pretty colours...

The pH Scale Goes From 0 to 14

1) The pH scale is a measure of how acidic or alkaline a solution is.
2) The lower the pH of a solution, the more acidic it is.
3) The higher the pH of a solution, the more alkaline it is.
4) A neutral substance (e.g. pure water) has pH 7.

Strong acids have pHs of 0-2, whilst strong alkalis have pHs of 12-14. There's more on acid and alkali strength on the next page.

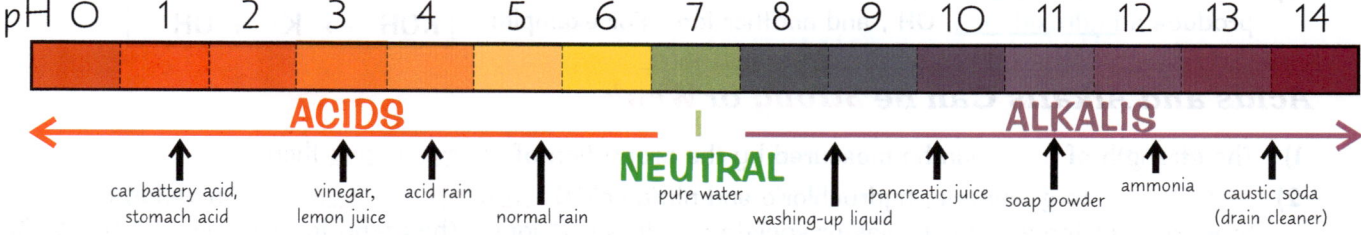

pH 0 1 2 3 4 5 6 7 8 9 10 11 12 13 14

ACIDS — NEUTRAL — ALKALIS

- car battery acid, stomach acid
- vinegar, lemon juice
- acid rain
- normal rain
- pure water
- washing-up liquid
- pancreatic juice
- soap powder
- ammonia
- caustic soda (drain cleaner)

You Can Measure the pH of a Solution

1) An indicator is a dye that changes colour depending on whether it's above or below a certain pH. Some indicators contain a mixture of dyes that means they gradually change colour over a broad range of pH. These are useful for estimating the pH of a solution. For example, universal indicator gives the colours shown above.
2) A pH probe attached to a pH meter can also be used to measure pH electronically. The probe is placed in the solution you are measuring and the pH is given on a digital display as a numerical value, meaning it's more accurate than an indicator.

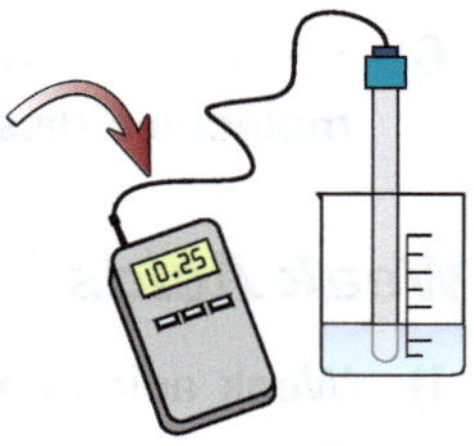

Acids and Bases Neutralise Each Other

1) An acid is a substance that forms aqueous solutions with a pH of less than 7. Acids form H^+ ions in water.
2) A base is a substance with a pH greater than 7.
3) An alkali is a base that dissolves in water to form a solution with a pH greater than 7. Alkalis form OH^- ions in water.

The reaction between acids and bases is called neutralisation:

$$\text{acid} + \text{base} \rightarrow \text{salt} + \text{water}$$

Neutralisation between acids and alkalis can be seen in terms of H^+ and OH^- ions like this:

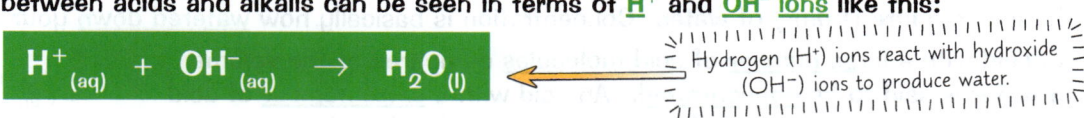

$$H^+_{(aq)} + OH^-_{(aq)} \rightarrow H_2O_{(l)}$$

Hydrogen (H^+) ions react with hydroxide (OH^-) ions to produce water.

When an acid neutralises a base (or vice versa), the products are neutral, i.e. they have a pH of 7. An indicator can be used to show that a neutralisation reaction is over.

Neutralisation reactions of strong acids and alkalis can be used to calculate the concentration of an acid or alkali by titration — there is more about this technique on page 71.

Indicators will tell you the pH.

This page should have all bases covered...

pHew, you finished the page... This stuff isn't too bad really, and pH is worth knowing about — it's important to the chemistry in our bodies. For example, here's an interesting(ish) fact — your skin is slightly acidic (pH 5.5).

Q1 A student uses universal indicator to test a sample of lemon juice with a pH of 3.
    What colour would you expect the indicator to turn? [1 mark]

Q2 The pH of an unknown solution is found to be 8. Is the solution acidic or alkaline? [1 mark]

Acid and Alkali Strength

Right then. More on acids and alkalis. Brace yourself...

Acids Produce Hydrogen Ions in Water

1) All acids can ionise (or dissociate) in solution. That means splitting up to produce a hydrogen ion, H$^+$, and another ion. For example:

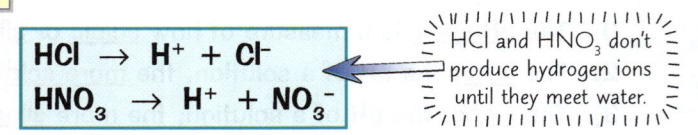

$$HCl \rightarrow H^+ + Cl^-$$
$$HNO_3 \rightarrow H^+ + NO_3^-$$

HCl and HNO$_3$ don't produce hydrogen ions until they meet water.

2) Alkalis ionise (or dissociate) in solution too. They split up to produce a hydroxide ion, OH$^-$, and another ion. For example:

$$NaOH \rightarrow Na^+ + OH^-$$
$$KOH \rightarrow K^+ + OH^-$$

Acids and Alkalis Can be Strong or Weak

1) The strength of acids can be measured by the proportion of hydrogen ions they release.
2) Strong acids (e.g. sulfuric, hydrochloric and nitric acids) ionise almost completely in water, i.e. a large proportion of the acid molecules dissociate to release H$^+$ ions. They tend to have low pHs (pH 0-2).
3) Weak acids (e.g. ethanoic, citric and carbonic acids) do not fully ionise in solution, i.e. only a small proportion of the acid molecules dissociate to release H$^+$ ions. Their pHs tend to be around 2-6.
4) The strength of alkalis can be measured by the proportion of hydroxide ions they release.
5) Strong alkalis ionise almost completely in water. A large proportion of the alkali molecules dissociate to release OH$^-$ ions. Strong alkalis have a pH of about 12-14.
6) Weak alkalis don't fully ionise in water. Only a small proportion of the alkali molecules dissociate to release OH$^-$ ions. Weak alkalis have a pH of about 8-12.

Weak Acids React in the Same Way as Strong Acids

1) Weak acids and strong acids react with metals, bases and carbonates in the same way.
2) E.g. ethanoic acid (a weak acid) reacts with sodium hydroxide to form sodium ethanoate (a salt) and water. Similarly, hydrochloric acid (a strong acid) reacts with sodium hydroxide to form sodium chloride (a salt) and water.
3) Reactions with weak acids don't happen as quickly as reactions with strong acids. They also give out less heat (they're less exothermic) than those with strong acids.

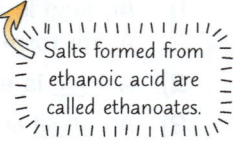

Salts formed from ethanoic acid are called ethanoates.

Don't Confuse Strong Acids with Concentrated Acids

1) Acid strength (i.e. strong or weak) tells you what proportion of the acid molecules ionise in water.
2) The concentration of an acid is different. Concentration measures how much acid there is in a litre (1 dm^3) of water. Concentration is basically how watered down your acid is.
3) An acid with a large number of acid molecules compared to the volume of water is said to be concentrated. An acid with a small number of acid molecules compared to the volume of water is said to be dilute.
4) Note that concentration describes the total number of dissolved acid molecules — not the number of acid molecules that produce hydrogen ions.
5) The more grams (or moles) of acid per dm^3, the more concentrated the acid is.
6) So you can have a dilute strong acid, or a concentrated weak acid.

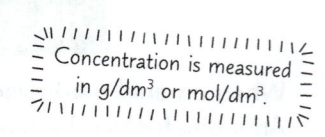

Concentration is measured in g/dm^3 or mol/dm^3.

Weak acid or strong acid? I know which goes better with chips...

Acids are acidic because of H$^+$ ions. And strong acids are strong because they let go of all their H$^+$ ions at the drop of a hat... Well, at the drop of a drop of water. The same goes for alkalis too — but they let go of OH$^-$ ions.

Q1 What ion is released when an alkali dissociates in water? [1 mark]

Q2 Explain the difference between a strong acid and a weak acid. [2 marks]

Unit 2b — Acids, Bases and Salts

Reactions of Acids

Now you've learnt the basics of what acids are, lets see what they can do...

Salts Form When Acids React with Bases

1) A salt is formed during a neutralisation reaction (a reaction between an acid and a base).
2) A neutralisation reaction is always exothermic (p.84)
3) In general, hydrochloric acid produces chloride salts, sulfuric acid produces sulfate salts and nitric acid produces nitrate salts.
4) You need to be able to remember what happens when you add acids to various bases...

Acid + Metal Oxide → Salt + Water

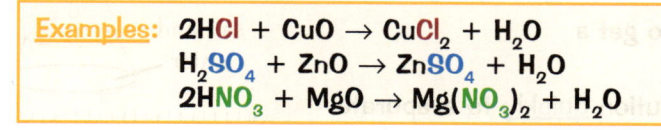

Examples:
$2HCl + CuO \rightarrow CuCl_2 + H_2O$ (Copper chloride)
$H_2SO_4 + ZnO \rightarrow ZnSO_4 + H_2O$ (Zinc sulfate)
$2HNO_3 + MgO \rightarrow Mg(NO_3)_2 + H_2O$ (Magnesium nitrate)

Metal oxides and metal hydroxides are bases.

Acid + Metal Hydroxide → Salt + Water

Examples:
$HCl + NaOH \rightarrow NaCl + H_2O$ (Sodium chloride)
$H_2SO_4 + Zn(OH)_2 \rightarrow ZnSO_4 + 2H_2O$ (Zinc sulfate)
$HNO_3 + KOH \rightarrow KNO_3 + H_2O$ (Potassium nitrate)

Salts Also Form When Acids React With Metals or Metal Carbonates

You also need to know what happens when you react an acid with a metal or a metal carbonate:

Acid + Metal → Salt + Hydrogen

Examples:
$2HCl + Mg \rightarrow MgCl_2 + H_2$ (Magnesium chloride)
$H_2SO_4 + Mg \rightarrow MgSO_4 + H_2$ (Magnesium sulfate)

The reaction of nitric acid with metals can be more complicated — you get a nitrate salt, but instead of hydrogen gas, the other products are usually a mixture of water, NO and NO_2.

Whether or not a metal will react with an acid depends on its position in the reactivity series compared to hydrogen — metals above hydrogen in the reactivity series will react with acids, metals below hydrogen will not. There's more on the reactivity series of metals on page 74.

Acid + Metal Carbonate → Salt + Water + Carbon Dioxide

Examples:
$2HCl + Na_2CO_3 \rightarrow 2NaCl + H_2O + CO_2$ (Sodium chloride)
$H_2SO_4 + K_2CO_3 \rightarrow K_2SO_4 + H_2O + CO_2$ (Potassium sulfate)
$2HNO_3 + ZnCO_3 \rightarrow Zn(NO_3)_2 + H_2O + CO_2$ (Zinc nitrate)

You can use this reaction as a test to see if an acid or carbonate is present — the solution will effervesce (fizz) as CO_2 is produced, and the gas will turn limewater milky (see page 48).

Test for Sulfate Ions Using Barium Chloride Solution

1) To test for sulfate ions in solution, first add some dilute hydrochloric acid or dilute nitric acid to the test sample — this stops any precipitation reactions not involving sulfate ions from taking place.
2) Then add some barium chloride solution. If there are sulfate ions in the solution, a white precipitate of barium sulfate will form:

barium ions + sulfate ions → barium sulfate
$Ba^{2+}_{(aq)} + SO_4^{2-}_{(aq)} \rightarrow BaSO_{4(s)}$

Nitrates — much cheaper than day-rates...

What a lot of reactions. Better take a peek back at page 17 for help with writing and balancing chemical equations.

Q1 Write a balanced chemical equation for the reaction of hydrochloric acid with calcium carbonate. [2 marks]

Unit 2b — Acids, Bases and Salts

Making Salts

Learning how salts are made — it's the moment you've been waiting for since the day you were born...

Making Soluble Salts Using an Acid and an Insoluble Reactant   PRACTICAL

1) You can make soluble salts (salts that dissolve in water) by reacting an acid with a metal, an insoluble base (normally a metal hydroxide or a metal oxide) or a metal carbonate. To get a particular salt, you need to pick the right reactants.
2) Add an excess of the insoluble substance to the acid — they will react to produce a soluble salt (plus either water, hydrogen, or water and carbon dioxide).
3) You will know when all the acid has reacted because the excess insoluble substance will just sink to the bottom of the flask.
   You sometimes need to heat the reaction mixture during this step to get everything to react faster.
4) Then filter off the excess insoluble substance to get a solution containing only salt and water.
5) To make small crystals of the salt, heat the solution quickly to evaporate off about two thirds of the solution and then leave the rest of the solution to cool to form crystals. Filter off the crystals and leave them to dry.
6) To make big crystals, leave the solution to evaporate slowly over a few days.

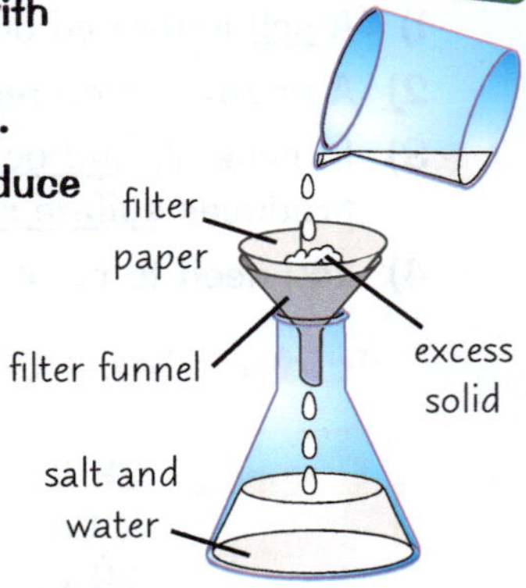

You can also check if the reaction is complete by putting a drop of the mixture onto indicator paper. If the solution is still acidic, then not all the acid will have reacted.

Examples: Adding zinc to sulfuric acid makes soluble zinc sulfate:
$Zn_{(s)} + H_2SO_{4(aq)} \rightarrow ZnSO_{4(aq)} + H_{2(g)}$

Adding copper(II) carbonate to sulfuric acid makes soluble copper(II) sulfate:
$CuCO_{3(s)} + H_2SO_{4(aq)} \rightarrow CuSO_{4(aq)} + H_2O_{(l)} + CO_{2(g)}$

Making Insoluble Salts — Precipitation Reactions

1) To make a clean, dry sample of an insoluble salt, you can use a precipitation reaction. You just need to pick the right two soluble salts to react and you get your insoluble salt.
2) E.g. to make lead chloride (insoluble), mix lead nitrate and sodium chloride (both soluble).

If you have an unknown insoluble salt, you could use a flame test to see what ion it contains (see p.35).

lead nitrate + sodium chloride → lead chloride + sodium nitrate
$Pb(NO_3)_{2(aq)} + 2NaCl_{(aq)} \rightarrow PbCl_{2(s)} + 2NaNO_{3(aq)}$

Remember that silver chloride, silver bromide, silver iodide (see p.35) and barium sulfate (p.69) are insoluble precipitates.

Method

1) Add one spatula of lead nitrate to a test tube. Add deionised water to dissolve the lead nitrate. Use deionised water to make sure there are no other ions about. Shake it thoroughly to ensure that all the lead nitrate has dissolved. Then, in a separate test tube, do the same with one spatula of sodium chloride.
2) Tip the two solutions into a small beaker, and give it a good stir to make sure it's all mixed together. The lead chloride should precipitate out.
3) Put a folded piece of filter paper into a filter funnel, and stick the funnel into a conical flask.
4) Pour the contents of the beaker into the middle of the filter paper.
5) The insoluble salt, lead chloride, will be collected on the filter paper.

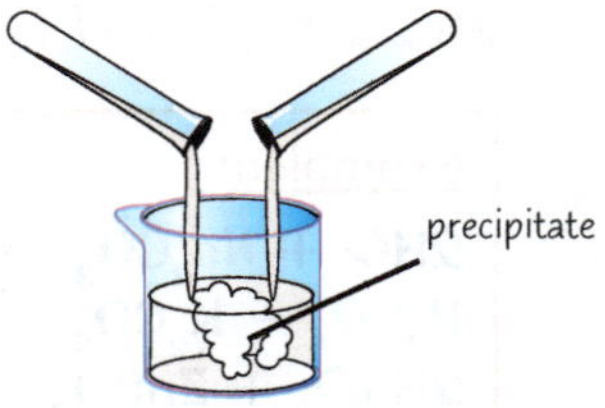

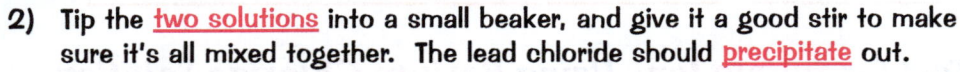

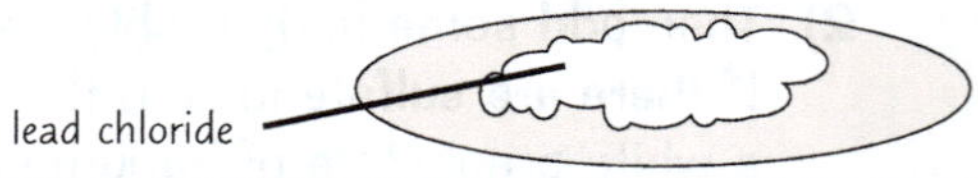

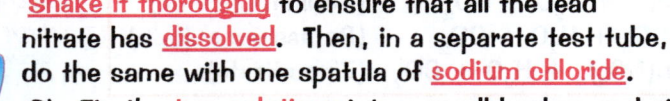

I was attacked by a nasty copper sulfate — it was a salt...

Making salts seems like a hassle. If I were you though, I'd just get my salts from a sachet at the local chippy...

Q1 Iron(III) nitrate is a soluble salt that can be made from iron(III) oxide (an insoluble base) and nitric acid. Suggest a method you could use to make a pure sample of iron(III) nitrate from these reactants. [3 marks]

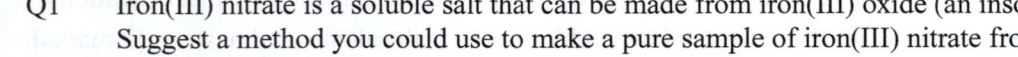

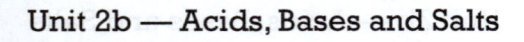

Unit 2b — Acids, Bases and Salts

Titrations

Another way of making salts is by titrations, pronounced 'tie-tray-shuns' (but try not spell it like that).

You Can Make Soluble Salts Using Acid/Alkali Reactions

1) Soluble salts can also be made by reacting an acid with an alkali.
2) But, in this case, you can't tell whether the reaction has finished — there's no signal that all the acid has been neutralised. You also can't just add an excess of alkali to the acid, because the salt is soluble and would be contaminated with the excess alkali.
3) Instead, you need to work out exactly the right volume of alkali to neutralise the acid. For this, you need to do a titration.

Titrations are Used to Find Out Concentrations   PRACTICAL

1) Say you want to find out the concentration of some alkali. Using a pipette and pipette filler, add a fixed volume of the alkali to a conical flask. Add two or three drops of indicator too.
   For a titration, use an indicator with a single, clear colour change (like phenolphthalein or methyl orange). Universal indicator is no good as its colour change is too gradual.

2) Use a funnel to fill a burette with a standard solution of an acid. Record the initial volume of the acid in the burette.

3) Using the burette, add the acid to the alkali a bit at a time — giving the conical flask a regular swirl. Go especially slowly when the end-point is about to be reached, (the point where the acid neutralises the alkali). At the end-point the indicator will change colour.

4) Record the final volume of acid in the burette and subtract it from the initial volume to calculate the volume of acid used to neutralise the alkali.

Pipette — Pipettes measure just one volume, very accurately. Fill the pipette to just above the line, then carefully drop the level down to the line.

You can also do titrations by adding alkali to acid.

Burette — Burettes measure different volumes and let you add the solution drop by drop.

acid

These marks down the side show the volume of acid used.

Conical flask containing alkali and indicator.

- You can tell if the acid is more concentrated than the alkali (or the other way round) by the relative volume that is needed to neutralise it.
- E.g. exactly 1 mole of hydrochloric acid neutralises exactly 1 mole of sodium hydroxide. So if it takes 30 cm^3 of hydrochloric acid to neutralise 25 cm^3 of sodium hydroxide, then the sodium hydroxide must be more concentrated than the hydrochloric acid.
- You can also calculate the actual concentrations of the acid and the alkali — see the next page.

5) Repeat the titration a couple of times and work out the mean of all the similar results. This way, the volume of acid needed for neutralisation will be measured as accurately as possible.

6) Once you know the measured volume of acid needed to neutralise the alkali, you can make the salt...

Making the Salt

- Carry out the reaction again using the same fixed volume of alkali (in a clean flask) and the accurate measured volume of acid needed to neutralise it.
- This time use no indicator, so the salt that is formed won't be contaminated with indicator.
- When the reaction is complete, the solution will only contain the salt and water.
- Then some of the water can be evaporated off slowly and the solution can be left to crystallise. Finally, filter off the salt and dry it — and you'll be left with a pure, dry salt.

What do you get when sailors do titrations? Sea Salt...

Titrations aren't too tricky really — you just need to be careful that you're doing them as carefully as you can.

Q1   How do you determine when the end-point of a titration has been reached?   [1 mark]

Unit 2b — Acids, Bases and Salts

Titration Calculations

I expect you're wondering what you can do with the results from a titration experiment (who wouldn't be?). Well, you'll be relieved to know that you can use them to calculate concentrations of acids or alkalis.

You Might Be Asked to Calculate the Concentration

Titrations let you find the volumes of two solutions that are needed to react together completely. If you know the concentration of one of the solutions, you can use the volumes from the titration experiment, along with the reaction equation, to find the concentration of the other solution.

Find the Concentration in mol/dm³

1) Concentration is the amount of a substance in a given volume of a solution. The units of concentration are usually mol/dm³ or g/dm³.
2) Here's a handy formula triangle you can use to find the concentration of a substance in mol/dm³. It's dead useful in titration calculations.

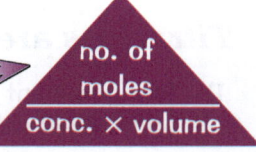

Formula triangle: no. of moles / conc. × volume

EXAMPLE: A student analysed a sample of sulfuric acid (H_2SO_4) of unknown concentration. She found by titration that it took an average of 25.0 cm³ of 0.100 mol/dm³ sodium hydroxide (NaOH) to neutralise 30.0 cm³ of the sulfuric acid. Find the concentration of the acid in mol/dm³. The balanced symbol equation for the reaction is:

$$2NaOH + H_2SO_4 \rightarrow Na_2SO_4 + 2H_2O$$

1) Work out how many moles of the "known" substance you have using the formula: no. of moles = conc. × volume.
   0.100 mol/dm³ × (25.0 / 1000) dm³ = 0.00250 moles of NaOH
2) Use the reaction equation to work out how many moles of the "unknown" substance you must have had.
   Using the equation, you can see that two moles of sodium hydroxide reacts with one mole of sulfuric acid. So 0.00250 moles of NaOH must have reacted with 0.00250 ÷ 2 = 0.00125 moles of H_2SO_4.
3) Work out the concentration of the "unknown" substance.
   Concentration = number of moles ÷ volume
   = 0.00125 mol ÷ (30.0 ÷ 1000) dm³ = 0.041666... mol/dm³ = 0.0417 mol/dm³

Make sure the volume is in dm³ by dividing volumes in cm³ by 1000.

Converting mol/dm³ to g/dm³

1) To find the concentration in g/dm³, start by finding the concentration in mol/dm³ using the steps above.
2) Then, convert the concentration in mol/dm³ to g/dm³ using the equation mass = moles × M_r.

You can also convert from g/dm³ to mol/dm³ by rearranging this equation to: moles = mass ÷ M_r.

EXAMPLE: What's the concentration, in g/dm³, of the sulfuric acid solution in the example above?

1) Work out the relative formula mass for the acid.
   $M_r(H_2SO_4)$ = (2 × 1.0) + 32.1 + (4 × 16.0) = 98.1
2) Convert the concentration in moles (that you've already worked out) into concentration in grams. So, in 1 dm³:
   Mass in grams = moles × relative formula mass = 0.041666... × 98.1 = 4.0875 g
   So the concentration in g/dm³ = 4.09 g/dm³

Don't round your answer until right at the end.

Titrations — you gotta concentrate...

These calculations look pretty scary. But if you get enough practice, then the fear will evaporate and you can tackle them with a smile on your face and a spring in your step. Better get cracking...

Q1 In a titration, 22.5 cm³ of 0.150 mol/dm³ potassium hydroxide (KOH) was needed to neutralise 25.0 cm³ of nitric acid (HNO_3). The balanced equation for the reaction is: $HNO_3 + KOH \rightarrow KNO_3 + H_2O$
Calculate the concentration of nitric acid in mol/dm³. [3 marks]

Unit 2b — Acids, Bases and Salts

Revision Questions for Unit 2b

Well, that wraps up Unit 2b — a nice short section. Don't be fooled though — there are still questions to do.
- Try these questions and tick off each one when you get it right.
- When you've done all the questions for a topic and are completely happy with it, tick off the topic.

Acids and Bases (p.67)

1) State whether the following pH values are acidic, alkaline or neutral.
   a) 9 b) 2 c) 6
2) Universal indicator is added to a strong alkali in solution. What colour would you expect the solution to go?
3) What is an acid?
4) Give the general word equation for the reaction between an acid and a base.
5) What type of reagent could be used to show that an acid or base has been completely neutralised?

Acid and Alkali Strength and the Reactions of Acids (p.68-69)

6) How can the strength of alkalis be measured?
7) What ions would hydrochloric acid, HCl, produce when in solution?
8) Do reactions with weak acids occur faster or slower than those with strong acids?
9) Is a neutralisation reaction exothermic or endothermic?
10) Write an equation to show how hydrochloric acid reacts with copper oxide.
11) What are the products of a reaction between a metal carbonate and an acid?
12) How can you test for sulfate ions?

Making Salts (p.70)

13) How can you make small crystals from a solution of a soluble salt and water?
14) Describe a method you could use to make a dry sample of an insoluble salt from two soluble salts.

Titrations (p.71-72)

15) How can titrations help you when you want to make a salt by reacting an acid with an alkali?
16) Explain why titrations should be repeated several times.
17) Why shouldn't you use an indicator when you're making a salt by reacting an acid with an alkali?
18) 50 cm^3 of hydrochloric acid, HCl, is needed to neutralise 30 cm^3 of sodium hydroxide, NaOH. Which is more concentrated — the hydrochloric acid or the sodium hydroxide?
19) What is the formula that links moles, concentration and volume?
20) What equation could you use to convert mol/dm^3 into g/dm^3?

Metal Ores and The Reactivity Series

A few unreactive metals, like gold, are found in the Earth as the metals themselves, rather than as a compound. The rest of the metals we get by extracting them from rocks — and I bet you're just itching to find out how...

Ores Contain Enough Metal to Make Extraction Worthwhile

1) A metal ore is a rock which contains enough metal to make it economically worthwhile extracting the metal from it. The metal ore is a metal compound — in many cases the ore is an oxide of the metal.

> Example: the main aluminium ore is called bauxite — it's a source of aluminium oxide (Al_2O_3).

You can tell what metals are in an ore by looking at its chemical formula.

2) Most of the metals that we use are found in their ores in the Earth's crust. The ores are mined and the metals can then be extracted from the ores.
3) Some unreactive metals, such as gold and silver, are present in the Earth's crust in their native forms (as uncombined elements). These metals can be mined straight out of the ground, but they usually need to be refined before they can be used.
4) The more reactive a metal, the harder they are to extract from their ores.

Some Metals can be Extracted by Reduction with Carbon

Oxidation can mean the reaction with, or addition of, oxygen. Reduction can be the removal of oxygen.

> E.g. $2Fe_2O_3 + 3C \rightarrow 4Fe + 3CO_2$
> - Iron oxide is reduced to iron (as oxygen is removed).
> - Carbon is oxidised to carbon dioxide (as oxygen is added).

Reduction and oxidation can also be to do with electrons (see page 76).

A metal can be extracted from its ore by reduction with carbon. The position of the metal in the reactivity series determines whether it can be extracted in this way.

- Metals higher than carbon in the reactivity series have to be extracted using electrolysis (see p.78) which is expensive.
- Metals below carbon in the reactivity series can be extracted by reduction using carbon. For example, iron oxide is reduced in a blast furnace to make iron.
- This is because carbon can only take the oxygen away from metals which are less reactive than carbon itself is.

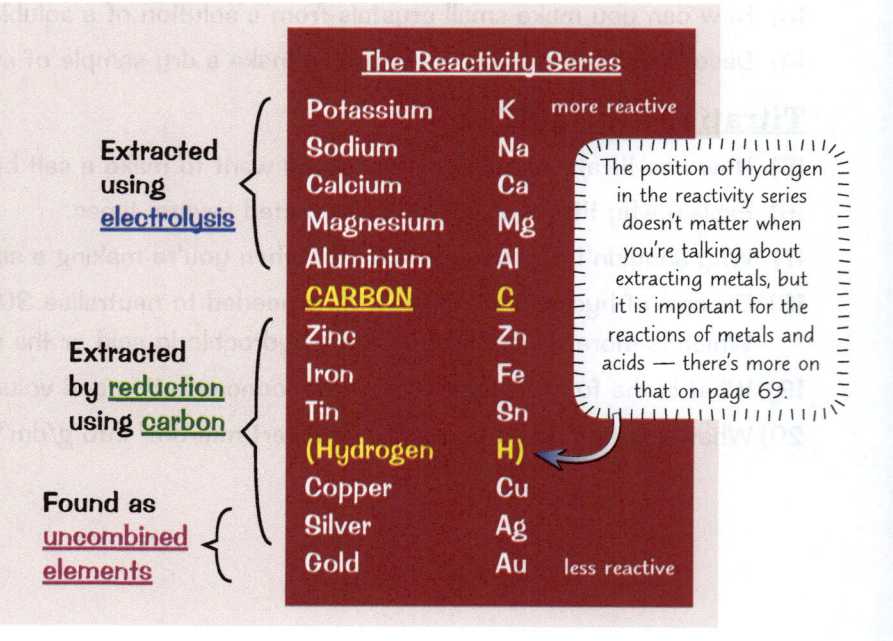

The Reactivity Series

Potassium	K	more reactive
Sodium	Na	
Calcium	Ca	
Magnesium	Mg	
Aluminium	Al	
CARBON	**C**	
Zinc	Zn	
Iron	Fe	
Tin	Sn	
(Hydrogen	H)	
Copper	Cu	
Silver	Ag	
Gold	Au	less reactive

Extracted using electrolysis

Extracted by reduction using carbon

Found as uncombined elements

The position of hydrogen in the reactivity series doesn't matter when you're talking about extracting metals, but it is important for the reactions of metals and acids — there's more on that on page 69.

[Please insert ore-ful pun here]...

Make sure you've got that reactivity series sorted in your head. If a metal's below carbon in the reactivity series, then it's less reactive than carbon and can be extracted from its ore by reduction using carbon. Phew... got it?

Q1 How would you extract tin from its metal ore? Explain your answer. [2 marks]

Q2 Write a balanced chemical equation to describe the reaction that occurs when carbon is used to extract zinc from its ore, zinc oxide (ZnO). [2 marks]

Extracting Iron

Iron is a very common element in the Earth's crust, but good iron ores are only found in a few select places around the world, such as Australia, Canada and Millom. Iron is extracted by reduction in a blast furnace.

The Raw Materials are Iron Ore, Coke and Limestone

1) The iron ore contains the iron — which is pretty important.
2) The coke is a fuel — it's almost pure carbon. It's used to produce carbon monoxide for the reduction of the iron(III) oxide to iron metal.
3) The limestone takes away impurities in the form of slag.

Reducing the Iron Ore to Iron:

1) Hot air is blasted into the furnace. This provides oxygen and makes the coke burn much faster than normal. This raises the temperature to about 1500 °C.
2) The coke burns in a combustion reaction and produces carbon dioxide:

$$C + O_2 \rightarrow CO_2$$
carbon + oxygen → carbon dioxide

3) The CO_2 then reacts with unburnt coke in a combustion reaction to form CO:

$$CO_2 + C \rightarrow 2CO$$
carbon dioxide + carbon → carbon monoxide

4) The carbon monoxide then reduces the iron ore to iron:

$$3CO + Fe_2O_3 \rightarrow 3CO_2 + 2Fe$$
carbon monoxide + iron(III) oxide → carbon dioxide + iron

5) The iron is molten at this temperature and it's also very dense, so it runs straight to the bottom of the furnace where it's tapped off.

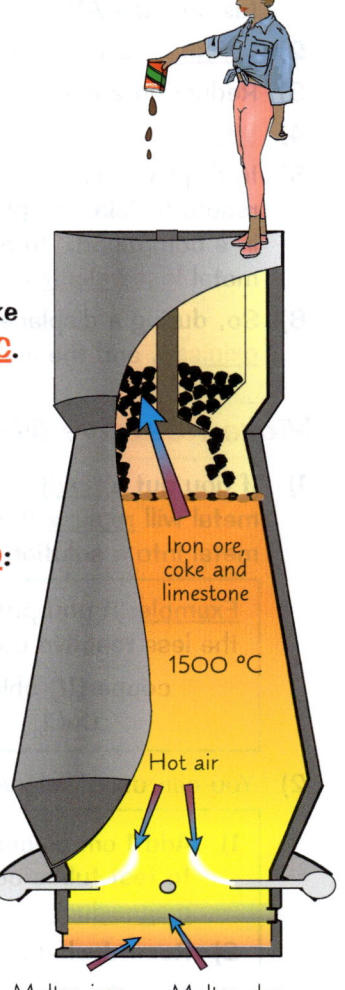

(Diagram labels: Iron ore, coke and limestone; 1500 °C; Hot air; Molten iron; Molten slag)

Removing the Impurities:

1) The main impurity is sand (silicon dioxide). This is still solid, even at 1500 °C, and would tend to stay mixed in with the iron. The limestone removes it.
2) The limestone is decomposed by the heat into calcium oxide and CO_2.

$$CaCO_3 \rightarrow CaO + CO_2$$
calcium carbonate → calcium oxide + carbon dioxide

3) The calcium oxide then reacts with the sand in a neutralisation reaction to form calcium silicate, or slag, which is molten and can be tapped off:

$$CaO + SiO_2 \rightarrow CaSiO_3$$
calcium oxide + silicon dioxide → calcium silicate (slag)

This is a continuous process — the iron ore, coke and limestone are continuously added to the furnace as the molten iron and molten slag are removed. This means that you don't need to get the furnace up to temperature each time as the reaction doesn't stop. This saves time and money.

Learn the facts about iron extraction — it's a blast...

This is all important and could be tested in the exam, including the equations. Cover it up and try repeating the facts back to yourself. If you're in a public place people might think you're mad. But that's OK.

Q1   Write the balanced equation for carbon monoxide reducing iron ore, Fe_2O_3, to iron.   [1 mark]

Unit 2c — Metals, Extraction and Energy

Metal Displacement Reactions

You can directly compare the reactivity of metals using displacement reactions. Exciting stuff I tell ya.

Displacement Reactions are Redox Reactions

1) As well as talking about reduction and oxidation in terms of the loss and gain of oxygen (as on page 74), you can also talk about them in terms of electrons.
2) Oxidation can be the loss of electrons, and reduction can be the gain of electrons.
3) Reduction and oxidation happen simultaneously — hence the name redox reactions.
4) Displacement reactions are examples of redox reactions.
5) In displacement reactions, a more reactive element reacts to take the place of a less reactive element in a compound. In metal displacement reactions, the more reactive metal loses electrons and the less reactive metal gains electrons.
6) So, during a displacement reaction, the more reactive metal is oxidised, and the less reactive metal is reduced. For example:

When dealing with electrons: Oxidation Is Loss, Reduction Is Gain. Remember it as OIL RIG.

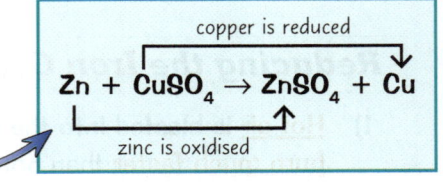

copper is reduced
$Zn + CuSO_4 \rightarrow ZnSO_4 + Cu$
zinc is oxidised

More Reactive Metals Displace Less Reactive Ones

PRACTICAL

1) If you put a reactive metal into a solution of a less reactive metal salt, the reactive metal will replace the less reactive metal in the salt. If you put a less reactive metal into a solution of a more reactive metal salt, nothing will happen.

Example: if you put an iron nail in a solution of copper(II) chloride, the more reactive iron "kicks out" the less reactive copper from the salt. You end up with iron(II) chloride solution and copper metal.

copper(II) chloride + iron → iron(II) chloride + copper
$CuCl_2$ + Fe → $FeCl_2$ + Cu

Copper is reduced and iron is oxidised.

2) You can use displacement reactions to work out where in the reactivity series a metal should go. E.g.

1) Add 1 cm pieces of copper, magnesium and zinc to test tubes containing 5 cm³ copper(II) sulfate, magnesium sulfate and zinc sulfate solutions.
2) Record whether any reactions happen.
3) The table shows the results you'd get.
4) You can use the table to work out an order of reactivity for the metals:

	copper(II) sulfate	magnesium sulfate	zinc sulfate
copper	no reaction	no reaction	no reaction
magnesium	magnesium sulfate and copper formed	no reaction	magnesium sulfate and zinc formed
zinc	zinc sulfate and copper formed	no reaction	no reaction

- Magnesium displaces both copper and zinc, so it must be more reactive than both.
- Copper is displaced by both magnesium and zinc, so it must be less reactive than both.
- Zinc can displace copper, but not magnesium, so it must go between them.

The order of reactivity, from most to least, is: magnesium, zinc, copper.

3) If you heat a reactive metal with a less reactive metal oxide, the more reactive metal will remove oxygen from it. This is called a competition reaction.

Example: if you heat iron(III) oxide with aluminium, the more reactive aluminium will remove the oxygen from the iron(III) oxide. You end up with aluminium oxide and iron metal.

iron(III) oxide + aluminium → aluminium oxide + iron
Fe_2O_3 + 2Al → Al_2O_3 + 2Fe

This is called the thermite reaction.

And that's why Iron Man never goes swimming in copper sulfate...

See, experiments aren't just for fun — they can give you a thrilling insight into the relative reactivities of elements.

Q1 State whether silver would displace iron from iron(II) chloride solution and explain your answer. [1 mark]

Unit 2c — Metals, Extraction and Energy

Electrolysis

Now I hope you're sitting comfortably. We're about to embark on some electrolysis. What a treat.

Electrolysis Means 'Splitting Up with Electricity'

1) During electrolysis, an electric current is passed through an electrolyte (a molten or dissolved ionic compound). The ions move towards the electrodes, where they react, and the compound decomposes.
2) The positive ions in the electrolyte will move towards the cathode (−ve electrode) and gain electrons (they are reduced).
3) The negative ions in the electrolyte will move towards the anode (+ve electrode) and lose electrons (they are oxidised).
4) This creates a flow of charge through the electrolyte as ions travel to the electrodes.
5) As ions gain or lose electrons, they form the uncharged element and are discharged from the electrolyte.

An electrolyte is just a liquid or solution that can conduct electricity. An electrode is a solid that conducts electricity and is submerged in the electrolyte.

Setting Up Electrolysis... **PRACTICAL**

You may have to predict and identify what's been made in an electrolysis experiment. To identify gaseous products, you need to set up the equipment as shown in the diagram.

1) The power supply is connected to the electrodes.
2) The end of the electrodes are placed inside test tubes.
3) Any gases produced at the electrodes can then be collected inside the test tubes.

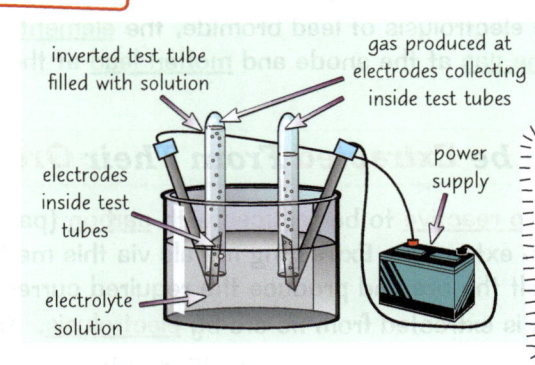

When drawing this set up, always label the d.c. power supply, wires and electrodes. The anode is on the same side as the longer line of the d.c. power supply.

Electrolysis Splits Water into Hydrogen and Oxygen

1) Water, H_2O, contains hydrogen ions (H^+) and hydroxide ions (OH^-).
2) When an electric current is passed through water, the ions move towards different electrodes.
3) Hydrogen ions are positive, so they are attracted towards the cathode (−ve electrode). At the cathode, the hydrogen ions are reduced and form hydrogen gas.
4) Hydroxide ions are negative, so they move towards the anode (+ve electrode). At the anode, the hydroxide ions are oxidised and form oxygen gas.

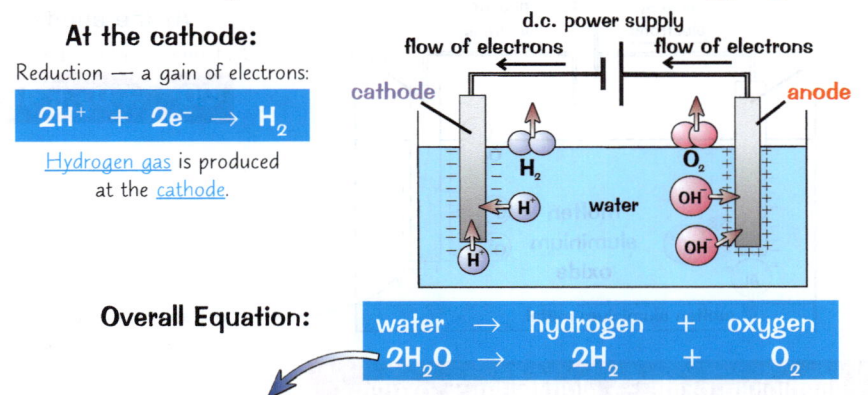

elec-toads

At the cathode:
Reduction — a gain of electrons:
$$2H^+ + 2e^- \rightarrow H_2$$
Hydrogen gas is produced at the cathode.

At the anode:
Oxidation — a loss of electrons
$$2OH^- \rightarrow O_2 + 2H^+ + 4e^-$$
Oxygen is produced at the anode.

You need to remember the equation for hydrogen ions at the cathode. The unbalanced equation for hydroxide ions at the anode will be given — but you will still need to know how to balance it.

Overall Equation:
water → hydrogen + oxygen
$2H_2O \rightarrow 2H_2 + O_2$

5) You can see from the equation that electrolysis of water forms two H_2 molecules for every O_2 molecule. So the volume of hydrogen gas formed is always twice the volume of oxygen gas formed.

Faster shopping at the supermarket — use Electrolleys...

Fed up with electrolysis? Probably best to take a short break before you turn over the page....

Q1 A student sets up an experiment for the electrolysis of water. He places the anode inside test tube A and the cathode inside test tube B. During the experiment, what gas will be collected in:
 a) test tube A? b) test tube B? [2 marks]

Unit 2c — Metals, Extraction and Energy

More on Electrolysis

What's that you say — you want more electrolysis? Well you should always give the people what they want...

Electrolysis of Molten Ionic Solids Forms Elements

The electrodes should be inert so they don't react with the electrolyte.

1) An ionic solid can't be electrolysed because the ions are in fixed positions and can't move.
2) Molten ionic compounds can be electrolysed because the ions can move freely and conduct electricity.
3) Molten ionic compounds, e.g. lead bromide ($PbBr_2$), are always broken up into their elements.
4) Positive metal ions gain electrons at the cathode (they are reduced).
   E.g. $Pb^{2+} + 2e^- \rightarrow Pb$
5) Negative non-metal ions lose electrons at the anode (they are oxidised).
   E.g. $2Br^- \rightarrow Br_2 + 2e^-$
6) So for the electrolysis of lead bromide, the elements formed are bromine gas at the anode and molten lead at the cathode.

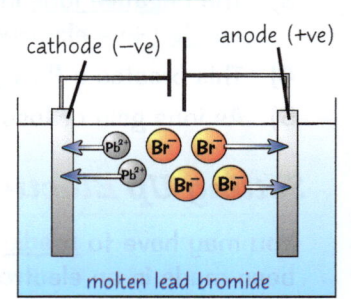

Metals can be Extracted From Their Ores Using Electrolysis

If a metal is too reactive to be reduced with carbon (page 74) or reacts with carbon, then electrolysis can be used to extract it. Extracting metals via this method is very expensive as lots of energy is required to melt the ore and produce the required current.

1) Aluminium is extracted from its ore by electrolysis. The ore contains alumina (aluminium oxide), Al_2O_3.
2) Aluminium oxide has a very high melting point, so it's dissolved in molten cryolite. Dissolving in cryolite needs a lower temperature than melting the aluminium oxide, so it reduces the energy needed for extraction.

Cryolite is an aluminium-based compound with a lower melting point than aluminium oxide.

3) The molten mixture contains free ions — so it'll conduct electricity.
4) The positive Al^{3+} ions are attracted to the cathode where they each pick up three electrons and turn into neutral aluminium atoms. These then sink to the bottom of the electrolysis tank.
5) The negative O^{2-} ions are attracted to the anode where they each lose two electrons. The neutral oxygen atoms will then combine to form O_2 molecules.

At the cathode:
Reduction — a gain of electrons:
$Al^{3+} + 3e^- \rightarrow Al$

Metals form positive ions, so they're attracted to the cathode.

Aluminium is produced at the cathode.

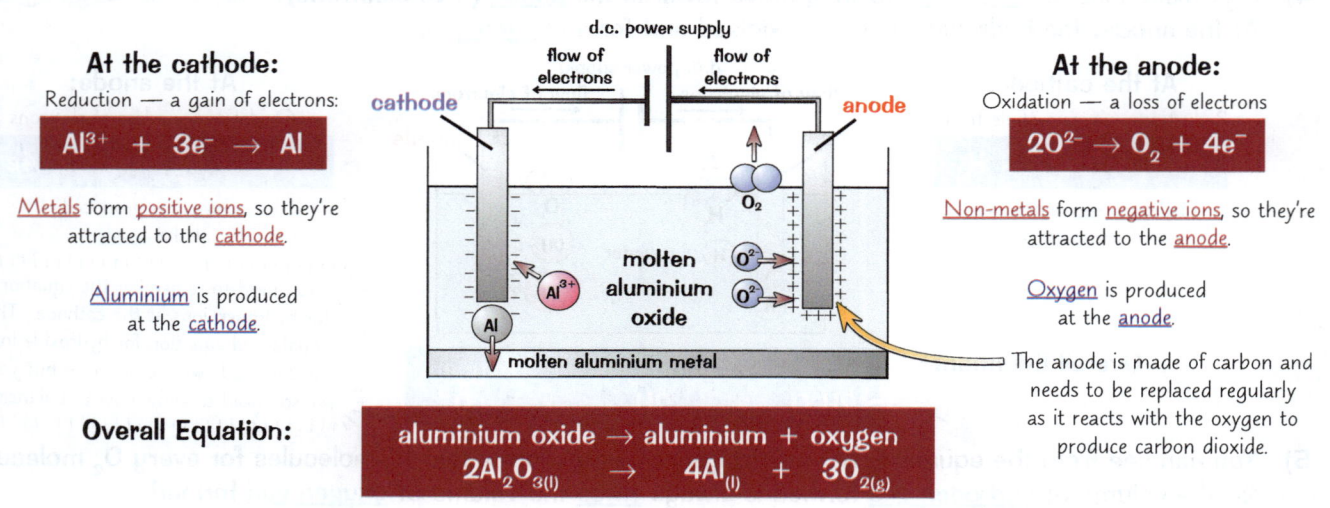

At the anode:
Oxidation — a loss of electrons
$2O^{2-} \rightarrow O_2 + 4e^-$

Non-metals form negative ions, so they're attracted to the anode.

Oxygen is produced at the anode.

The anode is made of carbon and needs to be replaced regularly as it reacts with the oxygen to produce carbon dioxide.

Overall Equation:
aluminium oxide → aluminium + oxygen
$2Al_2O_{3(l)} \rightarrow 4Al_{(l)} + 3O_{2(g)}$

Metal ions are reduced at the cathode — they're 5 for £1 there...

It might be useful for your exams to learn how to work out the products of the electrolysis of ionic compounds...

Q1   Briefly explain why solid sodium chloride cannot be electrolysed. [1 mark]

Q2   Explain why aluminium oxide is dissolved in molten cryolite before electrolysis. [3 marks]

Unit 2c — Metals, Extraction and Energy

Electrolysis of Aqueous Solutions

When you electrolyse an aqueous solution, you also have to factor in the ions in the water.

It May be Easier to Discharge Ions from Water than the Solute   PRACTICAL

1) In aqueous solutions, as well as the ions from the ionic compound, there will be hydrogen ions (H^+) and hydroxide ions (OH^-) from the water.
2) At the cathode, if H^+ ions and metal ions are present, hydrogen gas will be produced if the metal ions form an elemental metal that is more reactive than hydrogen (e.g. sodium ions). If the metal ions form an elemental metal that is less reactive than hydrogen (e.g. copper ions), a solid layer of the pure metal will be produced instead.
3) At the anode, if OH^- and halide ions (Cl^-, Br^-, I^-) are present, molecules of chlorine, bromine or iodine will be formed. If no halide ions are present, then the OH^- ions are discharged and oxygen will be formed.

A solution of copper(II) chloride ($CuCl_2$) contains four different ions: Cu^{2+}, Cl^-, H^+ and OH^-.

- Copper metal is less reactive than hydrogen. So at the cathode, copper metal is produced and coats the electrode.

  $Cu^{2+} + 2e^- \rightarrow Cu$

- The presence of chlorine ions in the solution means that chlorine gas is produced at the anode.

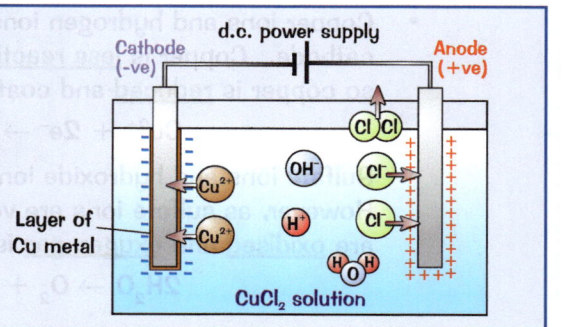

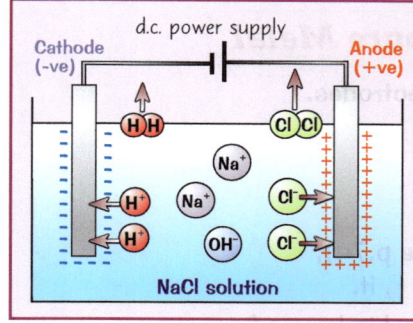

  $2Cl^- \rightarrow Cl_2 + 2e^-$

A solution of sodium chloride (NaCl) contains four different ions: Na^+, Cl^-, OH^- and H^+.

- Sodium metal is more reactive than hydrogen. So at the cathode, hydrogen gas is produced.

  $2H^+ + 2e^- \rightarrow H_2$

- Chloride ions are present in the solution. So at the anode chlorine gas is produced.

  $2Cl^- \rightarrow Cl_2 + 2e^-$

You should use inert (unreactive) electrodes when electrolysing an aqueous solution, e.g. graphite (carbon) electrodes. However, if oxygen is produced, you might find it reacts with the graphite electrodes, forming CO_2 gas.

You can set up an electrolysis experiment in the lab like the set-up on page 77. Once the experiment is finished you can test any gaseous products to work out what was produced.
- Hydrogen makes a "squeaky pop" with a lighted splint (see page 35).
- Oxygen will relight a glowing splint (see page 48).

Electrode Equations Show What's Happening at Each Electrode

You need to be able to write balanced equations for reactions occurring at the electrodes. The important thing to remember is that the charges must be the same on both sides of the equation. E.g. For the electrolysis of aqueous sodium chloride the electrode equations are:

Cathode: $2H^+ + 2e^- \rightarrow H_2$ — There are 2 positive (+1) hydrogen ions and 2 negative (−1) electrons on the left hand side. 2 − 2 = 0, so the right hand side must be uncharged — which it is, as hydrogen gas (H_2) is formed.

Anode: $2Cl^- \rightarrow Cl_2 + 2e^-$ or $2Cl^- - 2e^- \rightarrow Cl_2$

There are 2 negative (−1) chloride ions on the left hand side. So the right hand side must have a charge of −2. Uncharged chlorine gas is formed, so there must be 2 negative (−1) electrons on the right hand side.

I wrote a poem about my tabby — it was a cat ode...

So it's kinda confusing this electrolysis malarkey — you need to take it slow and make sure you get it.

Q1   An aqueous solution of potassium bromide, KBr, is electrolysed using inert electrodes. Write balanced equations for the reactions occurring at the anode and the cathode.   [2 marks]

Unit 2c — Metals, Extraction and Energy

Uses of Electrolysis

The products you get from electrolysis depend not only on your electrolyte, but on your electrodes too...

Electroplating is Applying a Metal Coating to an Object

1) Electroplating is coating the surface of a metal with another metal using electrolysis.
2) The cathode is the object you're going to electroplate, the anode is the metal you're using for the plating and your electrolyte is a solution containing the metal ions of the metal you're plating.

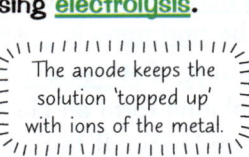

The anode keeps the solution 'topped up' with ions of the metal.

Electroplating with Copper — PRACTICAL

A solution of copper(II) sulfate ($CuSO_4$) contains four different ions: Cu^{2+}, SO_4^{2-}, H^+ and OH^-.

- Copper ions and hydrogen ions are attracted to the cathode. Copper is less reactive than hydrogen, so copper is reduced and coats the cathode.
  $$Cu^{2+} + 2e^- \rightarrow Cu$$
- Sulfate ions and hydroxide ions are attracted to the anode. However, as sulfate ions are very stable, hydroxide ions are oxidised and oxygen gas is produced.
  $$2H_2O \rightarrow O_2 + 4H^+ + 4e^-$$

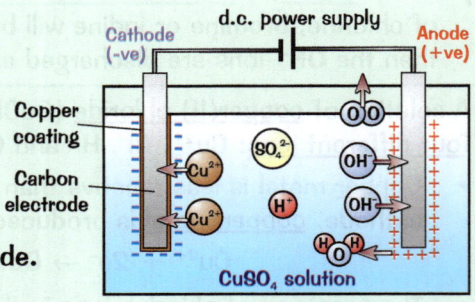

This is similar to how electroplating works in industry — you just replace the cathode with a conducting object that you want to coat with copper.

Purifying Means Removing Impurities from an Impure Metal

When purifying using electrolysis, pure metal builds up on one of the electrodes. The impurities from the metal then sink to the bottom of the solution.

Purifying Copper

Copper can be extracted from its ore by reduction with carbon (see p.74), but copper made in this way is impure. Electrolysis is used to purify it.

When copper is purified using electrolysis, the anode starts off as a big lump of impure copper and the cathode starts off as a thin piece of pure copper. The electrolyte is copper(II) sulfate. Here's what happens during the process:

- The impure copper anode is oxidised, dissolving into the electrolyte to form copper ions:
  $$Cu \rightarrow Cu^{2+} + 2e^-$$
- The copper ions are reduced at the pure copper cathode, and add to it as a layer of pure copper:
  $$Cu^{2+} + 2e^- \rightarrow Cu$$
- Any impurities from the impure copper anode sink to the bottom of the electrolysis tank, forming a sludge.

These two reactions mean the concentration of Cu^{2+} ions in solution is constant — they're produced and removed at the same rate.

Electrolysis of Sodium Chloride Produces Sodium Hydroxide

1) The main way sodium hydroxide is manufactured is by the electrolysis of aqueous sodium chloride (see page 79). In the electrolysis, hydrogen gas is produced at the cathode and chlorine gas is produced at the anode.
2) The sodium ions (Na^+) and the hydroxide ions (OH^-) in the solution don't react with the cathode or the anode. Instead, they form sodium hydroxide which is recovered by evaporation.

A hat, some handcuffs and a truncheon — 100% pure copper...

Phew, that really is the last page on electrolysis. Time to celebrate making it to the end with a question.

Q1 Explain how electrolysis is used to purify copper. [4 marks]

Unit 2c — Metals, Extraction and Energy

Sustainability of Metal Extraction

There's loads of things to take into account before building a metal extraction plant — where to build the plant, how to save fuel and energy costs, how to... oh the list is too long, just read the page.

It's Important to Choose the Right Site for a Metal Extraction Plant

There are lots of factors that affect where a metal extraction plant is set up. You have to take into account the economic benefits and sustainability of the extraction process when deciding on a site:

1) Plants are usually built near to the coast so raw materials can be easily imported into the plant.
2) Plants can't be built too close to urban areas — it's likely that local residents would oppose this. Metal extraction plants can create noise and air pollution, as well as a loss of natural landscape.
3) They need to be close enough to towns and cities that workers can travel easily from their homes.
4) Aluminium plants need a lot of electricity to run, so it's important that there is a direct power supply from a nearby power station.

> Anglesey Aluminium was an aluminium plant in Wales — when running it would use 10-15% of all the electricity used in Wales. When their closest power supply, Wylfa Power Station, was decommissioned, Anglesey Aluminium no longer had a guaranteed direct supply of electricity. This meant that the aluminium plant became uneconomical and had to close down.

5) The finished product from metal extraction plants needs to be transported all over the country (and possibly the world) to buyers. It's essential that the location has good transport links — nearby railway lines and motorways will influence the siting of a plant.

Metal Extraction Plants Need to be Sustainable

1) Metal extraction plants need be sustainable, both in economic and environmental terms.
2) Sometimes the cost of importing materials from other countries is lower than mining the raw materials near to the extraction plant.

> Wales has produced iron and steel for a very long time because all of the raw materials can be found there. However the plant at Port Talbot imports their raw materials instead. It isn't sustainable to use the raw materials available in Wales due to the cost and environmental impact of quarrying.

3) Extracting raw materials uses large amounts of energy, lots of which comes from burning fossil fuels.
4) Recycling materials saves energy as the process often only uses a small fraction of the energy needed to extract and refine the material from scratch. This reduces greenhouse gas emissions (p.47).
5) As there's a finite amount of most raw materials, recycling also conserves resources.
6) It's beneficial to the economy to recycle metals that are expensive to extract or buy.

Example: Recycling Aluminium

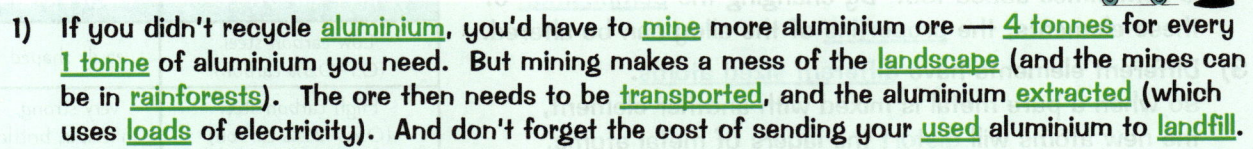

1) If you didn't recycle aluminium, you'd have to mine more aluminium ore — 4 tonnes for every 1 tonne of aluminium you need. But mining makes a mess of the landscape (and the mines can be in rainforests). The ore then needs to be transported, and the aluminium extracted (which uses loads of electricity). And don't forget the cost of sending your used aluminium to landfill.
2) It's a complex calculation, but recycling aluminium only uses about 5% of the energy that you'd need to extract the metal from aluminium ore.

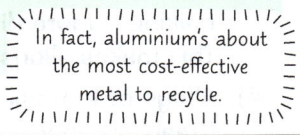

In fact, aluminium's about the most cost-effective metal to recycle.

Let's see if I can find a good joke to recycle here...

Sustainability's a hot topic. We don't have an infinite amount of materials to keep on making things from, so recycling is really important to make sure we don't run out of lots of important raw materials.

Q1 Give an advantage and a disadvantage of building a metal extraction plant near to a town. [2 marks]

Unit 2c — Metals, Extraction and Energy

Uses of Metals

Iron, aluminium, titanium and copper are some of the most used metals in the whole world. Time to learn why.

Iron, Aluminium, Titanium and Copper have Properties in Common

Iron, aluminium, titanium and copper have the same basic properties — they are all metals after all.

1) They are dense and lustrous (i.e. shiny) and have high melting points — iron melts at 1538 °C, aluminium melts at 660 °C, titanium melts at 1668 °C and copper melts at 1085 °C.
2) They have high tensile strength — they're strong and hard to break.
3) But they can also be hammered into a different shape (they're malleable).
4) They are good conductors of electricity and of heat energy too.

There's more on the properties of metals on page 59.

The Uses of Metals Depend on their Properties

- Iron has all the properties you'd expect a metal to have.
  Adding other materials to the iron can change its properties though (see below).
- Wrought iron is almost completely pure iron. It's malleable, so it's used to make gates and railings.
- The main problem with iron is that it corrodes easily (i.e. it rusts).

- Aluminium is also a typical metal. However, unlike iron, it doesn't corrode easily.
- The aluminium reacts very quickly with oxygen in the air to form aluminium oxide. A nice protective layer of aluminium oxide sticks firmly to the aluminium below and stops any further reaction taking place.
- Because aluminium doesn't corrode it's useful for products that come in contact with water, e.g. window frames. This also means it is non-toxic — it's good for food cans.
- Aluminium is also much less dense than iron, which makes it lighter.
- This makes it useful when the weight of the metal is important, e.g. in bicycle frames and aeroplanes.

- Copper is malleable and ductile, and it is an especially good conductor of heat and electricity.
- It is used in electrical components and wiring as it has low resistance and so is efficient at transferring electricity.
- It's also used in heating systems, such as underfloor heating, as it allows speedy transfer of heat to the surroundings.
- Copper also has an attractive colour and lustre (a bright, shiny glow) so it gets used as decoration.

- Titanium has a very low density and it doesn't corrode easily. It's also very hard.
- It is very lightweight, so it's used for bicycle frames and aeroplanes — like aluminium.

Pure Metals Don't Always Have the Properties Needed

1) The regular structure of many pure metals makes them soft — often too soft for everyday uses.
2) Alloys are made by mixing molten metals together. Carbon is sometimes added too. By changing the composition of these elements, the properties of the alloy can be altered.
3) Different elements have different sized atoms. So when a pure metal is mixed with another element, the new atoms will distort the layers of metal atoms, making it more difficult for them to slide over each other. This makes alloys harder than pure metals.
4) Alloys of iron called steels are often used instead of pure iron, since they are harder and stronger. Steels are made by adding small amounts of carbon and sometimes other metals to iron.

TYPE OF STEEL	PROPERTIES	USE
Low carbon steel (0.1–0.3% carbon)	easily shaped	car bodies
High carbon steel (0.22–2.5% carbon)	very strong, inflexible, brittle	bridges
Stainless steel (chromium added, and sometimes nickel)	corrosion-resistant, hard	cutlery

If Iron Man and the Silver Surfer teamed up, they'd be great alloys...

Different metals have different properties, which make them suited to different uses. The same goes for alloys too.

Q1   Give one use of steel.

[1 mark]

Unit 2c — Metals, Extraction and Energy

Transition Metals

Transition metals have plenty of different properties that you need to know — grab a cup of tea and read on...

The Transition Metals Sit in the Middle of the Periodic Table

A lot of everyday metals are transition metals (e.g. copper, iron, zinc, gold, silver, platinum) — but there are loads of others as well.

If you get asked about a transition metal you've never heard of — don't panic. These 'new' transition metals will follow all the properties you've already learnt for the others.

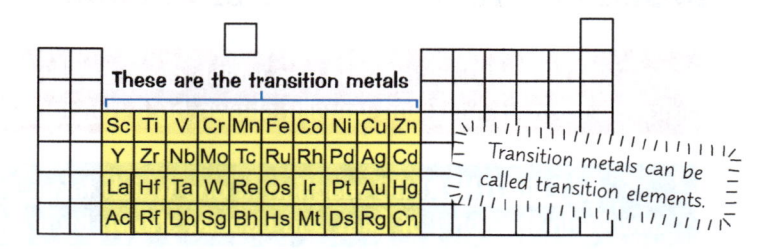

Transition metals can be called transition elements.

Transition Metals Have Typical Metallic Properties

1) The transition metals have all the typical properties of metals (see page 59) — they're relatively hard, strong, shiny and malleable materials that conduct heat and electricity well.
2) They have high melting and boiling points (except mercury, which is liquid at room temperature).
3) They have high densities.
4) Transition metals have more than one ion. For example, iron forms Fe^{2+} and Fe^{3+} ions.

Transition Metals and Their Compounds Make Good Catalysts

1) A catalyst speeds up the rate of a reaction without being changed or used up itself — see page 55 for more about catalysts.
2) Iron is the catalyst used in the Haber process for making ammonia.
3) Platinum is the catalyst used in catalytic converters.

Transition Metal Ions form Colourful Precipitates

1) The compounds and solutions of transition metals are colourful. What colour they are depends on what transition metal ion they contain — e.g. compounds and solutions containing: iron(II) (Fe^{2+}) ions are usually pale green, iron(III) (Fe^{3+}) ions are brown and copper(II) (Cu^{2+}) ions are often blue.
2) A transition metal can form a precipitate when it reacts with aqueous hydroxide ions. A precipitate is a solid, insoluble substance.
3) The precipitate is formed because the transition metal ions in the metal compound solution react with the hydroxide ions in the hydroxide solution.
4) The colour of the precipitate depends on the transition metal ion that it contains — e.g. a precipitate containing Fe^{2+} ions would be green.
5) Ions not included in precipitation reactions are called spectator ions (see page 35) and they are not included in the ionic equation for the reaction.

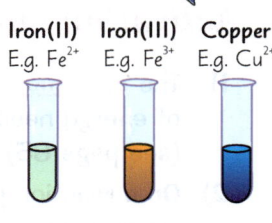

> **Example:** Copper(II) sulfate and sodium hydroxide react to form a copper(II) hydroxide precipitate.
> Full equation: $CuSO_{4(aq)} + 2NaOH_{(aq)} \rightarrow Cu(OH)_{2(s)} + Na_2SO_{4(aq)}$
> Writing out all the ions: $Cu^{2+}_{(aq)} + SO_4^{2-}_{(aq)} + 2Na^+_{(aq)} + 2OH^-_{(aq)} \rightarrow Cu(OH)_{2(s)} + Na_2SO_{4(aq)}$
> Here, the SO_4^{2-} and Na^+ ions are spectator ions as they don't take part in forming the precipitate. So the ionic equation is:
> $Cu^{2+}_{(aq)} + 2OH^-_{(aq)} \rightarrow Cu(OH)_{2(s)}$
>
> State symbols show the precipitate as a solid (s) and everything else in solution (aq).

It's hard to get more colourful than transition metal precipitates...

Transition metals are everywhere. They make good catalysts, iron's used to make steel for construction, copper's used in electrical wiring, and you can even use their pretty compounds to colour stained glass.

Q1 Explain how a scientist could tell apart solutions of iron(II) chloride and iron(III) chloride. [2 marks]

Unit 2c — Metals, Extraction and Energy

Endothermic and Exothermic Reactions

So, endothermic and exothermic reactions are all about taking in and giving out energy to the surroundings. I think endothermic reactions are a bit self-centred really — they just take, take, take...

Combustion reactions (p.90) and neutralisation reactions (p.67) are always exothermic.

Reactions are Exothermic or Endothermic

An **EXOTHERMIC** reaction is one which gives out energy to the surroundings, usually in the form of heat and usually shown by a rise in temperature of the surroundings.

An **ENDOTHERMIC** reaction is one which takes in energy from the surroundings, usually in the form of heat and usually shown by a fall in temperature of the surroundings.

Reaction Profiles Show if a Reaction's Exo- or Endothermic

Reaction profiles show the energy levels of the reactants and the products in a reaction. You can use them to work out if energy is released (exothermic) or taken in (endothermic).

1) This shows an exothermic reaction — the products are at a lower energy than the reactants.
2) The difference in height represents the energy given out in the reaction.

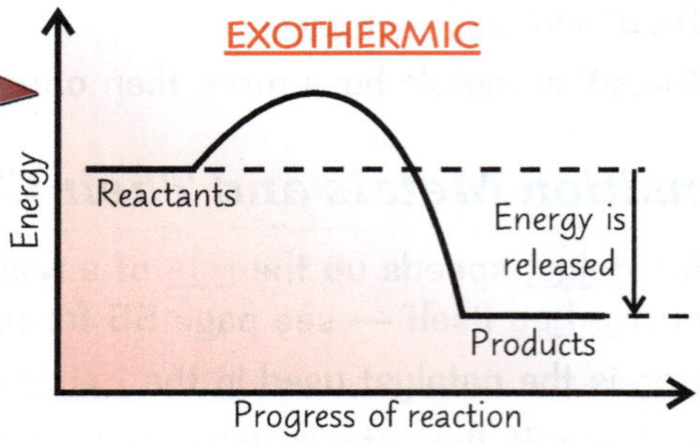

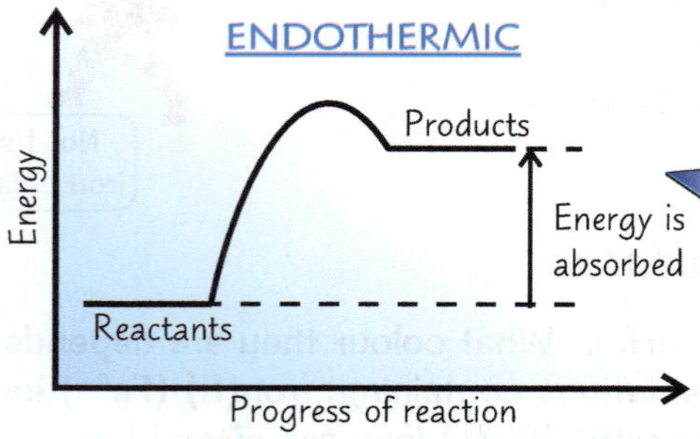

1) This shows an endothermic reaction because the products are at a higher energy than the reactants.
2) The difference in height represents the energy taken in during the reaction.

Activation Energy is the Energy Needed to Start a Reaction

1) The activation energy is the minimum amount of energy needed for bonds to break (see page 85) and for a reaction to start.
2) On a reaction profile, it's the energy difference between the reactants and the highest point on the curve.
3) It's a bit like having to climb up one side of a hill before you can ski/snowboard/sledge/fall down the other side.
4) If the energy input is less than the activation energy there won't be enough energy to start the reaction — so nothing will happen.

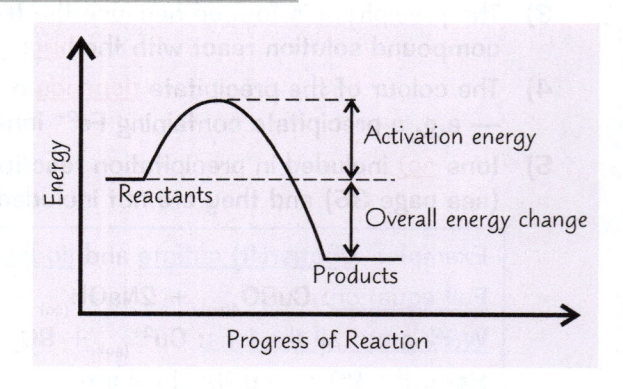

Endothermic reactions — they just get cooler and cooler...

Remember, "exo-" = exit, "-thermic" = heat, so an exothermic reaction is one that gives out heat — and endothermic means just the opposite. To make sure you really understand these terms, try this question.

Q1 A student carries out an experiment which results in a change in temperature of the reaction mixture. Use the energy profile for the reaction, shown on the right, to help explain whether the temperature of the reaction mixture increased or decreased. [2 marks]

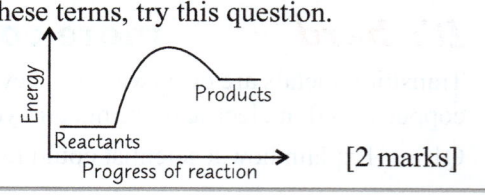

Unit 2c — Metals, Extraction and Energy

Bond Energies

Energy transfer in chemical reactions is all to do with making and breaking bonds.

Energy Must Always be Supplied to Break Bonds

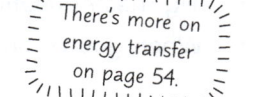

1) During a chemical reaction, old bonds are broken and new bonds are formed.
2) Energy must be supplied to break existing bonds — so bond breaking is an endothermic process.
3) Energy is released when new bonds are formed — so bond formation is an exothermic process.

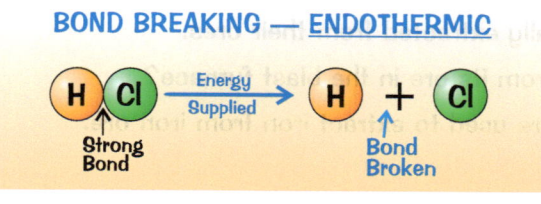

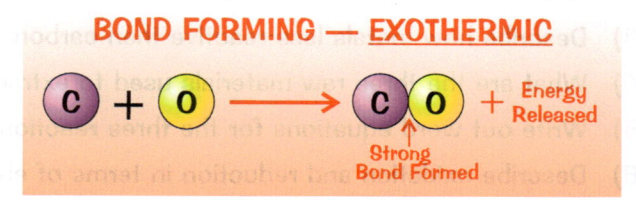

There's more on energy transfer on page 54.

BOND BREAKING — ENDOTHERMIC

H-Cl + Energy Supplied → H + Cl (Strong Bond / Bond Broken)

BOND FORMING — EXOTHERMIC

C + O → C-O + Energy Released (Strong Bond Formed)

4) In endothermic reactions, the energy used to break bonds is greater than the energy released by forming them.
5) In exothermic reactions, the energy released by forming bonds is greater than the energy breaking 'em.

Bond Energy Calculations — Need to be Practised

1) Every chemical bond has a particular bond energy associated with it. This bond energy varies slightly depending on the compound the bond occurs in.
2) You can use these known bond energies to calculate the overall energy change for a reaction.

$$\text{overall energy change} = \text{energy required to break bonds} - \text{energy released by forming bonds}$$

3) A positive energy change means an endothermic reaction and a negative energy change means an exothermic reaction.
4) You need to practise a few of these, but the basic idea is really very simple...

EXAMPLE: Using the bond energy values below, calculate the energy change for the following reaction, where hydrogen and chlorine react to produce hydrogen chloride:

$$H-H + Cl-Cl \rightarrow 2H-Cl$$

H—H: 436 kJ/mol   Cl—Cl: 242 kJ/mol   H—Cl: 431 kJ/mol

1) Work out the energy required to break the original bonds in the reactants.
   $(1 \times H-H) + (1 \times Cl-Cl) = 436 + 242$
   $= 678$ kJ/mol
2) Work out the energy released by forming the new bonds in the products.
   $(2 \times H-Cl) = 2 \times 431$
   $= 862$ kJ/mol
3) Work out the overall change.
   overall energy change = energy required to break bonds − energy released by forming bonds
   $= 678 - 862 = -184$ kJ/mol

In this reaction, the energy released by forming bonds is greater than the energy used to break them — so the reaction is exothermic.

A student and their mobile — a bond that can never be broken...

This stuff might look hard at the moment, but with a bit of practice it's dead easy and it'll win you easy marks if you understand all the theory behind it. See how you get on with this question:

Q1 During the Haber Process, N_2 reacts with H_2 in the following reaction: $N_2 + 3H_2 \rightarrow 2NH_3$
The bond energies for these molecules are:
N≡N: 941 kJ/mol
H—H: 436 kJ/mol
N—H: 391 kJ/mol

N≡N + H—H + H—H + H—H → N(H,H,H) + N(H,H,H)

Calculate the overall energy change for the reaction.   [3 marks]

Unit 2c — Metals, Extraction and Energy

Revision Questions for Unit 2c

Well, that's Unit 2c finished — now it's time for the greatest quiz on earth. Try not to get too excited...
- Try these questions and tick off each one when you get it right.
- When you've done all the questions for a topic and are completely happy with it, tick off the topic.

Extracting Metals From Their Ores (p.74-76)

1) What is a metal ore and where are they usually found?
2) How are metals more reactive than carbon usually extracted from their ores?
3) Describe how metals less reactive than carbon are usually extracted from their ores.
4) What are the three raw materials used to extract iron from its ore in the blast furnace?
5) Write out word equations for the three reactions that are used to extract iron from iron ore.
6) Describe oxidation and reduction in terms of electrons.
7) Describe what happens during a displacement reaction.

Electrolysis (p.77-80)

8) During electrolysis, which electrode are the positive ions attracted to?
9) Give the equation for the reaction occurring at the cathode during the electrolysis of water.
10) Write out ionic equations for the reactions occurring at each electrode during the electrolysis of aluminium oxide.
11) An aqueous solution is electrolysed. What product will be formed at the anode if no halide ions are present in the solution?
12) Describe why copper is produced at the cathode, instead of hydrogen, in the electrolysis of aqueous copper(II) chloride.
13) What does 'electroplating' mean?
14) Name the three products formed from the electrolysis of sodium chloride.

Metal Extraction Plants (p.81)

15) Why are metal extraction plants usually sited close to the coast?
16) Why do some metal extraction plants need a direct power supply from a nearby power station?
17) Why is it more sustainable to recycle metals than extract more of the raw materials?

Metals and Their Uses (p.82-83)

18) Give three properties that aluminium, copper, iron and titanium have in common.
19) What is an alloy?
20) Name an element that is added to iron to make steel.
21) a) Give two properties that transition metals have in common with most other metals.
    b) Give two typical properties of transition metals that they don't share with most other metals.
22) What colour are Fe^{3+} precipitates?

Reactions and Bond Energy (p.84-85)

23) What change in the temperature of the surroundings would you expect to observe in an exothermic reaction?
24) Draw a reaction profile for an endothermic reaction.
25) What is activation energy?
26) Is energy required for the breaking of bonds or the forming of bonds?
27) What is the equation for calculating the overall energy change for a reaction?

Unit 2c — Metals, Extraction and Energy

Unit 2d — Crude Oil, Fuels and Organic Chemistry

Fractional Distillation of Crude Oil

Fossil fuels like coal, oil and gas are called non-renewable fuels — they take so long to make that they're being used up much faster than they're being formed. They're finite resources — one day they'll run out.

Crude Oil is Separated into Different Hydrocarbon Fractions

1) Crude oil is our main source of hydrocarbons and is used as a raw material (sometimes called a feedstock) to create lots of useful substances used in the petrochemical industry.

2) It's formed underground, over millions of years (at high temperatures and pressures) from the buried remains of marine organisms. It's a non-renewable (finite) resource, so one day it will run out.

3) Crude oil is a complex mixture of lots of different hydrocarbons — compounds which contain just carbon and hydrogen. The hydrocarbons found in crude oil have their carbon atoms arranged in either chains or rings and are mostly alkanes (hydrocarbons with the general formula C_nH_{2n+2}).

4) Crude oil can be separated out into fractions — simpler, more useful mixtures containing groups of hydrocarbons of similar lengths (i.e. they have similar numbers of carbon and hydrogen atoms). The fractions from crude oil, e.g. petrol, kerosene and diesel, are examples of non-renewable fossil fuels.

5) The different fractions in crude oil are separated by fractional distillation. The oil is heated until most of it has turned into gas. The gases enter a fractionating column (and the liquid bit, bitumen, is drained off at the bottom).

6) In the column there's a temperature gradient (i.e. it's hot at the bottom and gets cooler as you go up).

7) The longer hydrocarbons have higher boiling points. They turn back into liquids and drain out of the column early on, when they're near the bottom. The shorter hydrocarbons have lower boiling points. They turn to liquid and drain out much later on, near to the top of the column where it's cooler.

8) You end up with the crude oil mixture separated out into different fractions. Each fraction contains a mixture of hydrocarbons, mostly alkanes with similar boiling points.

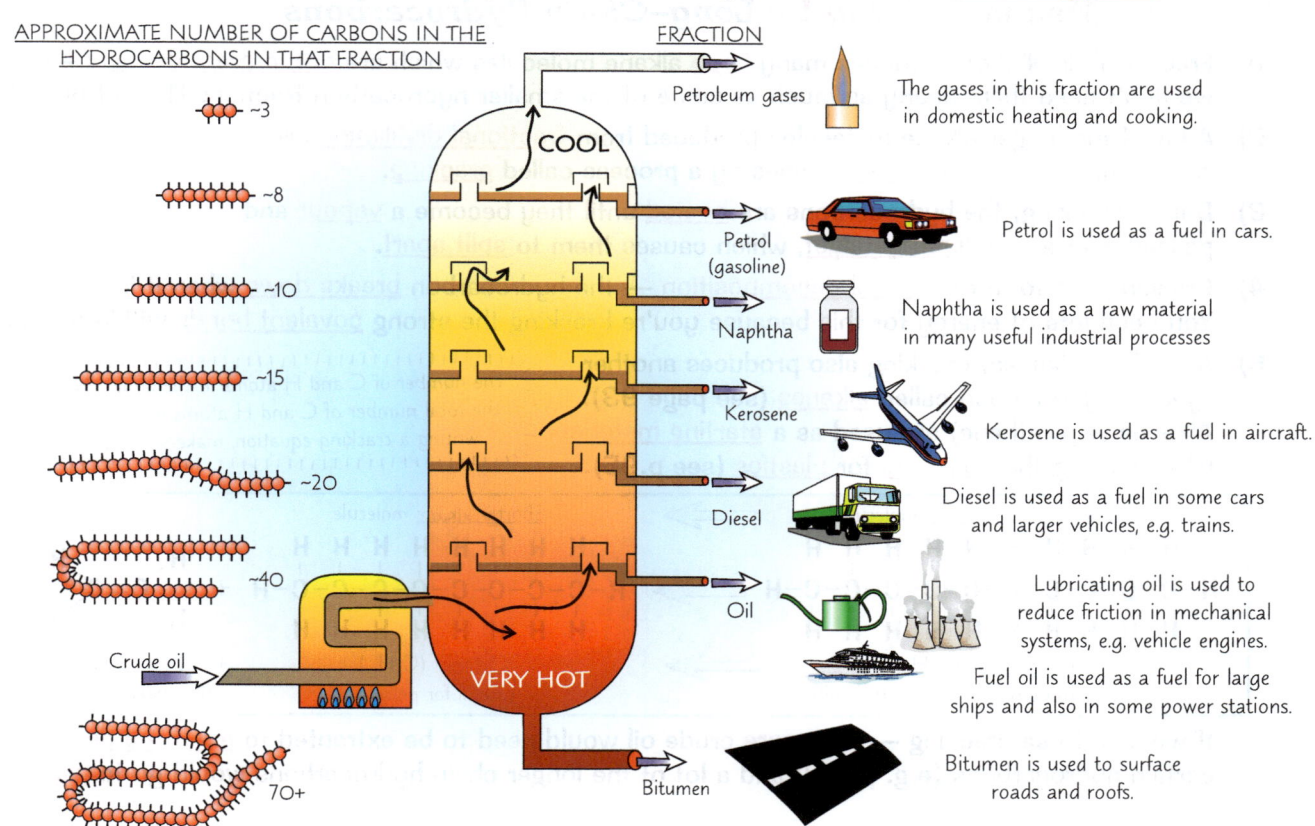

Approx. number of carbons	Fraction	Use
~3	Petroleum gases	The gases in this fraction are used in domestic heating and cooking.
~8	Petrol (gasoline)	Petrol is used as a fuel in cars.
~10	Naphtha	Naphtha is used as a raw material in many useful industrial processes
~15	Kerosene	Kerosene is used as a fuel in aircraft.
~20	Diesel	Diesel is used as a fuel in some cars and larger vehicles, e.g. trains.
~40	Oil	Lubricating oil is used to reduce friction in mechanical systems, e.g. vehicle engines. Fuel oil is used as a fuel for large ships and also in some power stations.
70+	Bitumen	Bitumen is used to surface roads and roofs.

How much petrol is there in crude oil? Just a fraction...

You'll need to know the names and uses of all the fractions for your exam, so best have a good read of this page.

Q1 Petrol drains further up a fractionating column than diesel. What does this suggest about the boiling points of the hydrocarbons which make up petrol compared to those in diesel? [1 mark]

Crude Oil and Cracking

Crude oil really improves our lives in lots of ways but we're using up our supplies way too quickly...

Crude Oil Provides Important Fuels for Modern Life

1) Crude oil provides the energy needed to do lots of vital things — generating electricity, heating homes...
2) Oil provides the fuel for most modern transport — cars, trains, planes, the lot. It also provides the raw materials needed to make various chemicals, including plastics.
3) However, crude oil supplies are limited and non-renewable.
4) New reserves are sometimes found, and new technology means we can get to oil that was once too difficult to extract. But one day we'll just run out.
5) Some people think we should stop using oil for fuel (where we have alternatives) and keep it for making plastics and other chemicals (e.g. medicines). This could lead to conflict for resources between the fuel and chemical industries.

But There Are Economic and Environmental Issues With Using It

1) As Earth's population increases, and as countries like India and China become more developed, more fossil fuels are burned to provide electricity — both for increased home use and to run manufacturing industries. This increasing use of crude oil isn't sustainable in the long run.
2) As the demand for fossil fuels increases, prices go up. It's not just heating and transport that get more expensive though — the prices of food and other goods are affected by energy costs too.
3) Burning fossil fuels also leads to environmental problems like global warming (p.47) and acid rain (p.48). The effects of these issues aren't just felt in the countries using the energy.

Cracking Means Splitting Up Long-Chain Hydrocarbons

1) Fractional distillation produces many large alkane molecules which are not in great demand — we don't need them nearly as much as some of the smaller hydrocarbon fractions like petrol and diesel.
2) A lot of the longer alkane molecules produced from fractional distillation are turned into smaller, more useful ones by a process called cracking.
3) During cracking, the hydrocarbons are heated until they become a vapour and passed over a powdered catalyst, which causes them to split apart.
4) Cracking is a form of thermal decomposition — the hydrocarbon breaks down when it is heated. You need lots of energy for this because you're breaking the strong covalent bonds within the molecule.
5) As well as alkanes, cracking also produces another type of hydrocarbon called alkenes (see page 93). Alkenes (e.g. ethene) are used as a starting material when making the polymers for plastics (see p.95).

The number of C and H atoms in the large alkane should equal the total number of C and H atoms in the products. So when writing a cracking equation, make sure both sides balance.

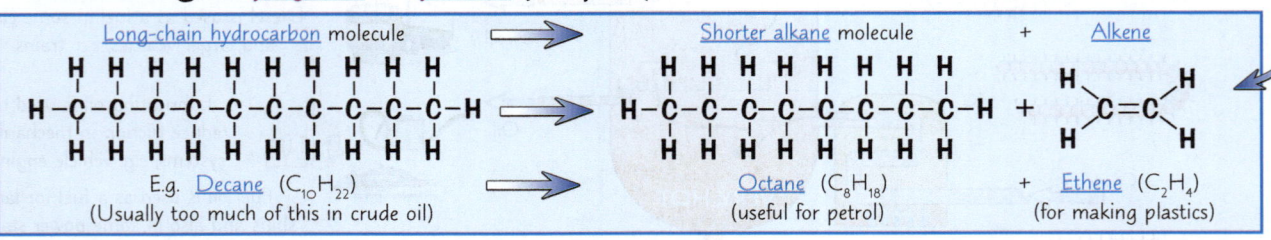

Long-chain hydrocarbon molecule ⟹ Shorter alkane molecule + Alkene

E.g. Decane ($C_{10}H_{22}$) ⟹ Octane (C_8H_{18}) + Ethene (C_2H_4)
(Usually too much of this in crude oil) (useful for petrol) (for making plastics)

6) If we didn't use cracking — lots more crude oil would need to be extracted to meet the demands for certain hydrocarbons (e.g. petrol) and a lot of the longer chain hydrocarbons would go to waste.

I'm not one to brag, but this really is a cracking page...

Demand for fossil fuels is rising, but supplies are running ever lower and prices are going up. That's why cracking is so important — we can eke out our resources until we've developed our technology to run on alternatives.

Q1   A molecule of dodecane, $C_{12}H_{26}$, was cracked, producing two products. One of the products had the molecular formula C_9H_{20}. Give the molecular formula for the other product.   [1 mark]

Unit 2d — Crude Oil, Fuels and Organic Chemistry

Hydrocarbons

The physical properties of crude oil fractions all depend on how big the hydrocarbons in that fraction are.

There are Trends in the Properties of Fractions

1) Crude oil fractions contain alkanes — see p.92.
2) For each additional carbon atom in the alkane molecule, there is an extra CH_2 unit in the molecular formula.
3) Different alkanes have similar chemical properties.
4) The physical properties of the alkanes vary between the different molecules. For example, the bigger a molecule is, the higher the boiling point will be (see below).
5) The properties of alkenes (p.93), which are also found in fractions, are related in a similar way.

Alkane	Molecular formula	Boiling point (°C)	Fraction in crude oil
Methane	CH_4	−162	Gases
Ethane	C_2H_6	−89	Gases
Dodecane	$C_{12}H_{26}$	216	Kerosene
Icosane	$C_{20}H_{42}$	343	Diesel
Tetracontane	$C_{40}H_{82}$	524	Fuel Oil

The Size of a Hydrocarbon Determines its Properties

1) The size of a hydrocarbon determines which fraction of crude oil it will separate into (see page 87).
2) Each fraction contains hydrocarbons (mostly alkanes) with similar numbers of carbon atoms, so all of the molecules in a fraction will have similar properties and behave in similar ways.
3) The physical properties are determined by the intermolecular forces that hold the chains together.

- The intermolecular forces of attraction break a lot more easily in small molecules than they do in bigger molecules. That's because the forces are much stronger between big molecules than they are between small molecules.
- It makes sense if you think about it — even if a big molecule can overcome the forces attracting it to another molecule at a few points along its length, it's still got lots of other places where the force is still strong enough to hold it in place.
- That's why big molecules have higher boiling points than small molecules.

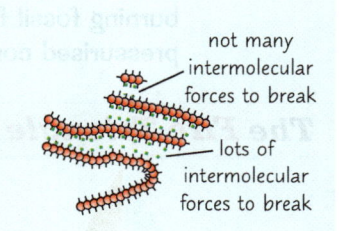

- Shorter hydrocarbons are easy to ignite because they have lower boiling points, so tend to be gases at room temperature.
- These gas molecules mix with oxygen in the air to produce a gas mixture which bursts into flames if it comes into contact with a spark.
- Longer hydrocarbons are usually liquids at room temperature. They have higher boiling points and are much harder to ignite.

- Viscosity measures how easily a substance flows.
- The stronger the force is between hydrocarbon molecules, the harder it is for the liquid to flow.
- Fractions containing longer hydrocarbons have a higher viscosity — they're thick like treacle.
- Fractions made up of shorter hydrocarbons have a low viscosity and are much runnier.

- Shorter hydrocarbons are more clean-burning than longer hydrocarbons.
- Because shorter hydrocarbons have fewer carbon atoms, less carbon is released when they're burnt.
- Shorter hydrocarbons burn with a blue flame, but when longer hydrocarbons are burned, the flame is yellow and smoky.

- The colours of the different fractions depend on chain length too.
- The fractions containing the shortest hydrocarbons (petroleum gases and petrol) are colourless.
- Fractions made up of medium-length hydrocarbons, such as naphtha, kerosene and diesel, are yellow.
- Fuel oil and bitumen, which have the longest hydrocarbons, are brown.

My sister has a high viscosity — she's pretty thick...

So there are trends in the properties of crude oil fractions — as the length of the hydrocarbons increases, boiling point and viscosity increase, ease of ignition and cleanliness of burn decrease, and the colour generally gets darker.

Q1 Explain why dodecane ($C_{12}H_{26}$) has a higher boiling point than methane (CH_4). [2 marks]

Unit 2d — Crude Oil, Fuels and Organic Chemistry

Burning Fuels

Combustion reactions can be really useful, but you've got to be able to stop them if things get out of hand...

Fuels Release Energy in Combustion Reactions

1) Hydrocarbons make great fuels because the combustion reactions that happen when you burn them in oxygen give out lots of energy — the reactions are very exothermic (see page 84).
2) When you burn hydrocarbons in plenty of oxygen, the only products are carbon dioxide and water — this is called complete combustion.

Hydrocarbon + oxygen → carbon dioxide + water
E.g. C_3H_8 + $5O_2$ → $3CO_2$ + $4H_2O$

Hydrogen Can be Used as a Clean, Renewable Fuel

Hydrogen gas has been used as rocket fuel for years, and is now being used in fuel cells to power cars.

Pros: Hydrogen is a very clean fuel. In a hydrogen fuel cell, hydrogen combines with oxygen to produce energy, and the only waste product is water — no nasty pollutants that cause global warming or acid rain (which are produced when fossil fuels are burnt). Hydrogen's obtained from water which is a renewable resource, so it's not going to run out (unlike fossil fuels). Hydrogen can even be obtained from the water produced by the cell when it's used in fuel cells.

hydrogen + oxygen → water
$2H_2$ + O_2 → $2H_2O$

Cons: You need a special, expensive engine. Hydrogen gas is produced from the electrolysis of water, which is expensive and uses large amounts of electricity — this electricity is often generated by burning fossil fuels, which produces pollutants. Also, hydrogen's hard to store (it requires large, pressurised containers) and it can be dangerous as it forms an explosive mixture with air.

The Fire Triangle Shows the Three Things Needed for a Fire to Burn

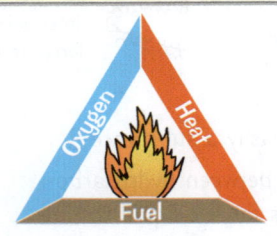

1) A fire needs fuel, oxygen and heat to burn.
2) Fire is just the combustion reaction between the fuel and the oxygen.
3) However, this reaction has a high activation energy, so can only start at high temperatures — you need heat too.

Check out page 84 if you're feeling uncertain about activation energy.

The fire triangle is used to prevent and to fight fires. A fire can only start and keep burning if all three elements from the fire triangle are present. If you take away one or more elements, the fire will go out (or won't start in the first place).

FUEL:
- In industry, safer alternatives to highly flammable materials are used wherever possible.
- Forest fires are often tackled by chopping down and removing trees in the path of the fire. Without these as a source of fuel, the fire (eventually) goes out.

OXYGEN:
- Covering a fire with a fire blanket or damp cloth stops the oxygen in the air from getting to it.
- Some fire extinguishers use foam or powder to block the oxygen in a similar way.
- Carbon dioxide fire extinguishers work by replacing the air (and so oxygen) around the fire.

HEAT:
- Storing flammable materials away from sources of heat is an important method of fire prevention.
- Pouring water over a fire, or spraying it from a hose or extinguisher, cools the fire down.

Water should never be used on fires involving electricity or flammable liquids — it just makes things worse.

I'm burning to know more...

The fire triangle could literally save your life. If that's not a good reason to learn this page, I don't know what is.

Q1   Explain how putting a fire blanket over a fire helps to put the fire out.   [2 marks]

Unit 2d — Crude Oil, Fuels and Organic Chemistry

Measuring Energy Changes — PRACTICAL

You can see for yourself just how exothermic combustion reactions are by doing this nice simple experiment (and a little bit of maths...). Probably not in your bedroom though — health and safety and all that...

You Can Measure the Energy Released in Combustion Reactions

To measure the amount of energy released when a fuel is burnt, you can simply burn the fuel and use the flame to heat up some water.

1) Put 100 cm³ of water into a conical flask and record its temperature.
2) Clamp the flask in place.
3) Weigh the spirit burner (filled with fuel) and the lid.
4) Put the spirit burner underneath the flask, and light the wick. Heat the water until the temperature has increased by about 40 °C.
5) Put out the flame using the burner lid, and measure the final temperature of the water.
6) Weigh the spirit burner and lid again.
7) You can then use the measurements you've taken to calculate the energy change (see below).

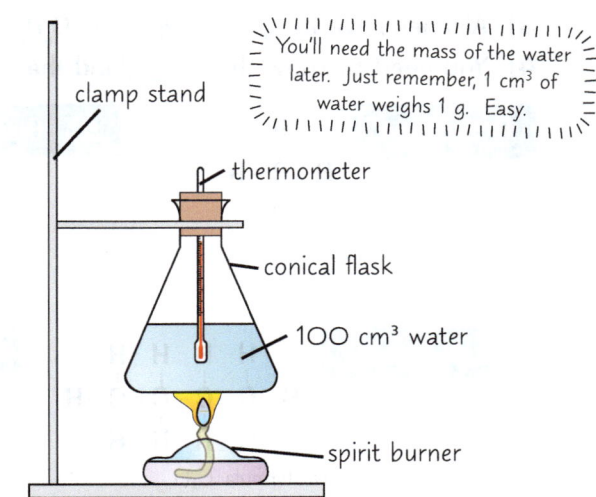

You'll need the mass of the water later. Just remember, 1 cm³ of water weighs 1 g. Easy.

Diagram labels: clamp stand, thermometer, conical flask, 100 cm³ water, spirit burner

You Calculate the Energy Released Per Gram of Fuel

1) The combustion experiment above involves heating water by burning a liquid fuel.
2) If you measure (i) how much fuel you've burned and (ii) the temperature change of the water, you can work out how much energy is supplied by each gram of fuel. You need this equation:

$$\text{Energy released from fuel per gram (J)} = \frac{\text{mass of water (g)} \times \text{temperature increase (°C)} \times 4.2 \text{ (J/g/°C)}}{\text{mass of fuel (g)}}$$

The more energy released per gram, the more efficient the fuel is.

This is the specific heat capacity of water — the amount of energy needed to raise the temperature of 1 gram of water by 1°C.

Example: to work out the heat energy change per gram of methylated spirit (meths):

Temperature of water in conical flask before heating = 21.5 °C
Temperature of water in conical flask after heating = 52.5 °C
⇒ Temperature rise of 100 g of water due to heating = **31.0 °C**

Mass of spirit burner + lid before heating = 69.25 g
Mass of spirit burner + lid after heating = 67.45 g
⇒ Mass of meths burnt = **1.80 g**

Using the equation above, the heat energy released per gram of fuel in this experiment
$$= \frac{100 \times 31 \times 4.2}{1.80} = 7230 \text{ J or } 7.23 \text{ kJ (3 s.f.)}$$

You'll be given this value in the exam.

Energy's wasted heating the flask, air, etc. So this figure will often be much lower than the actual energy content.

Specific revision capacity — biscuits per student per mark...

If you're using this method to compare different fuels, you need to make sure it's a fair test. So you want to use the same conical flask each time, keep it the same distance from the flame, use the same type of burner, etc., etc...

Q1 In an experiment, 0.2 g of butane is burnt and raises the temperature of 100 g of water by 18.7 °C. Use the formula above to calculate the energy in kJ given out per gram of butane burnt. [3 marks]

Unit 2d — Crude Oil, Fuels and Organic Chemistry

Alkanes

We're now going to look at the different types of hydrocarbons you can get. First up is the alkanes...

Alkanes are Saturated Hydrocarbons

1) Alkanes are hydrocarbons — they're chains of carbon atoms surrounded by hydrogen atoms.
2) Different alkanes have chains of different lengths.
3) Alkanes have the general formula C_nH_{2n+2}.
4) You need to know the names and the structural formulae of the first five alkanes.

Alkanes = C_nH_{2n+2}

n is just the number of carbon atoms there are in the molecule

1) Methane — Molecular formula: CH_4

2) Ethane — Molecular formula: C_2H_6

3) Propane — Molecular formula: C_3H_8

4) Butane — Molecular formula: C_4H_{10}

5) Pentane — Molecular formula: C_5H_{12}

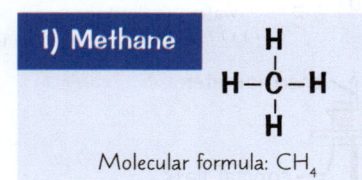

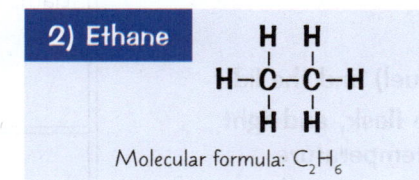

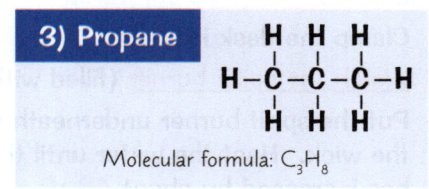

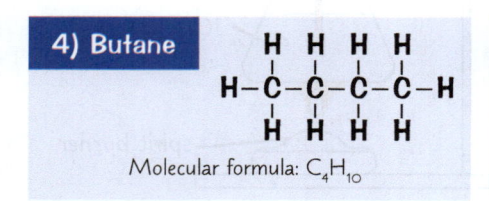

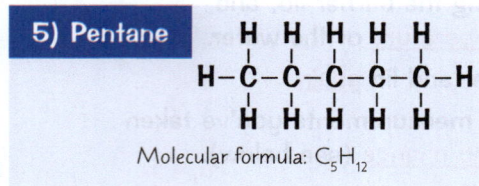

To help remember the names of the first four alkanes just remember: Mice Eat Peanut Butter. Pentane is five, just like a pentagon, so you'll have to remember that one on its own.

5) Carbon atoms must always form four bonds. This means they can bond to up to four other atoms.
6) The diagrams above show that all the atoms have formed bonds with as many other atoms as they can. There are only single bonds between the carbon atoms — this means the molecules are saturated.

In Isomers the Atoms Are Arranged Differently

1) Two molecules are isomers of one another if they have the same molecular formula but the atoms are arranged differently.
2) This means their structural formulae are different.
3) Isomers of alkanes have differently shaped carbon chains.
4) The carbons could be arranged as a straight chain or a branched chain (one of the carbons being bonded to more than two other carbons).

Alkane, Al saw, Al conquered. *Give it a rest, Alan!*

There Are Two Isomers of C_4H_{10} and Three Isomers of C_5H_{12}

And you need to be able to draw all of them.

C_4H_{10} has one straight chain isomer and one branched chain isomer.

C_5H_{12} has one straight chain and two different branched chain isomers

---

My brain during exam revision is a bit like alkanes — saturated...

I guess you're after a useful tip? OK here goes: Make sure you learn the general formula of alkanes and how to draw the first five alkanes. It could be super helpful in your exam, hint hint...

Q1 A molecule of the alkane octane contains eight carbon atoms. Give octane's molecular formula.   [1 mark]

Unit 2d — Crude Oil, Fuels and Organic Chemistry

Alkenes

Alkenes are another type of hydrocarbon. They are different to alkanes because they contain a double bond.

Alkenes Have a C=C Double Bond

1) Alkenes are hydrocarbons which have a double bond between two of the carbon atoms in their chain.
2) They are unsaturated molecules because they can make more bonds — the double bond can open up, allowing the two carbon atoms to bond with other atoms (see below). This is an addition reaction.
3) The first three alkenes are ethene (with two carbon atoms), propene (three Cs) and butene (four Cs).
4) Alkenes have the general formula: C_nH_{2n} — they have twice as many hydrogens as carbons.

Alkenes = C_nH_{2n}

1) Ethene
Molecular Formula: C_2H_4

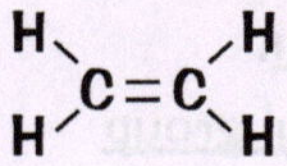

2) Propene
Molecular Formula: C_3H_6

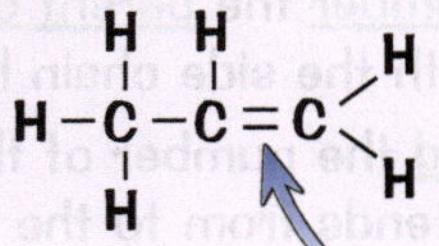

This is a double bond — so each carbon atom is still making four bonds.

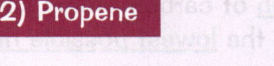

3) Butene
There are two different structures for butene — these are isomers (see previous page).

But-1-ene — Molecular Formula: C_4H_8
But-2-ene — Molecular Formula: C_4H_8

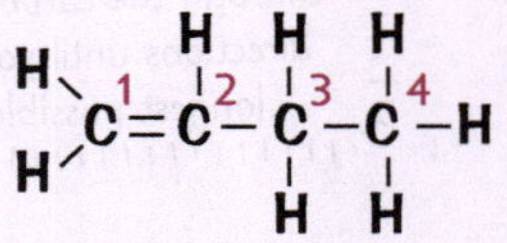

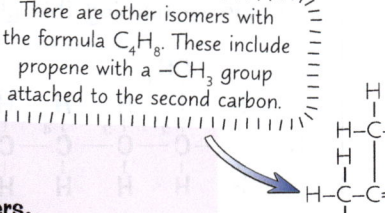

There are other isomers with the formula C_4H_8. These include propene with a –CH_3 group attached to the second carbon.

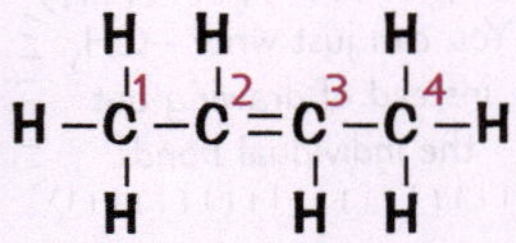

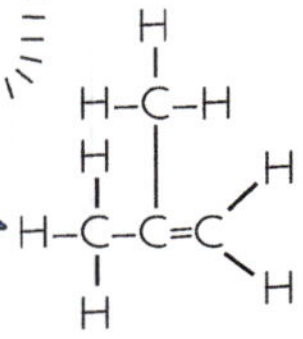

- But-1-ene and but-2-ene are the systematic names for these isomers.
- You find the systematic name by numbering the carbon chain so that one of the carbons in the C=C group has the lowest possible number.
- In but-1-ene the C=C group starts at carbon 1 and in but-2-ene it starts at carbon 2.

Alkenes Can React with Hydrogen...

Hydrogen can react with the double-bonded carbons to open up the double bond and form the equivalent, saturated, alkane.
The alkene is reacted with hydrogen in the presence of a catalyst:

R is just the rest of the molecule. It isn't involved in the reaction so it doesn't matter what it's like.

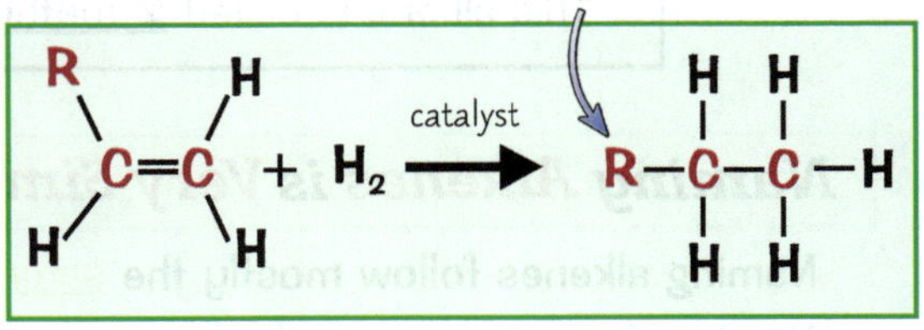

$RCH=CH_2 + H_2 \xrightarrow{catalyst} R-CH_2-CH_3$

...And Also with Bromine

1) Alkenes will also react in addition reactions with bromine. The molecules formed are saturated bromoalkanes, with the C=C carbons each becoming bonded to a bromine atom.
2) For example, bromine and ethene react together to form dibromoethane:

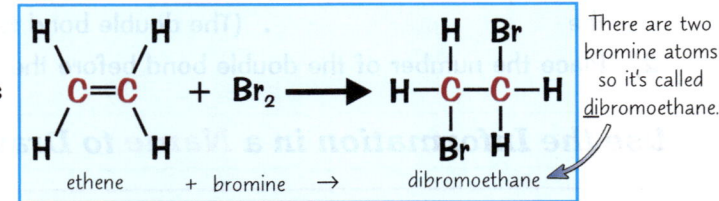

ethene + bromine → dibromoethane

There are two bromine atoms so it's called dibromoethane.

The addition of bromine to a double bond can be used to test for alkenes. Bromine water is used rather than pure bromine, as it is safer and easier to handle.

1) When the orange-brown bromine water is added to a saturated compound, like an alkane, no reaction will happen and it'll stay orange-brown.
2) If it's added to an alkene the bromine will add across the double bond, making a colourless dibromo-compound — so the bromine water is decolourised.

bromine water + an alkene → SHAKE → solution goes colourless

Double the carbon bonds, double the fun...

Don't go mixing up your alkanes and alkenes — remember, the double bond in alkenes makes them 'kene' to react.

Q1 Give the structural formula of the product of the reaction between propene and hydrogen. [1 mark]

Unit 2d — Crude Oil, Fuels and Organic Chemistry

Naming Other Alkanes and Alkenes

No, you can't just call them Barry or Chloe. There are rules to this stuff...

The Names of Alkanes depends on What and Where the Alkyl Group is

1) Not all alkanes have a straight chain of carbon atoms. Sometimes there will be a branch in the chain.
2) A branch in the chain is called a side chain. In an alkane, it is an alkyl group. Alkyl groups are named based on their number of carbons followed by '-yl', e.g. methyl (-CH$_3$), ethyl (-C$_2$H$_5$), etc.
3) The longest chain of carbon atoms in the molecule is called the parent chain — this bit is named like normal alkanes, e.g. methane, ethane, etc.
4) Naming an alkane with a side chain can be a bit of a challenge, but it can be done using these 3 steps:

   Step 1 — Number the parent chain of carbon atoms so that the carbon with the side chain has the lowest possible number.

   Step 2 — Add the number of the carbon atom which the alkyl group extends from to the front of the alkyl group's name.

   Step 3 — Place the name of the alkyl group in front of the name of the parent chain.

Sometimes, the chain of carbon atoms is bent, so it's not so easy to see the parent chain. In this case, just count through the carbons from all directions until you find the longest possible chain.

Example — naming this alkane:

You can just write –CH$_3$ instead of drawing out the individual bonds.

STEP 1: The longest chain of carbons is five atoms long — this is the parent chain. The left hand side is closer to the side chain than the right hand side, so start numbering the carbons from this direction.

STEP 2: The alkyl group extends from the 2nd carbon. It is the methyl group, CH$_3$. So, the alkane's name will begin with 2-methyl.

STEP 3: There are five carbons in the parent chain so the parent chain is pentane. Place 2-methyl in front of the name of the parent chain. So...

This alkane is called **2-methylpentane**.

2-methylpentane has the molecular formula C$_6$H$_{14}$. It's an isomer of 3-methylpentane, as they have the same molecular formula but different structural formulae (try drawing it out and you'll see for yourself).

Naming Alkenes is Very Similar to Naming Alkanes

Naming alkenes follow mostly the same rules as naming alkanes, except...
1) For Step 2, number the parent chain so that one of the carbons in the C=C bond has the lowest possible number. (The double bond takes priority over any side chains.)
2) Place the number of the double bond before the '-ene' (see p.93).

Let's call her... 2-methyprop-1-ene.

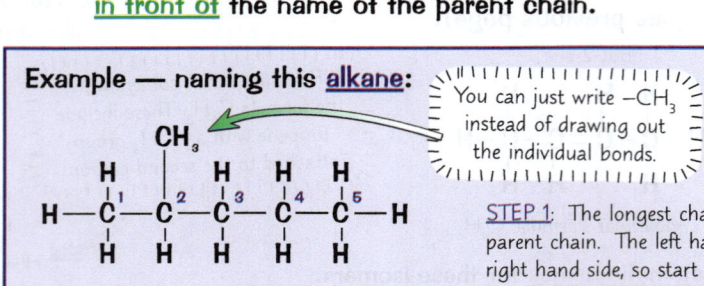

Use the Information in a Name to Draw the Structure

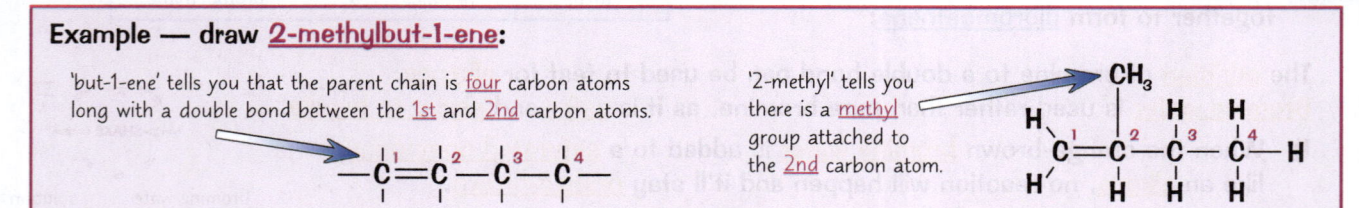

Example — draw **2-methylbut-1-ene**:

'but-1-ene' tells you that the parent chain is four carbon atoms long with a double bond between the 1st and 2nd carbon atoms.

'2-methyl' tells you there is a methyl group attached to the 2nd carbon atom.

An alkene that does everything — it must be 2-good-2-be-true...

Remember, the name of the alkyl group goes before the name of the parent chain. You wouldn't want to name an alkene such as 2-methylbut-1-ene as but-1-ene-2-methyl — it just wouldn't have the same ring to it.

Q1 Draw the structural formula of 3-ethylpentane. [1 mark]

Unit 2d — Crude Oil, Fuels and Organic Chemistry

Addition Polymers

Polymers are made by joining lots of little molecules together in long chains. Magic.

Addition Polymers are Made From Unsaturated Monomers

1) Polymers are long molecules made by joining up lots of small repeating units called monomers. The monomers that make up addition polymers have a double covalent bond — this makes them very reactive.
2) Lots of unsaturated monomer molecules (alkenes — see last page) can open up their double bonds and join together to form polymer chains. This is called addition polymerisation.
3) The name of the polymer comes from the type of monomer it's made from — you just put brackets around it and stick the word "poly" in front of it. So propene becomes poly(propene), etc.
4) To get the formula of the polymer, you just put the formula of the monomer in brackets and put a little 'n' after it. So C_3H_6 becomes $(C_3H_6)_n$. Simple.

Ethene (C_2H_4) becomes poly(ethene) — $(C_2H_4)_n$:

The 'n' represents 'any number' — it just means you start with lots of ethene molecules.

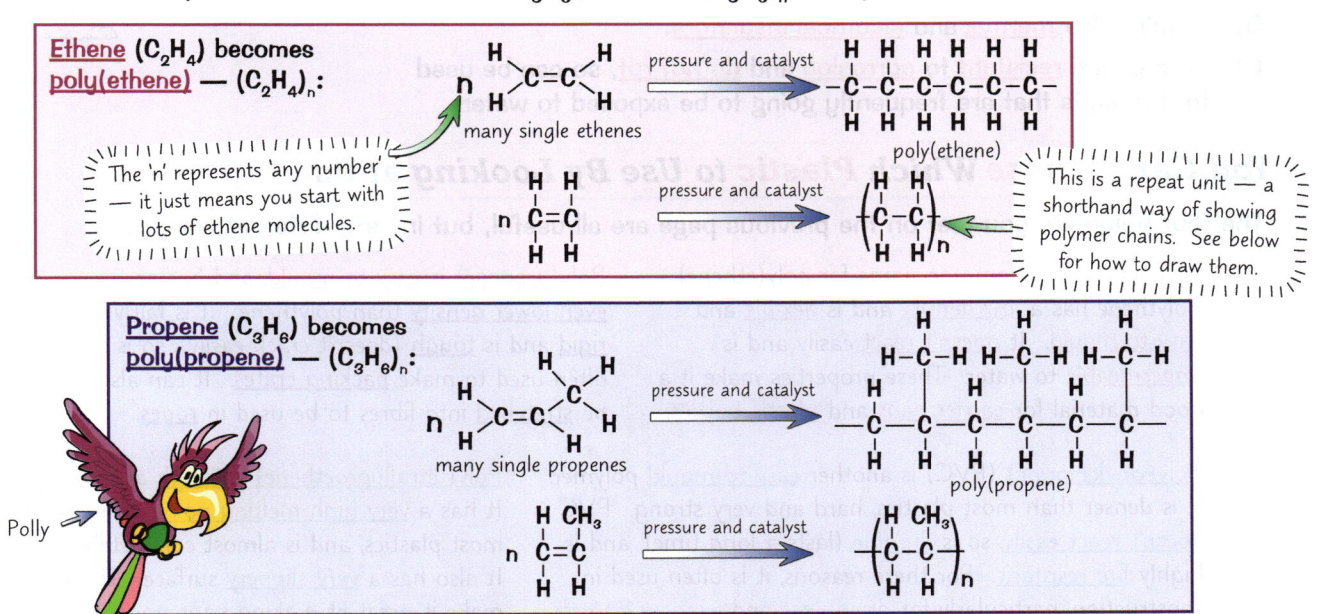

This is a repeat unit — a shorthand way of showing polymer chains. See below for how to draw them.

Propene (C_3H_6) becomes poly(propene) — $(C_3H_6)_n$:

Polly

Vinyl chloride (C_2H_3Cl) becomes poly(vinyl chloride) — $(C_2H_3Cl)_n$:

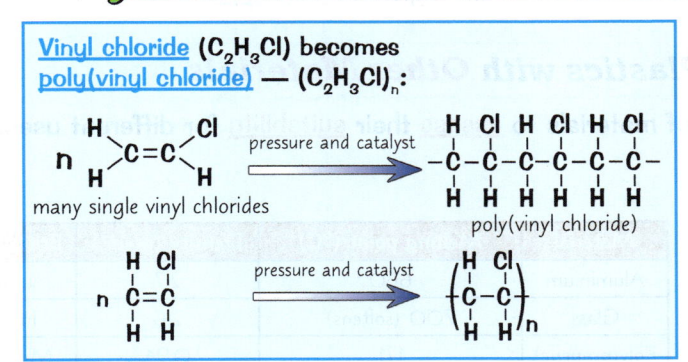

Tetrafluoroethene (C_2F_4) becomes poly(tetrafluoroethene) — $(C_2F_4)_n$:

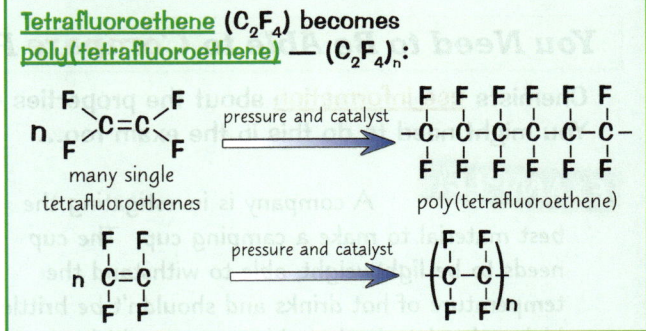

5) Drawing the structural formula of an addition polymer from the structural formula of its monomer is easy. Join the carbons together in a row with no double bonds between them, stick a pair of brackets around the repeating bit, and put an 'n' after it (to show that there are lots of monomers). You should also draw a bond going through the brackets at each end — this shows the chain continues.
6) To get from the structural formula of the polymer to the structural formula of the monomer, just do the reverse. Draw out the repeating bit, get rid of the two bonds going through the brackets and put a double bond between the carbons.

Which polymer is good for making a cuppa? Poly(putthekettleon)...

You'll need to be able to draw the structural formulae of all of the monomers and polymers shown on this page.

Q1   Explain why propene can undergo addition polymerisation but propane cannot.   [2 marks]

Unit 2d — Crude Oil, Fuels and Organic Chemistry

Uses of Plastics

Materials made up of lots of individual polymer molecules are known as plastics.
You need to know all about their properties and uses.

Plastics Are Really Adaptable

Plastics have lots of different properties that make them useful in a wide range of applications.
1) They're often cheaper than most other materials.
2) They're generally strong.
3) They tend to be less dense than most metals or ceramics, so they're often used when designing products that need to have a low mass.
4) Some plastics are flexible, so they can be bent without breaking, and can be easily moulded into almost any shape.
5) They're also thermal and electrical insulators.
6) Plastics are resistant to corrosion and do not rot, so can be used for products that are frequently going to be exposed to water.

You Can Choose Which Plastic to Use By Looking at Its Properties

The four polymers you met on the previous page are all useful, but in very different ways...

Polythene is the common name for poly(ethene). Polythene has a low density and is flexible and easy to mould. It doesn't react easily and is impermeable to water. These properties make it a good material for carrier bags and plastic bottles.

Poly(propene) is easy to mould, and has an even lower density than polythene. It is fairly rigid and is tough (doesn't crack easily), so is often used to make packing crates. It can also be stretched into fibres to be used in ropes.

Poly(vinylchloride) (PVC) is another easy-to-mould polymer. It is denser than most plastics, hard and very strong. PVC doesn't react easily, so is durable (lasts a long time), and is highly fire resistant. For these reasons, it is often used in construction, particularly for drainpipes and window frames.

Poly(tetrafluoroethene) is tough and strong. It has a very high melting point compared to most plastics, and is almost completely unreactive. It also has a very slippery surface. These properties make it great at making pans non-stick.

You Need to Be Able to Compare Plastics with Other Materials

Chemists use information about the properties of materials to assess their suitability for different uses. You might need to do this in the exam too...

EXAMPLE: A company is investigating the best material to make a camping cup. The cup needs to be lightweight, able to withstand the temperature of hot drinks and shouldn't be brittle. Using the data in the table, suggest which material from the table the company should use.

Material	Melting point (°C)	Density (g/cm^3)	Brittleness
Aluminium	660	2.7	Low
Glass	700 (softens)	2.6	High
Poly(propene)	171	0.94	Medium
LDPE	110 (but softens from 80)	0.92	Medium

- Aluminium can be ruled out — it has a high melting point and isn't brittle but it's the densest material.
- Glass has a high softening point and is less dense than aluminium, but it's brittle, so breaks easily.
- The density and brittleness of LDPE and poly(propene) are similar, but LDPE starts softening at 80 °C. A hot drink could be up to 100 °C, so LDPE wouldn't be any good.
- Poly(propene) melts above 100 °C, is lightweight and not too brittle.
So poly(propene) is the best material for the job.

My PVC skirt didn't produce the reaction I'd hoped for...

Plastics can be used for all kinds of things, but you need to make sure you get the right one for the job.

Q1 State two properties of poly(tetrafluoroethene) which make it suitable for coating non-stick pans. [2 marks]

Unit 2d — Crude Oil, Fuels and Organic Chemistry

Disposing of Polymers

It's easy to throw away old plastic bottles and plastic packaging without giving it much thought — but we need to think about the impact it's having on the environment today and the availability of plastics in the future.

Polymers are Made From Crude Oil

1) Plastics are a type of polymer which are made from crude oil. Crude oil is a finite resource — eventually, it will all get used up and run out.
2) The more we use up our crude oil resources, the more expensive crude oil will become — this will then increase the price of crude oil products.
3) Crude oil isn't just used to make plastics — we need it for lots of different things, such as petrol for cars and heating our homes. As resources dry up, we will face the dilemma of how to use the remaining oil. One way we can help delay this problem is by recycling our polymers.

The Disposal of Polymers Comes with Many Problems

In the UK, over 2 million tonnes of plastic waste are generated each year. It's important to find ways to get rid of this waste while minimising environmental damage.

Disposal of Polymers in Landfill Sites:
1) A lot of plastics get dumped in landfill sites. This is usually when different polymers are too difficult or expensive to separate and recycle.
2) Lots of valuable land is quickly getting used up for use as landfill sites.
3) Most polymers are non-biodegradable — they're not broken down by microorganisms. This means that they will sit in landfill for years and years and years and years...

Disposal of Polymers by Combustion:
1) Burning plastics produces a lot of energy and this can be used to generate electricity. But it's not all rainbows and smiles...
2) If not carefully controlled, toxic gases can be released from the combustion of plastics. For example, when polymers that contain chlorine (such as PVC) are burned, they produce HCl — this has to be removed.
3) Carbon dioxide is also produced and this contributes to global warming.

Recycling Polymers Has Both Pros and Cons

1) Recycling polymers is a great way to limit the amount of crude oil we're using and avoid the environmental impact of burning and landfills.
2) Unfortunately, recycling is not as simple as throwing all the plastic rubbish together and then melting and remoulding it all...

Stop trying to recycle your sister, Molly.

ADVANTAGES	DISADVANTAGES
• Reduces the amount of non-biodegradable waste filling up landfill sites. • Reduces emissions of greenhouse and toxic gases which can be released from burning polymers. • Recycling generally uses up less water and energy resources than when making new plastics. • Reduces the amount of crude oil needed to produce more plastics. • Recycling generally saves money and creates jobs.	• Polymers must be separated by type before they can be melted and reformed into a new product — this can be difficult and expensive. • If polymers are mixed together, the quality of the final recycled polymer product could be reduced. • Polymers can only be recycled a finite number of times. Over time, the strength of the polymer can decrease. • Melting polymers can release dangerous gases into the atmosphere. These are harmful to plants and animals.

I hear plastic cars are the way forward — they don't break down...

So, if you didn't realise how important recycling polymers was, you should definitely know now. I, for one, can't imagine a life without plastics or petrol, but if we carry on the way we are going, it could soon become reality...

Q1 Give two disadvantages of burning waste plastics. [2 marks]

Q2 Explain why the price of polymer products could increase if we don't recycle polymers. [3 marks]

Unit 2d — Crude Oil, Fuels and Organic Chemistry

Alcohols

This page is about *different* types of alcohol — and that's not just beer, wine and other pub favourites...

Alcohols Have an '-OH' Functional Group and End in '-ol'

1) The general formula of an alcohol is $C_nH_{2n+1}OH$. So an alcohol with 2 carbons has the formula C_2H_5OH.
2) All alcohols contain an -OH functional group. These are the names of the first 5:

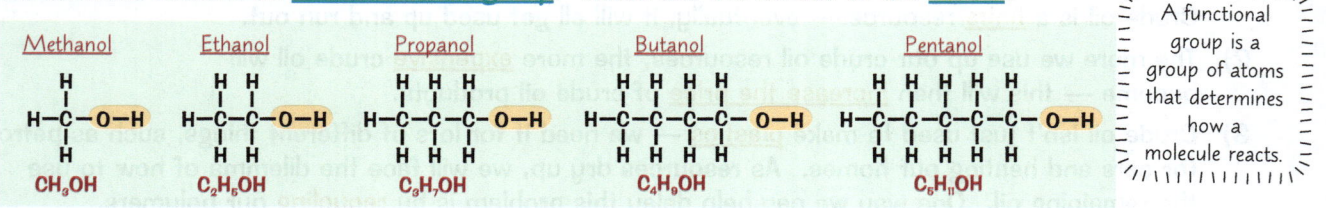

Methanol	Ethanol	Propanol	Butanol	Pentanol
CH_3OH	C_2H_5OH	C_3H_7OH	C_4H_9OH	$C_5H_{11}OH$

A functional group is a group of atoms that determines how a molecule reacts.

3) The basic naming system is the same as for alkanes — but replace the final '-e' with '-ol'.
4) The position of the -OH functional group is shown by the name of the isomer. E.g. butan-1-ol has the -OH on the 1st carbon atom and butan-2-ol has the -OH on the 2nd carbon atom.
5) To name an alcohol, number the parent chain so that the -OH functional group is on the lowest numbered carbon possible. Then use the rules on page 94 to name any alkyl groups.

Two isomers of pentanol...
Pentan-2-ol   3-methylbutan-2-ol

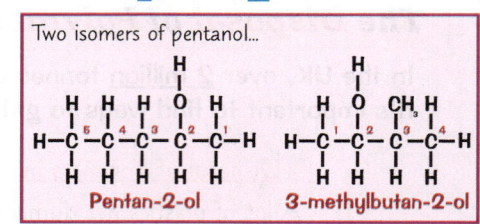

Ethanol can be made by Fermentation

Ethanol is the alcohol found in alcoholic drinks such as wine or beer. It's usually made using fermentation.

1) Fermentation uses an enzyme in yeast to convert sugars (e.g. glucose) into ethanol and carbon dioxide.

$$glucose \xrightarrow{yeast} ethanol + carbon\ dioxide$$
$$C_6H_{12}O_6 \rightarrow 2C_2H_5OH + 2CO_2$$

2) Enzymes are naturally occurring catalysts — they speed up reactions (see p.55).
3) The enzyme in yeast works best at a temperature of around 37 °C, in a slightly acidic solution and under anaerobic conditions (no oxygen). Fermentation therefore happens fastest under these conditions.
4) The ethanol produced by fermentation can be distilled to make spirits, such as vodka and whisky.
5) There are other ways of producing ethanol, e.g. you can make it by reacting ethene with steam. This process is used in industry as it is a much quicker and efficient way of producing ethanol.

Microbial Oxidation forms Carboxylic Acids from Alcohols

1) Some microorganisms are able to use alcohols as an energy source. To do this, they use oxygen in the air to oxidise alcohols.
2) The microbial oxidation of alcohols produces carboxylic acids. These have more oxygen and less hydrogen than the alcohols they're made from.
3) For example, the oxidation of ethanol produces ethanoic acid:

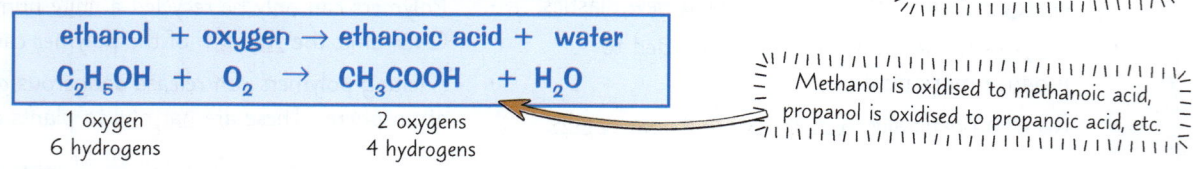

$$ethanol + oxygen \rightarrow ethanoic\ acid + water$$
$$C_2H_5OH + O_2 \rightarrow CH_3COOH + H_2O$$

1 oxygen, 6 hydrogens → 2 oxygens, 4 hydrogens

Carboxylic acids are a homologous series. This means they each have the same general formula and the same functional group (-COOH).

Methanol is oxidised to methanoic acid, propanol is oxidised to propanoic acid, etc.

4) This reaction occurs quite slowly, and is the reason why beer and wine can taste "off" if they are left exposed to the air for a couple of days (as ethanoic acid tastes sour).

Yeast and alcohol — this'll be your bread and butter-anol...

For the exams, it might be jolly useful to learn the structures of alcohols... In fact, it might be essential...

Q1 Draw the structural formula of 2-methylpropan-1-ol. [1 mark]

Unit 2d — Crude Oil, Fuels and Organic Chemistry

Uses of Ethanol

Spoiler alert: something that you can both drink and use as a fuel probably isn't all that good for you...

Misuse of Alcohol can be Dangerous and Expensive

1) The alcohol found in alcoholic drinks is ethanol (made from fermentation — see previous page).
2) Drinking alcoholic drinks can risk damaging your health. The UK government issues guidelines for the amount people can drink while keeping the risk low. The recommended maximum number of units of alcohol to be consumed per week is: **14 units for both men and women.**

Units are a measure of how much alcohol is in a drink. One standard 25 ml measure of vodka = 1 unit. One standard glass of wine = 2 units.

3) Up until 2016, the guidelines said that men could drink 21 units of alcohol per week and women could drink 14 units. However, the guidelines were recently reduced for men to keep the risk of cancer, heart disease and other health problems as low as possible.
4) Health problems can be caused by binge drinking (when you drink lots of alcohol in a short amount of time) and by misusing alcohol over a long period of time.

Possible health problems from binge drinking:
1) Alcohol poisoning.
2) Headaches, vomiting and dehydration.
3) Accidents resulting in injury.
4) Chance of death (by an accident or by some other means, such as a fatal overdose).

Possible health problems from longer-term misuse of alcohol:
1) Damage to organs such as the brain, heart and liver.
2) Increased blood pressure and cholesterol levels, which are major causes of heart attacks and strokes.
3) Longer term mental health problems, such as depression.

5) Regular binge drinking and long-term alcohol misuse can both lead to social problems:
   1) Increased strain on relationships, which can lead to a family break-up or divorce.
   2) Financial problems. E.g. a drinker may find themselves unemployed as a result of their drinking problems.
   3) Increased involvement with violence. Drinking alcohol can cause a rise in aggression.
6) The tax raised from the sale of alcoholic drinks generates a serious amount of money for the government (around £11 billion per year). However, it doesn't cover the cost spent treating alcohol-related issues.
7) A lot of money is spent on dealing with issues which result from alcohol misuse (between £21-52 billion per year). This includes spending on healthcare, for treating alcohol-related illnesses, and spending on law enforcement, for dealing with domestic and violent crimes linked with alcohol.

Ethanol is Used as a Solvent and as a Fuel

1) Ethanol can be used as a solvent in industry. This is because it can dissolve most things water can dissolve, but it can also dissolve substances that water can't dissolve — e.g. hydrocarbons, oils and fats.
2) Bioethanol is a biofuel that is produced from the fermentation of plants such as sugar cane. Bioethanol has both benefits and drawbacks...

ADVANTAGES
- It can be created quickly (compared to fossil fuels).
- It is renewable (as it's made from sugar cane).
- It is cheaper than fossil fuels.
- It creates employment and boosts economy.
- It is almost carbon neutral.

DISADVANTAGES
- Growing sugar cane for bioethanol reduces the land available to grow food crops, so could cause food shortages.
- Growing sugar cane relies on a good climate — something which cannot be controlled.
- Processes used to transport bioethanol cost money and produce carbon dioxide.

Alcohol — drink too much and it's likely tequila...

Ethanol really is a multi-purpose compound. Make sure you know the pros and cons of the uses here.

Q1 Give two social problems which may arise if an adult misuses alcohol over a long period of time. [2 marks]

Unit 2d — Crude Oil, Fuels and Organic Chemistry

Testing for Alcohols and Infrared Spectroscopy

This page shows two ways to test for alcohols and other organic molecules (molecules that contain carbon). One test involves a colour change and the other is infrared spectroscopy — how spectacular...

Alcohol Makes Potassium Dichromate(VI) Solution Change Colour

1) To test if a liquid contains alcohol, add a few drops of the liquid to potassium dichromate(VI) solution in sulfuric acid. Then, gently heat the mixture.

2) If the mixture turns green, it contains alcohol. If the mixture remains orange, it doesn't.

3) Older models of the breathalyser used this test to determine whether a driver was over the drink-driving limit.

Potassium dichromate(VI) is a hazardous chemical — if you use it, make sure you are wearing gloves and safety goggles.

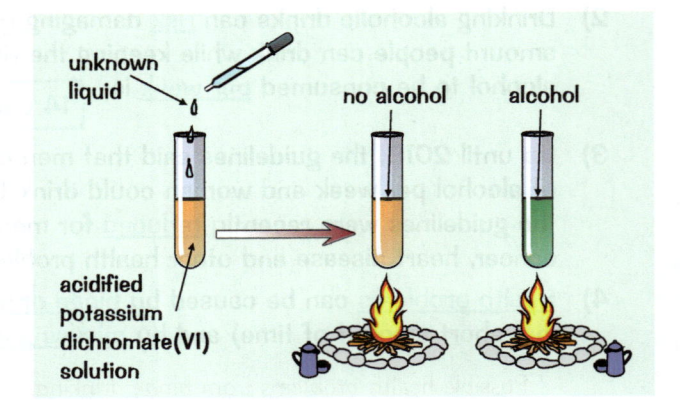

Infrared Spectroscopy Identifies Bonds in Organic Molecules

1) You can use infrared (IR) spectroscopy to identify the presence of certain bonds in organic molecules.

2) In IR spectroscopy, a beam of IR radiation is passed through a sample.

3) Bonds between different atoms in the sample absorb different frequencies of IR radiation.

4) The frequencies are converted to a wavenumber, and an IR graph called a spectrum is produced. The spectrum has peaks in wavenumber, which can show what bonds are present in the sample. This table shows what peaks are produced by different bonds:

Bond	Where it's found	Wavenumber (cm^{-1})
O–H (alcohols)	alcohols	3230 - 3550
C–H	most organic molecules	2850 - 3300
O–H (acids)	carboxylic acids	2500 - 3000
C=O	carboxylic acids	1680 - 1750
C=C	alkenes	1620 - 1680
C–O	alcohols, carboxylic acids	1000 - 1300
C–C	most organic molecules	750 - 1100

Don't panic — you don't need to recall how IR spectroscopy works, or the values of these wavenumbers. However, you do need to know how it's used.

5) Since the frequencies absorbed by different bonds are already known, the peaks on the graph can be used to identify what type of molecule is in the sample.

6) E.g. for the spectrum on the right, there is a peak at 3000 cm^{-1}, which suggests the sample contains a O–H (acids) bond, and a peak at 1720 cm^{-1}, which suggests the sample contains a C=O bond. Together, this information tells you that the sample is a carboxylic acid.

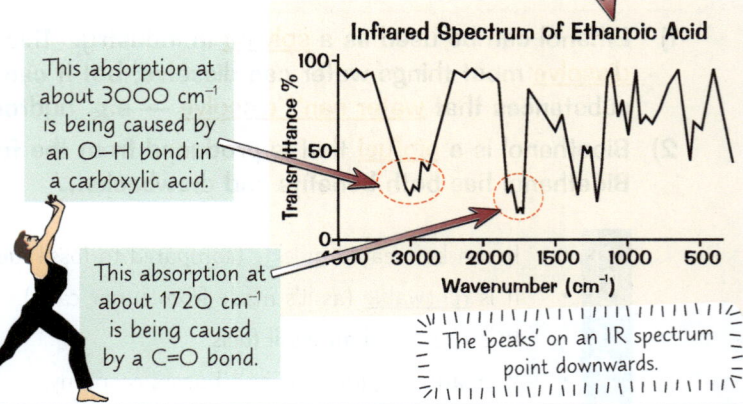

This absorption at about 3000 cm^{-1} is being caused by an O–H bond in a carboxylic acid.

This absorption at about 1720 cm^{-1} is being caused by a C=O bond.

The 'peaks' on an IR spectrum point downwards.

If you see green, there's alcohol at the scene...

... if you see orange, there's no alcohol (and no rhyme — how sad).

Q1 A carboxylic acid is added to potassium dichromate(VI) solution. What colour will the mixture be after heating? [1 mark]

Q2 Describe how IR spectra could be used to distinguish between an alkane and an alkene. [2 marks]

Unit 2d — Crude Oil, Fuels and Organic Chemistry

Revision Questions for Unit 2d

Phew! That unit was a wild ride. Time to see how much you can remember...
- Try these questions and tick off each one when you get it right.
- When you've done all the questions for a topic and are completely happy with it, tick off the topic.

Crude Oil and its Fractions (p.87-89)

1) How is crude oil formed?
2) What is a fraction in terms of crude oil?
3) Put these fractions in order of increasing chain length: kerosene, petroleum gases, bitumen, petrol.
4) Give two environmental issues that arise from burning fossil fuels.
5) What is the purpose of cracking?
6) How do the boiling points of the alkanes change as the size of the molecule increases?
7) Are longer or shorter hydrocarbons associated with a low viscosity?

Burning Fuels (p.90-91)

8) Give the products of the complete combustion of a hydrocarbon.
9) Give two advantages and two disadvantages of using hydrogen as a fuel.
10) Name the three sides of the fire triangle.
11) Draw a diagram of the set-up you would use to measure the energy transferred when a fuel is burnt.

Alkanes and Alkenes (p.92-94)

12) Give the general formula of alkanes.
13) List the first five alkanes.
14) Draw all the isomers of C_5H_{12}.
15) Explain why alkenes are known as unsaturated molecules.
16) Name the alkene that contains three carbon atoms.
17) What is used to test for alkenes?
18) How many carbon atoms are in the parent chain of 2-methylpentane?
19) Draw the structural formula of 2-methylbut-1-ene.

Polymers (p.95-97)

20) What is a monomer?
21) Draw the repeat unit of poly(vinylchloride).
22) List three properties of poly(ethene).
23) Give a disadvantage associated with the disposal of polymers in landfills.

Alcohols and Infrared Spectroscopy (p.98-100)

24) Name the first five alcohols.
25) Give the balanced symbol equation for the fermentation of sugar into ethanol.
26) What are the products of the microbial oxidation of ethanol?
27) What is the recommended maximum number of units of alcohol to be consumed per week?
28) Describe two health problems associated with long-term misuse of alcohol.
29) How can the production of bioethanol cause food shortages?
30) Name a solution that can be used to test for alcohols.
31) Name the method that is used to identify bonds in organic molecules.

Unit 2d — Crude Oil, Fuels and Organic Chemistry

Reversible Reactions

Some reactions can go backwards. Honestly, that's all you need — well almost...

Reversible Reactions Go In Both Directions

1) This equation shows a reversible reaction. You can tell it's reversible because of the ⇌ symbol.

$$A + B \rightleftharpoons C + D$$

2) The reactants (A and B) react and form the products (C and D) in the forward reaction. The products also react to form the reactants again. Both reactions happen at the same time.
3) As reactants react, their concentrations fall — so the forward reaction will slow down (see page 54). But as more and more products are made and their concentrations rise, the backward reaction will speed up.
4) When the reactions are going at the same rate, the concentration of the reactants and products won't change (this is known as equilibrium).
5) There might still be a greater concentration of reactants than products (or vice versa...). If there are more products than reactants, the reaction is going in the forwards direction. If there are more reactants than products then the reaction is going in the backwards direction.

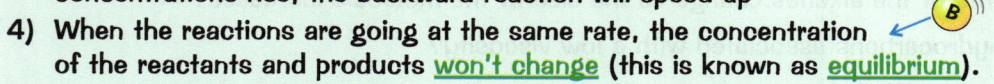

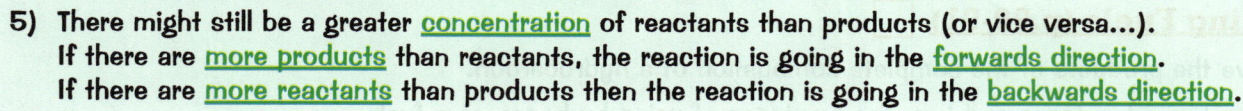

Reversible Reactions Can Be Endothermic and Exothermic

1) In reversible reactions, if the reaction is endothermic in one direction, it will be exothermic in the other.
2) The energy transferred from the surroundings by the endothermic reaction is equal to the energy transferred to the surroundings during the exothermic reaction.
3) A good example is the thermal decomposition of hydrated cobalt(II) chloride:

'Anhydrous' just means 'without water', and 'hydrated' means 'with water'.

See page 84 for more on endothermic and exothermic reactions.

$$\text{hydrated cobalt(II) chloride} \underset{\text{exothermic}}{\overset{\text{endothermic}}{\rightleftharpoons}} \text{anhydrous cobalt(II) chloride} + \text{water}$$

If you heat pink hydrated cobalt(II) chloride crystals, it drives the water off and leaves blue anhydrous cobalt(II) chloride crystals. This is endothermic.

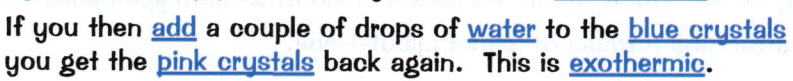

If you then add a couple of drops of water to the blue crystals you get the pink crystals back again. This is exothermic.

Reaction Conditions Determine The Reaction's Direction

The direction of the reaction depends on the reaction conditions (the temperature, and the pressure or concentration of the reactants and products).

Ammonium chloride breaks down to form ammonia and hydrogen chloride. The hydrogen chloride can then react with the ammonia to make ammonium chloride again. The reaction equation is:

$$\text{ammonium chloride} \underset{\text{cool}}{\overset{\text{heat}}{\rightleftharpoons}} \text{ammonia} + \text{hydrogen chloride}$$

If you heat this reaction, it goes in the forwards direction. You'll get more ammonia and hydrogen chloride.

When you heat a reaction, it will go in the endothermic direction (which in this case is the forwards direction).

If you cool it, it will go in the backwards direction. You'll get more ammonium chloride.

...yrtsimehc fo trap etiruovaf ym era snoitcaer elbisreveR

Make sure you understand everything on this page before you move on to the next one. Trust me, it'll help.

Q1 The reversible reaction between water and anhydrous copper(II) sulfate gives out heat. Is the reverse of this reaction exothermic or endothermic? Explain your answer. [2 marks]

The Haber Process

This is an important industrial process. It produces ammonia (NH$_3$), which is used to make fertilisers.

Nitrogen and Hydrogen are Needed to Make Ammonia

The Haber process is used to make ammonia from hydrogen and nitrogen using the following reaction:

$$N_{2(g)} + 3H_{2(g)} \rightleftharpoons 2NH_{3(g)} \text{ (+ heat)}$$
nitrogen   hydrogen   ammonia

1) The nitrogen is obtained easily from the air, which is 78% nitrogen.
2) The hydrogen mainly comes from reacting methane (from natural gas) with steam to form hydrogen and carbon dioxide.
3) The reactant gases are passed over an iron catalyst. A high temperature (350 - 450 °C) and a high pressure (150 - 200 atmospheres) are used.
4) Because the reaction is reversible (it occurs in both directions), some of the ammonia produced converts back into hydrogen and nitrogen again.
5) The ammonia is formed as a gas, but as it cools in the condenser it liquefies and is removed. The unused hydrogen (H$_2$), and nitrogen, (N$_2$), are recycled, so nothing is wasted.
6) The ammonia produced can then be used to make ammonium nitrate — a very nitrogen-rich fertiliser.

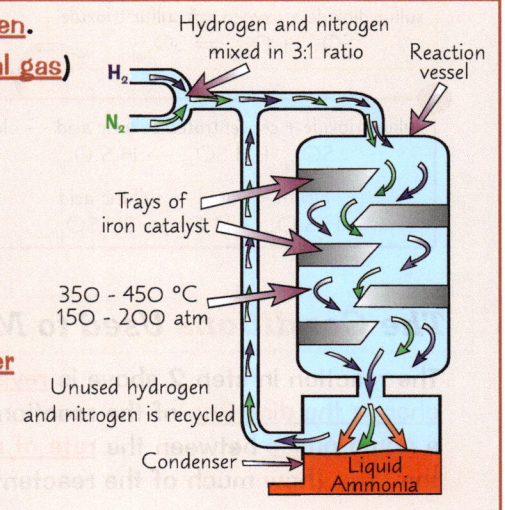

The Reaction is Reversible, So There's a Compromise to be Made

1) You might remember from pages 54-55 that certain conditions, such as the temperature and pressure, can affect the rate of a reaction. These factors can also affect the direction of a reversible reaction.
2) High temperatures move the direction of the reaction away from ammonia and towards nitrogen and hydrogen — they favour the backwards reaction. Lower temperatures turn a greater proportion of hydrogen and nitrogen into ammonia — they increase the yield.
3) The trouble is, lower temperatures mean a slower rate of reaction. The temperature chosen is a compromise between the rate and direction of the reaction.

A low yield of ammonia can be tolerated because unused reactants go through the process again.

4) Higher pressures shift the reaction in the forward direction. So the pressure is set as high as possible, without making the process too expensive or too dangerous to build and maintain. Hence, the 150 to 200 atmospheres operating pressure range is a compromise.
5) And finally, the iron catalyst makes the reaction go faster, but it doesn't affect the direction (or the yield of ammonia).
6) These conditions are chosen so that the process maximises the amount of ammonia produced in a given time.

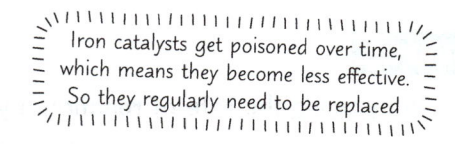

Iron catalysts get poisoned over time, which means they become less effective. So they regularly need to be replaced.

You Can Test For Ammonia Gas Using Damp Red Litmus Paper

1) Alkalis turn damp red litmus paper blue.
2) Ammonia forms an alkaline solution when it dissolves in water. So ammonia gas turns damp red litmus paper blue.

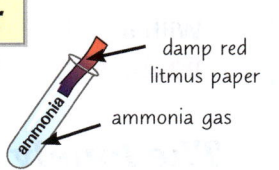

You need to learn this stuff — go on, Haber go at it...

The trickiest bit of this page is remembering that temperature is raised to make ammonia quickly, not make more of it. Remember that industries must consider costs — a higher pressure may give a better yield, but it's not cheap.

Q1   What are the industrial conditions used in the Haber process and why are they used?   [3 marks]

Unit 2e — Reversible Reactions and Industrial Processes

The Contact Process

And here's another example where getting the conditions right makes you more product. Whoop.

The Contact Process is Used to Make Sulfuric Acid

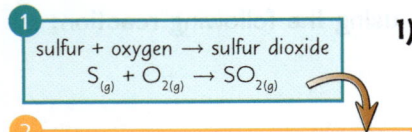

1 sulfur + oxygen → sulfur dioxide
$S_{(g)} + O_{2(g)} → SO_{2(g)}$

2 sulfur dioxide + oxygen ⇌ sulfur trioxide
$SO_{2(g)} + O_{2(g)} ⇌ SO_{3(g)}$

3 sulfur trioxide + concentrated sulfuric acid → oleum
$SO_{3(g)} + H_2SO_{4(l)} → H_2S_2O_{7(l)}$

oleum + water → sulfuric acid
$H_2S_2O_{7(l)} + H_2O_{(l)} → 2H_2SO_{4(l)}$

1) The first stage is to make sulfur dioxide (SO_2) — usually by burning sulfur in air.

2) Sulfur dioxide is then oxidised (with the help of a catalyst) to make sulfur trioxide (SO_3).

3) Oleum is then made by dissolving sulfur trioxide in concentrated sulfuric acid. The oleum is then converted to sulfuric acid by adding water.

Adding sulfur trioxide to water produces a lot of heat, so it's added to concentrated sulfuric acid instead. This produces less heat so the process is safer and easier to manage.

The Conditions Used to Make SO₃ are Carefully Chosen

The reaction in step 2 above is reversible. So, the reaction conditions can be controlled to change the direction of the reaction. The conditions used in industry for the Contact process are a compromise between the rate of reaction (how fast the reaction happens — see page 50), the yield (how much of the reactants are converted to products — see page 21) and cost.

TEMPERATURE
1) Low temperatures are needed to oxidise sulfur dioxide and form sulfur trioxide.
2) This is because low temperatures favour the forward reaction, producing more sulfur trioxide.
3) Unfortunately, reducing the temperature slows the reaction right down — not much good.
4) So a compromise temperature of 450 °C is used. This gets an acceptable yield quite quickly.

PRESSURE
1) Higher pressures shift the reversible oxidation reaction in the forward direction.
2) So to get a higher yield of product, you'd think the pressure should be increased.
3) But increasing the pressure is expensive (and luckily the conditions already favour the forward reaction, so it's not really necessary).
4) In fact, the reaction is usually carried out at, or just above, atmospheric pressure.

CATALYST
1) To increase the rate of reaction a vanadium pentoxide catalyst (V_2O_5) is used.
2) It DOESN'T change the direction of the reaction.

This isn't the sort of contact process I wanted to learn about...

With a fairly high temperature, a low pressure and a vanadium pentoxide catalyst, the reaction goes pretty quickly without reducing the yield of SO_3 too much. And that's how chemistry works in real life.

The lonely hearts column — go on, start the contact process...

It seems odd, but remember that SO_3 is added to concentrated H_2SO_4 to make, erm... H_2SO_4.

Q1 Describe how you could alter the pressure of the reaction to increase the yield of sulfur trioxide in the second stage of the synthesis of sulfuric acid. [1 mark]

Q2 Write balanced chemical equations, including state symbols, to show how sulfuric acid is formed from sulfur trioxide in the third stage of the Contact process. [4 marks]

Unit 2e — Reversible Reactions and Industrial Processes

Uses of Sulfuric Acid

Sulfuric acid is some seriously dangerous stuff. So of course, that makes it really useful.

Most Sulfuric Acid Produced is Used to Make Fertilisers

1) Ammonium sulfate is a fertiliser made from ammonia and sulfuric acid. It's used in agriculture to improve crop yields (see next page).
2) It's also used to make paints, dyes, plastics, fibres, and detergents.

Sulfuric Acid Dehydrates Salts and Sugars

All solid salts consist of a lattice of positive and negative ions (see page 61).

1) In some salts, water molecules are incorporated in the lattice too.
3) The water in a lattice is called water of crystallisation.
4) A solid salt containing water of crystallisation is hydrated.

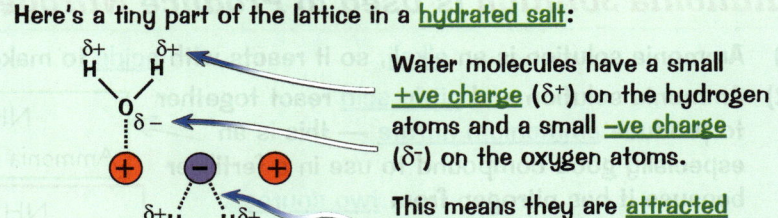

Here's a tiny part of the lattice in a hydrated salt:

Water molecules have a small +ve charge (δ^+) on the hydrogen atoms and a small −ve charge (δ^-) on the oxygen atoms.

This means they are attracted to the ions in the lattice and are held in place.

5) If a salt doesn't contain any water of crystallisation, the salt is anhydrous.
6) Concentrated sulfuric acid is really good at removing the water of crystallisation from hydrated salts, such as copper(II) sulfate. It also removes the 'elements of water' from sugars, such as sucrose.

Dehydration of hydrated copper(II) sulfate

1) When you add concentrated sulfuric acid to hydrated copper(II) sulfate crystals, the water of crystallisation is removed.
2) The blue hydrated crystals turn into white, anhydrous copper(II) sulfate powder.
3) The reaction is very exothermic, so lots of heat is given off.

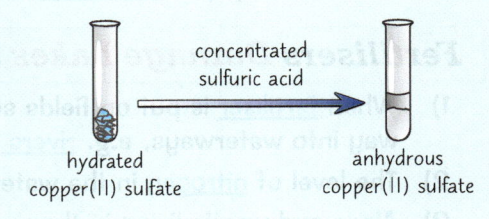

Dehydration of sugars

1) When concentrated sulfuric acid is mixed with a sugar, the mixture first turns yellow, then brown.
2) Sulfuric acid removes hydrogen and oxygen (the 'elements of water') from sugar, forming water. Solid carbon is left behind, which turns the solution black.
3) The water which is formed dilutes the sulfuric acid and generates a lot of heat, which boils the water.
4) The steam produced by boiling water causes the carbon to rise up out of the beaker.

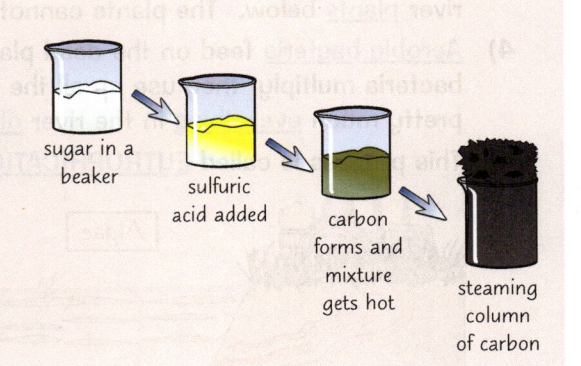

Sulfuric acid — much more useful than a chocolate fire guard...

And there you have it... make sure you can recall some of the uses of sulfuric acid in the exam. You'll also need to be able to describe how it acts as a dehydrating agent.

Q1   Describe the observations made when concentrated sulfuric acid is added to sugar.   [3 marks]

Unit 2e — Reversible Reactions and Industrial Processes

Nitrogenous Fertilisers

Fertilisers allow us to keep growing crops on the same land every year — thanks to our old friend ammonia.

Nitrogenous Fertilisers Provide Plants with Nitrogen

1) The world's population is increasing, so there is more demand for food.
2) Nitrogenous fertilisers help meet this increasing demand because they help plants grow faster and bigger. They do this by increasing the nitrogen in the soil (or replacing that which has been used up).
3) Nitrogenous fertilisers are made to an exact recipe, so farmers know exactly how much nitrogen is in them. They're produced in larger quantities than traditional fertilisers like manure.
4) Ammonium salts such as ammonium nitrate and ammonium sulfate are two common fertilisers.

Ammonia Solution is Used to Produce Nitrogen-Containing Compounds

1) Ammonia solution is an alkali, so it reacts with acids to make ammonium salts in neutralisation reactions.
2) Ammonia solution and nitric acid react together to produce ammonium nitrate — this is an especially good compound to use in a fertiliser because it has nitrogen from two sources.

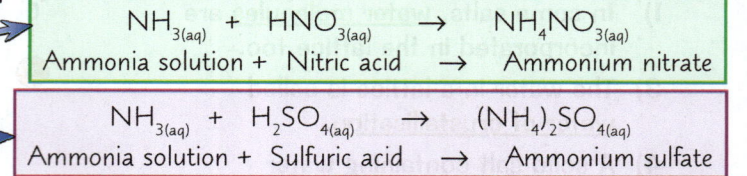

$$NH_{3(aq)} + HNO_{3(aq)} \rightarrow NH_4NO_{3(aq)}$$
Ammonia solution + Nitric acid → Ammonium nitrate

3) Ammonium sulfate is made when ammonia is neutralised by sulfuric acid.

$$NH_{3(aq)} + H_2SO_{4(aq)} \rightarrow (NH_4)_2SO_{4(aq)}$$
Ammonia solution + Sulfuric acid → Ammonium sulfate

4) Ammonium salts contain ammonium ions (NH_4^+). You can test for ammonium ions by adding a source of OH^- ions (usually $NaOH_{(aq)}$) to a solution of a salt and gently heating it. If ammonia gas is given off, it means that there are ammonium ions present.
5) You can test whether the gas given off is ammonia by holding a piece of damp red litmus paper over it. If the litmus paper turns blue, then the gas is ammonia (see page 103).

Fertilisers Damage Lakes and Rivers — Eutrophication

1) When fertiliser is put on fields some of it runs off and finds its way into waterways, e.g. rivers and streams.
2) The level of nitrogen in the waterway increases.
3) Algae and weeds living in the river water use the nutrients to grow and multiply rapidly. The algae form an algal bloom (a carpet of algae near the surface of the river). This blocks off the light to the river plants below. The plants cannot photosynthesise, so they have no food and they die.
4) Aerobic bacteria feed on the dead plants and start to multiply. As the bacteria multiply, they use up all the oxygen in the water. As a result pretty much everything in the river dies (including fish and insects).

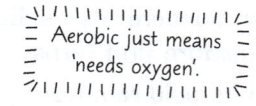

Aerobic just means 'needs oxygen'.

5) This process is called EUTROPHICATION, which basically means 'too much of a good thing'.

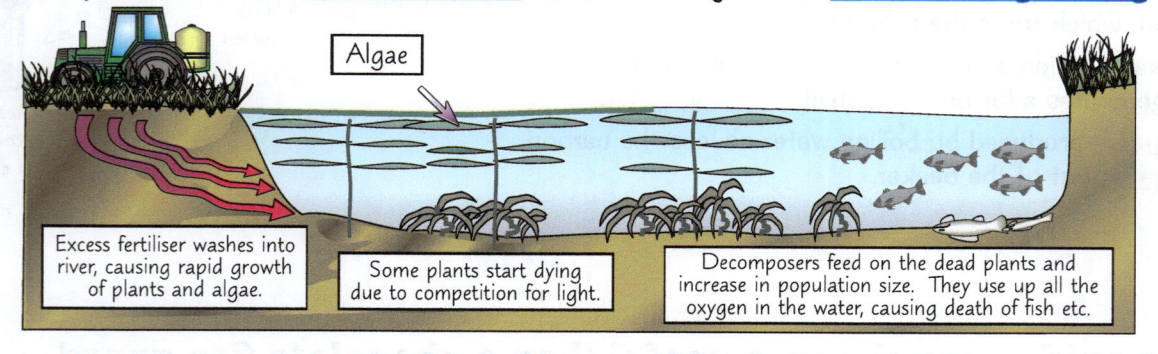

Excess fertiliser washes into river, causing rapid growth of plants and algae.

Some plants start dying due to competition for light.

Decomposers feed on the dead plants and increase in population size. They use up all the oxygen in the water, causing death of fish etc.

There's nowt wrong wi' just spreadin' muck on it...

Nitrogenous fertilisers are great, but not perfect. Make sure you know why.

Q1 Rupert has a sample of a fertiliser. How could he show that it contains ammonium ions? [3 marks]

Unit 2e — Reversible Reactions and Industrial Processes

Revision Questions for Unit 2e

Woohoo — you did it. But before you run off, time to have a go at a few questions.
- Try these questions and tick off each one when you get it right.
- When you've done all the questions for a topic and are completely happy with it, tick off the topic.

Reversible Reactions (p.102)

1) What symbol is used in equations to show that a reaction is reversible?
2) What does it mean if a reversible reaction is going in the forward direction?
3) Give three factors that can affect the direction of a reversible reaction.
4) True or false? If the forward reaction is endothermic, the reverse reaction is also endothermic.

The Haber Process (p.103)

5) What is the balanced symbol equation for the Haber process?
6) From what source is the hydrogen in the Haber process obtained?
7) What happens to unused hydrogen and nitrogen in the Haber process?
8) How does the iron catalyst affect the direction of the reversible reaction in the Haber process?
9) Describe the chemical test for ammonia gas.

The Contact Process and Uses of Sulfuric Acid (p.104-105)

10) Write word equations for the three stages of the Contact process.
11) Why is sulfur trioxide dissolved in concentrated sulfuric acid rather than in water in the Contact process?
12) Why is the temperature used in the second stage of the Contact process a compromise?
13) What catalyst is used in the Contact process?
14) Give three uses of sulfuric acid.
15) Describe what you would observe if hydrated copper(II) sulfate was mixed with concentrated sulfuric acid.

Nitrogenous Fertilisers (p.106)

16) Why do plants need nitrogen?
17) Name two nitrogenous fertilisers.
18) Describe the chemical test for ammonium ions.
19) Explain how fertilisers can be harmful to organisms in rivers and streams.

Unit 2e — Reversible Reactions and Industrial Processes

Measuring Techniques

Safety specs out and lab coats on, it's time to find out about the skills you'll need in experiments...

Mass Should Be Measured Using a Balance

1) To measure mass, start by putting the container you're measuring the substance into on the balance.
2) Set the balance to exactly zero and then start adding your substance.
3) It's no good carefully measuring out your substance if it's not all transferred to your reaction vessel — the volume in the reaction vessel won't be the same as your measurement. Here are a couple of methods you can use to make sure that none gets left in your weighing container...

- If you're dissolving a mass of a solid in a solvent to make a solution, you could wash any remaining solid into the new container using the solvent. This way you know that all the solid you weighed has been transferred.
- You could set the balance to zero before you put your weighing container on the balance. Then reweigh the weighing container after you've transferred the substance. Use the difference in mass to work out exactly how much substance you've transferred.

Different Ways to Measure Liquids

There are a few methods you might use to measure the volume of a liquid. Whichever method you use, always read the volume from the bottom of the meniscus (the curved upper surface of the liquid) when it's at eye level.

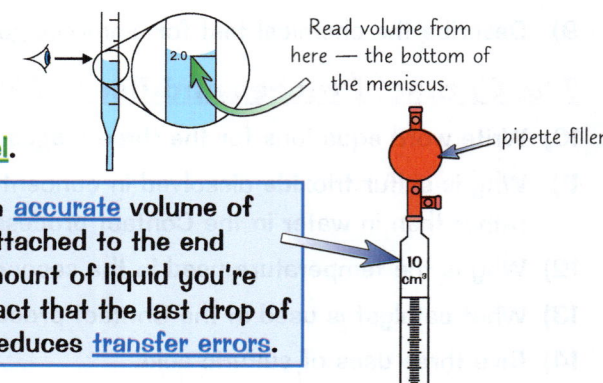

Read volume from here — the bottom of the meniscus.

pipette filler

Pipettes are long, narrow tubes that are used to suck up an accurate volume of liquid and transfer it to another container. A pipette filler attached to the end of the pipette is used so that you can safely control the amount of liquid you're drawing up. Pipettes are often calibrated to allow for the fact that the last drop of liquid stays in the pipette when the liquid is ejected. This reduces transfer errors.

Measuring cylinders are the most common way to measure out a liquid. They come in all different sizes. Make sure you choose one that's the right size for the measurement you want to make. It's no good using a huge 1000 cm³ cylinder to measure out 2 cm³ of a liquid — the graduations will be too big, and you'll end up with massive errors. It'd be much better to use one that measures up to 10 cm³.

If you only want a couple of drops of liquid, and don't need it to be accurately measured, you can use a dropping pipette to transfer it. For example, this is how you'd add a couple of drops of indicator into a mixture.

Gas Syringes Measure Gas Volumes

1) Gases can be measured with a gas syringe. They should be measured at room temperature and pressure as the volume of a gas changes with temperature and pressure. You should also use a gas syringe that's the right size for the measurement you're making. Before you use the syringe, you should make sure it's completely sealed and that the plunger moves smoothly.
2) Alternatively, you can use an upturned measuring cylinder filled with water. The gas will displace the water so you can read the volume off the scale — see page 110.
3) Another method to measure the amount of gas is to count the bubbles produced during a reaction. This method is less accurate, but will give you relative amounts of gas to compare results.
4) When you're measuring the volume of a gas, you need to make sure that the equipment is set up so that none of the gas can escape, otherwise your results won't be accurate.

Experimentus apparatus...

Wizardry won't help you here, unfortunately. It's best you just get your head down and learn this stuff.

Practical Skills

Measuring Techniques and Safety

With all these measuring techniques, you'll be able to tackle experiments like a pro. But that's only half the job. You also need to know the safety precautions you should be taking before you start an experiment...

Measure pH to Find Out How Acidic or Alkaline a Solution is

You need to be able to decide the best method for measuring pH, depending on what your experiment is.

1) Indicators are dyes that change colour depending on whether they're in an acid or an alkali.
2) Universal indicator is a mixture of indicators that changes colour gradually as pH changes. It doesn't show a sudden colour change. It's useful for estimating the pH of a solution based on its colour.
3) Indicators can be soaked into paper and strips of this paper can be used for testing pH. If you use a dropping pipette to spot a small amount of a solution onto some indicator paper, it will change colour depending on the pH of the solution.

> Blue litmus paper turns red in acidic conditions and red litmus paper turns blue in basic conditions. Universal indicator paper can be used to estimate the pH based on its colour.

4) Indicator paper is useful when you don't want to change the colour of all of the substance, or if the substance is already coloured so might obscure the colour of the indicator. You can also hold a piece of damp indicator paper in a gas sample to test its pH.
5) pH probes are attached to pH meters which have a digital display that gives a numerical value for the pH of a solution. They're used to give an accurate value of pH.

Make Sure You're Working Safely in the Lab

1) Make sure that you're wearing sensible clothing when you're in the lab (e.g. open shoes won't protect your feet from spillages). When you're doing an experiment, you should wear a lab coat to protect your skin and clothing. Depending on the experiment, you may need to also wear safety goggles and gloves.
2) You also need to be aware of general safety in the lab, e.g. keep anything flammable away from lit Bunsen burners, don't directly touch any hot equipment, handle glassware carefully so it doesn't break, etc.
3) You should follow any instructions that your teacher gives you carefully. But here are some basic principles for dealing with chemicals and equipment...

Be Careful When You're Using Chemicals...

1) The chemicals you're using may be hazardous — for example, they might be flammable (catch fire easily), or they might irritate or burn your skin if it comes into contact with them.
2) Make sure you're working in an area that's well ventilated and if you're doing an experiment that might produce nasty gases (such as chlorine), you should carry out the experiment in a fume hood so that the gas can't escape out into the room you're working in.
3) Never directly touch any chemicals (even if you're wearing gloves). Use a spatula to transfer solids between containers. Carefully pour liquids between containers, using a funnel to avoid spillages.
4) Be careful when you're mixing chemicals, as a reaction might occur. If you're diluting a liquid, add the concentrated substance to the water (not the other way around) or the mixture could get very hot.

...and Equipment

1) Stop equipment falling by using clamp stands.
2) When heating materials, make sure to let them cool before moving them, or wear insulated gloves while handling them.

Safety first...

I know — lab safety isn't the most exciting topic. But it's mega important. Not only will it stop you from blowing your eyebrows off, it'll help you pick up more marks in the exam. And that IS worth getting excited about...

Practical Skills

Setting Up Experiments

Setting up the equipment for an experiment correctly is <u>important</u>. <u>Drawing</u> it neatly can come in handy too...

To Collect Gases, the System Needs to be Sealed

1) There are times when you might want to <u>collect</u> the gas produced by a reaction. For example, to investigate the <u>rate</u> of reaction.
2) The most accurate way to measure the volume of a gas that's been produced is to collect it in a <u>gas syringe</u> (see page 108).
3) You could also collect it by <u>displacing water</u> from a measuring cylinder. Here's how you do it...

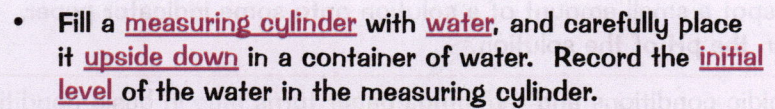

- Fill a <u>measuring cylinder</u> with <u>water</u>, and carefully place it <u>upside down</u> in a container of water. Record the <u>initial level</u> of the water in the measuring cylinder.
- Position a <u>delivery tube</u> coming <u>from</u> the reaction vessel so that it's <u>inside</u> the measuring cylinder, pointing upwards. Any gas that's produced will pass <u>through</u> the delivery tube and <u>into</u> the <u>measuring cylinder</u>. As the gas enters the measuring cylinder, the <u>water</u> is <u>pushed out</u>.
- Record the <u>level of water</u> in the measuring cylinder and use this value, along with your <u>initial value</u>, to calculate the <u>volume</u> of gas produced.

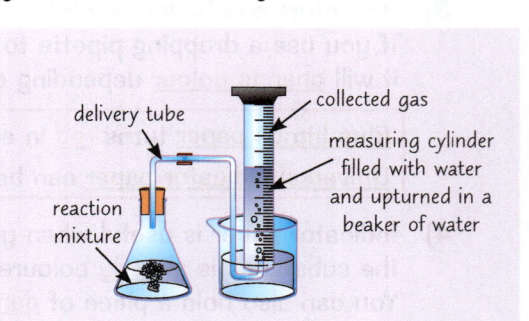

If the delivery tube is underneath the measuring cylinder rather than inside it then some of the gas might escape out into the air.

4) This method is <u>less accurate</u> than using a gas syringe to measure the volume of gas produced. This is because some gases can <u>dissolve</u> in water, so less gas ends up in the measuring cylinder than is <u>actually produced</u>.
5) If you just want to <u>collect</u> a sample to test (and don't need to measure a volume), you can collect it over water, as above, using a <u>test tube</u>. Once the test tube is full of gas, you can stopper it and store the gas for later.

Remember — when you're measuring a gas, your equipment has to be sealed or some gas could escape and your results wouldn't be accurate.

Make Sure You Can Draw Diagrams of Your Equipment

1) When you're writing out a <u>method</u> for your experiment, it's always a good idea to draw a <u>labelled diagram</u> showing how your apparatus will be <u>set up</u>.
2) The easiest way to do this is to use a scientific drawing, where each piece of apparatus is drawn as if you're looking at its <u>cross-section</u>. You can simplify a Bunsen burner though. For example:

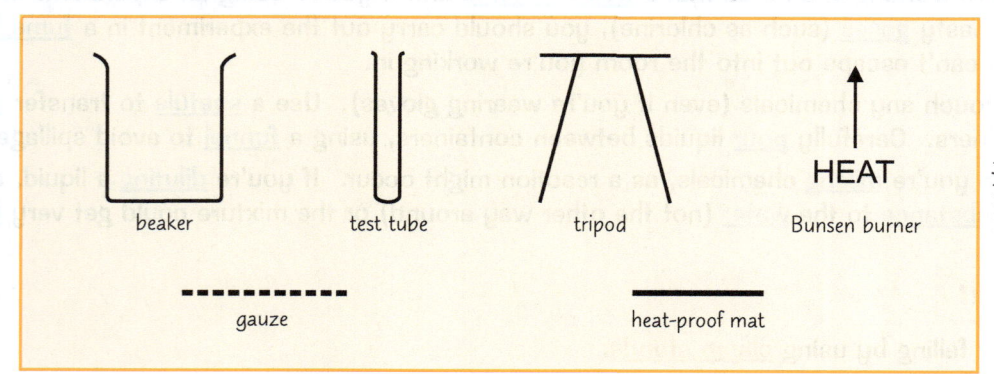

beaker   test tube   tripod   Bunsen burner

gauze   heat-proof mat

The pieces of glassware are drawn without tops so they aren't sealed. If you want to draw a closed system, remember to draw a bung in the top.

Science exams — they're a set-up...

It may seem like science exams are a devious ploy by the creatures of darkness to set you up for misery and heartache... and maybe they are. But whether they are or not, you need to know each of the experimental set-ups on these pages. It'll be worth it in the end, when you ace the exam and smite the evil ones with your top grades...

Practical Skills

Heating Substances

Heating a reaction isn't as simple as wrapping it up in a lumpy wool jumper and a stripy scarf. There's more than one way to do it, and you need to be able to decide on the best, and the safest, method.

Bunsen Burners Have a Naked Flame

Bunsen burners are good for heating things quickly. You can easily adjust how strongly they're heating. But you need to be careful not to use them if you're heating flammable compounds as the flame means the substance would be at risk of catching fire.

Here's how to use a Bunsen burner...

- Connect the Bunsen burner to a gas tap, and check that the hole is closed. Place it on a heatproof mat.
- Light a splint and hold it over the Bunsen burner. Now, turn on the gas. The Bunsen burner should light with a yellow flame.
- The more open the hole is, the more strongly the Bunsen burner will heat your substance. Open the hole to the amount you want. As you open the hole more, the flame should turn more blue.
- The hottest part of the flame is just above the blue cone, so you should heat things here.
- If your Bunsen burner is alight but not heating anything, make sure you close the hole so that the flame becomes yellow and clearly visible.
- If you're heating something so that the container (e.g. a test tube) is in the flame, you should hold the vessel at the top, furthest away from the substance (and so the flame) using a pair of tongs.
- If you're heating something over the flame (e.g. an evaporating dish), you should put a tripod and gauze over the Bunsen burner before you light it, and place the vessel on this.

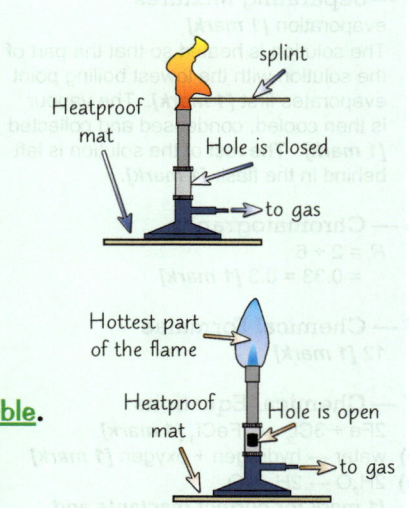

The Temperature of Water Baths and Electric Heaters Can Be Set

1) A water bath is a container filled with water that can be heated to a specific temperature. A simple water bath can be made by heating a beaker of water over a Bunsen burner and monitoring the temperature with a thermometer. However, it is difficult to keep the temperature of the water constant.

2) An electric water bath will monitor and adjust the temperature for you. Here's how you use one:

- Set the temperature on the water bath, and allow the water to heat up.
- Place the vessel containing your substance in the water bath using a pair of tongs. The level of the water outside the vessel should be just above the level of the substance inside the vessel. The substance will then be warmed to the same temperature as the water.

As the substance in the vessel is surrounded by water, the heating is very even. Water boils at 100 °C though, so you can't use a water bath to heat something to a higher temperature than this — the water won't get hot enough.

Handle any glassware you've heated with tongs until you're sure it's cooled down.

3) Electric heaters are often made up of a metal plate that can be heated to a certain temperature. The vessel containing the substance you want to heat is placed on top of the hot plate. You can heat substances to higher temperatures than you can in a water bath but, as the vessel is only heated from below, you'll usually have to stir the substance inside to make sure it's heated evenly.

A bath and an electric heater — how I spend my January nights...

You know, I used to have a science teacher who'd play power ballads when the Bunsen burners were alight and sway at the front of the class like she was at a gig. You think I made that up, but it's true.

Practical Skills

Answers

Unit 1a — The Nature of Substances and Chemical Reactions

p.13 — Elements, Compounds and Mixtures
Q1 a) compound *[1 mark]*
b) element *[1 mark]*
c) mixture *[1 mark]*

p.14 — Separating Mixtures
Q1 evaporation *[1 mark]*
Q2 The solution is heated so that the part of the solution with the lowest boiling point evaporates first *[1 mark]*. The vapour is then cooled, condensed and collected *[1 mark]*. The rest of the solution is left behind in the flask *[1 mark]*.

p.15 — Chromatography
Q1 $R_f = 2 \div 6$
= 0.33 or 0.3 *[1 mark]*

p.16 — Chemical Formulae
Q1 12 *[1 mark]*

p.17 — Chemical Equations
Q1 $2Fe + 3Cl_2 \rightarrow 2FeCl_3$ *[1 mark]*
Q2 a) water → hydrogen + oxygen *[1 mark]*
b) $2H_2O \rightarrow 2H_2 + O_2$
[1 mark for correct reactants and products, 1 mark for a correctly balanced equation]

p.18 — Chemical Reactions
Q1 E.g. colour change / temperature change / effervescence *[1 mark]*.

p.19 — Relative Formula Mass
Q1 a) A_r of H = 1 and A_r of O = 16
M_r of H_2O = (2 × 1) + 16 = 18 *[1 mark]*
b) A_r of Li = 7, A_r of O = 16 and A_r of H = 1
So M_r of LiOH = 7 + 16 + 1 = 24 *[1 mark]*
c) A_r of H = 1, A_r of S = 32 and A_r of O = 16
M_r of H_2SO_4 = (2 × 1) + 32 + (4 × 16) = 98 *[1 mark]*
Q2 A_r of K = 39, A_r of O = 16 and A_r of H = 1
M_r of KOH = 39 + 16 + 1 = 56 *[1 mark]*
$\frac{39}{56} \times 100 = 70\%$ (2 s.f.) *[1 mark]*

p.20 — The Mole
Q1 M_r of H_2O = 16 + (2 × 1) = 18 *[1 mark]*
number of moles = mass ÷ M_r
number of moles = 90 g ÷ 18 = 5 moles *[1 mark]*
Q2 M_r of Na_2SO_4 = (23 × 2) + 32 + (16 × 4) = 142 *[1 mark]*
mass = number of moles × M_r
mass = 0.20 × 142 = 28 g (to 2 s.f.) *[1 mark]*

p.21 — Calculating Masses in Reactions
Q1 a) M_r(KBr) = 39 + 80 = 119
M_r(Br_2) = 80 × 2 = 160 *[1 mark]*
moles of KBr = mass ÷ M_r = 23.8 ÷ 119 = 0.200 moles *[1 mark]*
From the equation, 2 moles of KBr react to produce 1 mole of Br_2. So 0.200 moles of KBr will produce (0.200 ÷ 2) = 0.100 moles of Br_2 *[1 mark]*.
So mass of Br_2 = moles × M_r = 0.100 × 160 = 16.0 g *[1 mark]*
b) Percentage yield
= actual yield ÷ theoretical yield × 100
= 12.4 g ÷ 16.0 g × 100 *[1 mark]*
= 77.5% *[1 mark]*

p.22 — Calculating Formulae from Reacting Masses
Q1 moles of sulfur = 40.0 ÷ 32 = 1.25
moles of oxygen = 60.0 ÷ 16 = 3.75 *[1 mark]*
Divide by the smallest number (1.25):
sulfur = 1.25 ÷ 1.25 = 1
oxygen = 3.75 ÷ 1.25 = 3
Ratio of S : O = 1 : 3
So simplest formula = SO_3 *[1 mark]*
Q2 mass of oxygen = 45.6 − 13.9 = 31.7 g *[1 mark]*
moles = mass ÷ M_r
moles of oxygen = 31.7 ÷ 16 = 1.98125
moles of nitrogen = 13.9 ÷ 14 = 0.99... *[1 mark]*
Divide by the smallest number (0.99...).
oxygen = 1.98125 ÷ 0.99... = 2
nitrogen = 0.99... ÷ 0.99... = 1
Ratio of O : N = 2 : 1.
So simplest formula = NO_2 *[1 mark]*

p.23 — Calculating Formulae from Reacting Masses
Q1 Heat a crucible until it's red hot, leave it to cool, and then weigh it, along with its lid *[1 mark]*. Add a sample of the metal that you're investigating and reweigh the crucible, lid and contents *[1 mark]*. Heat the crucible strongly for around 10 minutes, with the lid on but leaving a small gap for oxygen to get in *[1 mark]*. Allow the crucible to cool and reweigh the crucible, lid and contents *[1 mark]*.

Unit 1b — Atomic Structure and the Periodic Table

p.25 — The Atom
Q1 electrons = 19 *[1 mark]*,
protons = 19 *[1 mark]*,
neutrons = 39 − 19 = 20 *[1 mark]*

p.26 — Ions, Isotopes and Relative Atomic Mass
Q1 a) Bromine-79: 35 protons, 35 electrons and (79 − 35 =) 44 neutrons *[1 mark]*.
Bromine-81: 35 protons, 35 electrons and (81 − 35 =) 46 neutrons *[1 mark]*.
b) 35 + 1 = 36 electrons *[1 mark]*

p.27 — The Periodic Table
Q1 2 *[1 mark]*
Q2 Both chlorine and bromine have the same number of electrons in their outer shell *[1 mark]*.
You know this because they're both in the same group.
Q3 E.g. potassium forms 1+ ions because it's in the same group as sodium / has the same number of electrons in its outer shell, so will react in a similar way *[1 mark]*.

p.28 — Electron Shells
Q1 2.8.3 or

[1 mark]
Q2 Group 2 *[1 mark]*
Period 4 *[1 mark]*

p.29 — Group 1 — The Alkali Metals
Q1 Reactivity increases down Group 1 *[1 mark]*. As you go down the group, the outer electron is further away from the nucleus *[1 mark]*. This means the attraction between the nucleus and the electron decreases, so the electron is more easily removed *[1 mark]*.

p.30 — Reactions of the Alkali Metals
Q1 lithium *[1 mark]*
Q2 $2Na + 2H_2O \rightarrow 2NaOH + H_2$
[1 mark for correct reactants and products, 1 mark for correctly balanced equation.]

p.31 — Group 7 — The Halogens
Q1 Bromine would be a solid at this temperature *[1 mark]*. The melting points of the halogens increase as you go down the group, so at the melting point of chlorine, bromine would still be solid *[1 mark]*.

p.32 — Reactions of the Halogens
Q1 $2Na + I_2 \rightarrow 2NaI$
[1 mark for correct reactants and products, 1 mark for correctly balanced equation]
Q2 $2Fe + 3Cl_2 \rightarrow 2FeCl_3$
[1 mark for correct reactants and products, 1 mark for correctly balanced equation]

p.33 — Halogen Displacement Reactions
Q1 Bromine water *[1 mark]*.

p.34 — Group 0 — The Noble Gases
Q1 They have a full outer shell of electrons. *[1 mark]*

p.35 — Tests for Ions and Hydrogen
Q1 Barium *[1 mark]*

Answers

Answers

Unit 1c — Water and the Earth

p.37 — Water Treatment
Q1 A sedimentation process is used which involves larger particles settling at the bottom of the water tank due to gravity *[1 mark]*.
The water is then filtered through gravel and sand to filter out smaller solid objects *[1 mark]*.
Finally, chlorine gas is bubbled through the water to kill harmful bacteria *[1 mark]*.

p.38 — Distillation and Desalination
Q1 Distillation requires the sea water to be heated. This requires a lot of energy and therefore a lot of money *[1 mark]*.

p.39 — Solubility Curves
Q1 The ability of a substance to dissolve in a solvent *[1 mark]*.
Q2 46 g per 100 g of water *[1 mark]*.

p.40 — Investigating Solubility
Q1 E.g. weigh out an excess of the solid and add it to a boiling tube containing a known volume of water to make a saturated solution *[1 mark]*. Stir the solution and place the boiling tube in a water bath set to 40 °C for 5 minutes *[1 mark]*. Filter out the excess solid using filter paper *[1 mark]*. Dry and weigh the excess solid that was removed from the solution *[1 mark]*. To find the solubility of the solid in g per 100 g of water, you would then divide the mass of solid dissolved in the solution by the mass of water and multiply by 100 *[1 mark]*.

p.41 — Water Hardness
Q1 The columns contain sodium ions attached to a resin *[1 mark]*. When water runs through the column, the calcium or magnesium ions in the water are exchanged for sodium ions, making the water soft *[1 mark]*.

p.42 — Measuring Water Hardness
Q1 E.g. add soap solution 1 cm³ at a time to set volumes of the three water samples *[1 mark]* and shake for 5 seconds each time until a lasting lather is formed *[1 mark]*. Boil fresh samples of water and repeat the experiment *[1 mark]*. Distilled water will need the least soap to form a lasting lather, and will do so before and after boiling *[1 mark]*. Temporary hard water will need lots of soap to give a good lather before boiling but much less after boiling *[1 mark]*. Permanent hard water will need lots of soap to give a lather before and after boiling *[1 mark]*.

p.43 — The Earth's Structure
Q1 Iron *[1 mark]*

p.44 — Plate Tectonics
Q1 E.g. matching layers in the rocks on different continents / fossils of very similar plants and animals found on different continents / jigsaw-like fit of some continents (Africa and South America) *[1 mark]*

p.45 — Plate Boundaries
Q1 Constructive plate boundaries are found where two plates are moving away from each other *[1 mark]*. Magma (molten rock) rises from the mantle to fill the gap and cools, creating new crust *[1 mark]*.

p.46 — The Atmosphere
Q1 Green plants evolved and removed CO_2 from the atmosphere through photosynthesis *[1 mark]*. Some of the early CO_2 dissolved into the oceans *[1 mark]*. Much of the remaining CO_2 got locked up in fossil fuels and sedimentary rocks *[1 mark]*.

p.47 — Greenhouse Gases and Climate Change
Q1 E.g. flooding due to rising sea levels / increased rainfall in some areas / droughts due to hotter, drier weather in some areas *[1 mark]*.

p.48 — Reducing Pollution and Tests for Gases
Q1 E.g. the company could invest in a scheme to offset the carbon dioxide they emit / use carbon capture and storage to capture the carbon dioxide before it's released into the atmosphere / plan how to reduce its emissions in future by reducing energy usage or using renewable energy *[1 mark]*.
Q2 Any two from e.g. causes lakes to become acidic and harm aquatic life / kills trees (and other plants) / damages limestone buildings / corrodes metal structures faster *[2 marks]*.

Unit 1d — Rate of Chemical Change and Thermal Decomposition

p.50 — Reaction Rates
Q1 E.g. put a conical flask on a mass balance and add your reactants *[1 mark]*. As gas is produced from the reaction, measure how quickly the reading on the balance drops until the balance stops changing *[1 mark]*. Plot the results in a graph of change in mass against time *[1 mark]*.
Q2 E.g. it gives more accurate results than human judgement *[1 mark]*.

p.51 — Rate Experiments Involving Gases
Q1 E.g. place a measured volume of hydrochloric acid of a known concentration in a conical flask. Add a known mass of calcium carbonate in the form of marble chips *[1 mark]*. Use a gas syringe to take readings of the volume of gas produced at regular time intervals *[1 mark]*. Repeat the experiment with the same volume and concentration of acid and the same mass of calcium carbonate but increase the surface area by crunching the marble chips up *[1 mark]*.

p.52 — Rate Experiments Involving Precipitation
Q1 The time taken would decrease *[1 mark]*.

p.53 — Calculating Rates
Q1 E.g.

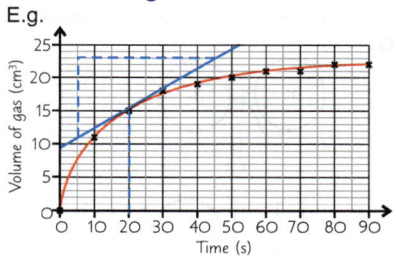

[1 mark]
E.g. Change in $y = 23 - 11 = 12$
Change in $x = 45 - 5 = 40$
Gradient $= 12 \div 40 = 0.30$ cm³/s
[1 mark for a rate between 0.25 cm³/s and 0.40 cm³/s]

p.54 — Factors Affecting Rate of Reaction
Q1 The energy transferred during a collision *[1 mark]* and the collision frequency *[1 mark]*.
Q2 Breaking a solid into smaller pieces will increase the surface area to volume ratio *[1 mark]*. This means that particles of the other reactant will have more area to work on *[1 mark]*. This increases the frequency of collisions and speeds up the rate of reaction *[1 mark]*.

p.55 — More Factors Affecting Rate of Reaction
Q1 In industrial processes there may be impurities present *[1 mark]*, which cause catalysts to lose their activity and work less effectively over time *[1 mark]*.

p.56 — Thermal Decomposition
Q1 Sodium carbonate is very stable *[1 mark]* and doesn't decompose when heated with a Bunsen burner *[1 mark]*. This means that there is no carbon dioxide produced so the limewater doesn't turn milky *[1 mark]*.

p.57 — Limestone
Q1 Calcium oxide undergoes an exothermic reaction with water, so the temperature increases *[1 mark]*. Calcium hydroxide is produced, which forms an alkaline solution, so the pH increases *[1 mark]*.

Answers

Unit 2a — Bonding, Structure and Properties

p.59 — Metallic Bonding
Q1 Copper is a good electrical conductor *[1 mark]* as it contains delocalised electrons which are able to carry an electrical charge *[1 mark]*.
Q2 Magnesium is made up of Mg^{2+} ions and sodium is made up of Na^+ ions *[1 mark]*. The greater number of delocalised electrons in magnesium means the electrostatic forces of attraction are stronger *[1 mark]* and so they need more energy to be broken *[1 mark]*.

p.60 — Ionic Bonding
Q1 A calcium atom loses two electron to form a Ca^{2+} ion *[1 mark]*. Each fluorine atom gains an electron to form an F^- ion *[1 mark]*. The oppositely charged ions are attracted to each other by electrostatic attraction *[1 mark]*.
Q2 *[1 mark for showing electron transferred from potassium to bromine, 1 mark for correct outer shell electron configurations (with or without inner shells), 1 mark for correct charges on ions]*

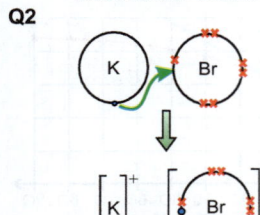

p.61 — Ionic Compounds
Q1 A lot of energy is needed to break the strong ionic bonds / electrostatic forces of attraction *[1 mark]*.

p.62 — Simple Molecules
Q1 *[1 mark for correct diagram (with or without inner shells)]*

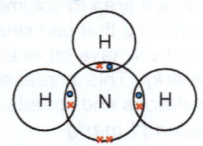

p.63 — Giant Covalent Structures and Fullerenes
Q1 Each carbon atom in graphite forms three covalent bonds and has one electron that is delocalised and can carry charge *[1 mark]*. Each carbon atom in diamond forms four covalent bonds and so diamond has no delocalised electrons, meaning it cannot carry charge *[1 mark]*.

p.64 — Nanoparticles
Q1 E.g. sun cream / self-cleaning glass *[1 mark]*

p.65 — Smart Materials
Q1 Heat both samples / place both samples in hot water *[1 mark]*. The shape memory alloy will return to its original shape *[1 mark]*.

Unit 2b — Acids, Bases and Salts

p.67 — Acids and Bases
Q1 orange *[1 mark]*
Q2 alkaline *[1 mark]*

p.68 — Acid and Alkali Strength
Q1 hydroxide ions / OH^- *[1 mark]*
Q2 A strong acid ionises/dissociates almost completely in water *[1 mark]*. A weak acid only ionises/dissociates partially in water *[1 mark]*.

p.69 — Reactions of Acids
Q1 $2HCl + CaCO_3 \rightarrow CaCl_2 + H_2O + CO_2$
[1 mark for correct reactants and products, 1 mark for a correctly balanced equation]

p.70 — Making Salts
Q1 E.g. React the base, iron(III) oxide, with the acid, nitric acid. Keep on adding base until all the acid has been neutralised — at this point, no more base will react and it will sink to the bottom of the flask *[1 mark]*. Then, filter out the excess solid using filter paper, and collect the solution of salt and water *[1 mark]*. Then, gently evaporate off some of the water from your salt and water solution and leave to allow the salt to crystallise *[1 mark]*.

p.71 — Titrations
Q1 The indicator will have just changed colour *[1 mark]*.

p.72 — Titration Calculations
Q1 Moles of KOH = $0.150 \times (22.5 \div 1000)$
= 0.003375 *[1 mark]*
From the reaction equation, 1 mole of KOH reacts with 1 mole of HNO_3, so 0.003375 mol of KOH reacts with 0.003375 mol of HNO_3 *[1 mark]*.
Concentration of HNO_3
= $(0.003375) \div (25.0 \div 1000)$
= 0.135 mol/dm³ *[1 mark]*

Unit 2c — Metals, Extraction and Energy

p.74 — Metal Ores and The Reactivity Series
Q1 Tin is less reactive than carbon *[1 mark]* so you could extract tin from its ore by reducing it with carbon *[1 mark]*.
Q2 E.g. $2ZnO + C \rightarrow 2Zn + CO_2$
[1 mark for correct reactants and products, 1 mark for balanced equation]

p.75 — Extracting Iron
Q1 $3CO + Fe_2O_3 \rightarrow 3CO_2 + 2Fe$ *[1 mark]*

p.76 — Metal Displacement Reactions
Q1 Silver would not displace iron from iron(II) chloride solution, because it's below iron in the reactivity series/less reactive than iron *[1 mark]*.

p.77 — Electrolysis
Q1 a) oxygen gas/O_2 *[1 mark]*
b) hydrogen gas/H_2 *[1 mark]*

p.78 — More on Electrolysis
Q1 The ions in solid sodium chloride are in fixed positions, so cannot move to conduct electricity *[1 mark]*.
Q2 Aluminium oxide has a very high melting point. Dissolving aluminium oxide in molten cryolite can be done at a lower temperature *[1 mark]*. This reduces the energy needed for aluminium extraction *[1 mark]* and therefore lowers the cost of extraction *[1 mark]*.

p.79 — Electrolysis of Aqueous Solutions
Q1 At the anode: $2Br^- \rightarrow Br_2 + 2e^-$ *[1 mark]*
At the cathode: $2H^+ + 2e^- \rightarrow H_2$ *[1 mark]*

p.80 — Uses of Electrolysis
Q1 The anode is a big lump of impure copper *[1 mark]* and the cathode is a thin piece of pure copper *[1 mark]*. During the electrolysis, the impure copper is oxidised and dissolves into the electrolyte to form copper ions *[1 mark]*. These copper ions move to the cathode where they are reduced and coat the cathode with a pure layer of copper *[1 mark]*.

p.81 — Sustainability of Metal Extraction
Q1 Advantage: building the plant near to a town means that workers can travel easily from their homes *[1 mark]*. Disadvantage: the plant might create noise/air pollution/a loss of the natural landscape so local residents might oppose the build *[1 mark]*.

p.82 — Uses of Metals
Q1 E.g. car bodies / bridges / cutlery *[1 mark]*

p.83 — Transition Metals
Q1 The iron(II) chloride would be green *[1 mark]* and the iron(III) chloride would be brown *[1 mark]*.

p.84 — Endothermic and Exothermic Reactions
Q1 The products are at a higher energy than the reactants so the reaction must be endothermic *[1 mark]*. This means the reaction mixture must have decreased in temperature *[1 mark]*.

Answers

p.85 — Bond Energies
Q1 Energy required to break original bonds:
(1 × N≡N) + (3 × H–H)
= 941 + (3 × 436) = 941 + 1308
= 2249 kJ/mol *[1 mark]*
Energy released by forming new bonds:
(6 × N–H) = 6 × 391 = 2346 kJ/mol
[1 mark]
Overall energy change:
2249 – 2346 = –97 kJ/mol *[1 mark]*

Unit 2d — Crude Oil, Fuels and Organic Chemistry

p.87 — Fractional Distillation of Crude Oil
Q1 It suggests that the hydrocarbons in petrol have lower boiling points than those in diesel *[1 mark]*.

p.88 — Crude Oil and Cracking
Q1 C_3H_6 *[1 mark]*

p.89 — Hydrocarbons
Q1 Dodecane molecules are much bigger/longer than methane molecules *[1 mark]* and so there are more/stronger intermolecular forces between dodecane molecules than between methane molecules *[1 mark]*.

p.90 — Burning Fuels
Q1 A fire needs fuel, oxygen and heat to burn *[1 mark]*. Putting a blanket over the fire blocks oxygen from getting to it, and so the fire cannot keep burning *[1 mark]*.

p.91 — Measuring Energy Changes
Q1 Energy released per gram of fuel
$= \dfrac{100 \times 18.7 \times 4.2}{0.2}$ *[1 mark]*
= 39 270 J *[1 mark]*
= 40 kJ (2 s.f.) *[1 mark]*

p.92 — Alkanes
Q1 C_8H_{18} *[1 mark]*

p.93 — Alkenes
Q1

(displayed structural formula of propene) *[1 mark]*

p.94 — Naming Other Alkanes and Alkenes
Q1 E.g.

(displayed structural formula with a C_2H_5 branch) *[1 mark]*

p.95 — Addition Polymers
Q1 Propene has a double covalent bond *[1 mark]* which can open up to join to other monomers *[1 mark]*.

p.96 — Uses of Plastics
Q1 Any two from: e.g. it has a high melting point. / It is almost completely unreactive. / It has a very slippery surface. *[2 marks]*

p.97 — Disposing of Polymers
Q1 E.g. if not controlled, toxic gases can be released from burning plastics / carbon dioxide is released when plastics are burned which contributes to global warming *[2 marks]*.
Q2 Polymers are made from crude oil *[1 mark]*. Crude oil is a finite resource *[1 mark]* so the more of it we use up, the more expensive it will become and this will increase the price of polymer products *[1 mark]*.

p.98 — Alcohols
Q1 E.g.

(displayed structural formula of propan-1-ol with a CH_3 branch shown) *[1 mark]*

p.99 — Uses of Ethanol
Q1 Any two from: e.g. could lead to a break-up in family and friend relationships / could lead to unemployment / could lead to increased involvement in violence. *[2 marks]*

p.100 — Testing for Alcohols and Infrared Spectroscopy
Q1 Orange *[1 mark]*
Q2 An alkene has a carbon-carbon double bond (C=C) *[1 mark]*. So, the spectrum of an alkene will contain a peak in the region of carbon-carbon double bond wavenumbers (1620-1680 cm^{-1}), but a spectrum of an alkane will not *[1 mark]*.

Unit 2e — Reversible Reactions and Industrial Processes

p.102 — Reversible Reactions
Q1 Adding water to anhydrous copper sulfate gives out heat, so it is exothermic *[1 mark]*. This means the reverse of this reaction must be endothermic *[1 mark]*.

p.103 — The Haber Process
Q1 A temperature between 350° and 450° is used because this is high enough to ensure a fast rate of reaction without decreasing the yield of ammonia by too much *[1 mark]*. A pressure between 150 and 200 atm is used in order to maximise the rate and the yield of ammonia. A higher pressure would be too expensive *[1 mark]*. An iron catalyst is used in order to speed up the rate of the reaction *[1 mark]*.

p.104 — The Contact Process
Q1 You could increase the pressure *[1 mark]*.
Q2 $SO_{3(g)} + H_2SO_{4(l)} \rightarrow H_2S_2O_{7(l)}$
$H_2S_2O_{7(l)} + H_2O_{(l)} \rightarrow 2H_2SO_{4(l)}$
[1 mark for each correct equation, 1 mark for correct state symbols in each equation]

p.105 — Uses of Sulfuric Acid
Q1 The mixture of sugar and sulfuric acid would first turn yellow, then darken to brown and eventually black *[1 mark]*. The mixture would get hot and begin to steam *[1 mark]*, causing a spongy black column of carbon to rise out of the beaker *[1 mark]*.

p.106 — Nitrogenous Fertilisers
Q1 Rupert could dissolve the fertiliser in sodium hydroxide solution *[1 mark]* and gently warm it *[1 mark]*. If the fertiliser contained ammonium ions, ammonia gas would be given off which would turn damp red litmus paper blue *[1 mark]*.

Index

A
accuracy 7
acid rain 48
acids 67-69
  reactions of 69-71
activation energy 84
addition polymers 95
addition reactions 93
alcohols 98-100
  test for 100
alkali metals 29, 30
alkalis 67, 68
  reactions of 71
alkanes 88, 92, 94
alkenes 88, 93-95
  test for 93
alkyl groups 94
alloys 65, 82
alumina 78
aluminium 78, 82
ammonia 103, 106
  making 103
  test for 103
ammonium chloride 40
anodes 77-80
anomalous results 7
apparatus 110
  drawing 110
atmosphere 46, 47
atomic number 25, 26
atoms 13, 25, 26
averages (means) 8
Avogadro constant 20

B
balancing equations 17
bar charts 8
bases 67-71
  reactions of 69-71
bias 4
bioethanol 99
biofuels 99
blast furnaces 75
bond energies 85
bonds
  covalent 62
  ionic 60
  metallic 59
bromine water 93
Bunsen burners 111
burettes 42

C
calcium ions 41
calculating masses 21
cancer 37
carbon 63, 74
  giant covalent structures 63
carbon dioxide 56
  in the atmosphere 46, 47
  test for 48
carbonate ions 41
carbonates 56
carboxylic acids 98
catalysts 55, 83, 104
cathodes 77-80
chemical reactions 18
chlorination 37
chromatography 15
climate change 47
coke 75
collisions (particle theory) 54
combustion reactions 75, 90
  measuring 91
compounds 13
concentrated acids 68
concentration 68, 71, 72
  effect on rate 51, 54
conclusions 11
conservative boundaries 45
constructive boundaries 45
Contact process 104
continental drift 44
control variables 6
convection currents 43
copper 82
  purification of 80
core (of the Earth) 43
correlations 11
covalent bonds 62
cracking 88
crude oil 87, 88, 97
crust (of the Earth) 43, 45
crystals 70

D
dehydration 105
delocalised electrons 59, 63
dependent variables 6
desalination 38
destructive boundaries 45
diamond 63
displacement reactions 32, 33, 76
distillation 14, 38
dot and cross diagrams 60, 62
double bonds 93
drinking water 37

E
earthquakes 43, 45
effervescence 18
electric heaters 111
electrodes 77-80
electrolysis 77-80
  of copper(II) chloride 79
  of sodium chloride 79
electrolytes 77
electron shells 28
electronic structures 28
electrons 25, 60, 62
elements 13
endothermic reactions 84, 85, 102
energy changes 91
equations 17
errors 7
ethanol 98, 99
evaluations 12
evaporation 14
exothermic reactions 84, 85, 102
extraction of metals
  74, 75, 78, 81
  aluminium 78, 81
  electrolysis 78
  iron 75
  reduction with carbon 74

F
fair tests 6
fermentation 98
fertilisers 105, 106
filtration 14, 37
fire triangle 90
flame tests 35
fluoride 37
formulae 16
  calculating 22, 23
fractional distillation 87
fractions 87, 89
fuels 90
fullerenes 63
functional groups 98

G
gas syringes 108
gases
  collecting 110
  syringes 108
  tests for 48
giant covalent structures 63
giant ionic lattices 61
gradients 9, 53
graphene 63
graphite 63
graphs 9
greenhouse effect 47
greenhouse gases 47
  reducing 48
Group 0 elements 34
  uses 34
Group 1 elements 29, 30
  reactions 30
Group 7 elements 31-33
  reactions 32, 33
  reactivity 31-33
  uses 31

H
Haber process 103
halide ions
  test for 35
halides 79
halogens 31-33
  reactions 32, 33
  reactivity 31-33
  uses 31
hard water 41, 42
hazards 5
hydrated salt 105
hydrocarbons 87-90, 92, 93
hydrogen
  as a fuel 90
  ions 68
  test for 35
hydrogencarbonate 41
hypotheses 3, 6

I
independent variables 6
indicators 67, 109
infertility 37
infrared spectroscopy 100
insoluble salts 70
intermolecular forces 89
ion exchange columns 41
ionic bonds 60
ionic compounds 16, 61
  formulae 16
  properties 61
ionic equations 35
ionisation of acids 68
ions 26, 60, 61
iron 75, 82
  extraction 75
  halides 32
  ores 75
isomers 92-94, 98
isotopes 26

Index

L
limescale 41
limestone 57, 75
limewater 48, 56, 57
lithosphere 43

M
magnesium ions 41
making salts 70
mantle (of the Earth) 43, 45
mass number 25, 26
means (averages) 8
measuring
  cylinders 108
  mass 108
  pH 109
  rates of reaction 50-52
  techniques 108, 109
  volumes 108
metal carbonates 56
metal ions
  test for 35
metallic bonds 59
metals 59, 83
  extraction plants 81
  properties 59
  reactions 69, 76
  uses 82
microbial oxidation 98
mixtures 13
  separating 14, 15
molecular formulae 16
moles 20
monomers 95

N
nanoparticles 64
nanotubes 63
neutralisation reactions
    67, 69-71, 75
neutrons 25, 26
nitrogen (in the atmosphere) 46
noble gases (uses of) 34
nuclei (of atoms) 25

O
oleum 104
ores 74, 75, 78
oxidation 76, 77
oxygen
  in the atmosphere 46
  test for 48

P
Pangaea 44
particle theory 54
percentage mass 19
percentage yield 21
periodic table 27
permanent hardness 41
pH 67, 68
  probes 109
photochromic pigments 65
pipettes 108
plastics 96
plate boundaries 43, 45
  conservative 45
  constructive 45
  destructive 45
plate tectonics 44
plates
  continental 45
  oceanic 45
polymer gels 65
polymers 95-97
potassium dichromate(VI) 100
precipitates 41
precipitation reactions 50, 52, 70
precision 7
predictions 3, 6
pressure 54
properties of
  hydrocarbons 89
  metals 82
  transition metals 83
protons 25, 26
purification of copper 80

Q
quarrying 57
quicklime 57

R
random errors 7
range (of data) 8, 12
rates of reaction 50-55
  graphs 53
reaction profiles 84
reactivity series 74
recycling 81, 97
redox reactions 76
reduction 74-77
relative atomic mass 19, 26
relative formula mass 19
repeatability 6, 7
reproducibility 6, 7
resolution 7
reversible reactions 102-104
R_f values 15

S
safety
  chemicals 109
  equipment 109
salts 69-71, 105
saturated compounds 92
saturated solutions 39
scale 41
scientific drawings 110
sea water 38
sedimentation 37
separating solutions 38
shape memory
  alloys 65
  polymers 65
significant figures 8
simple covalent structures 62
simple distillation 14, 38
simple molecular structures 62
slaked lime 57
smart materials 65
soft water 41
solubility 39, 40
  calculating 40
  curves 39
  investigating 40
soluble salts 70, 71
solutes 39
solvents 39
spectator ions 83
steel 82
strong acids 68
structural formulae 16
sugars 105
sulfates
  test for 69
sulfur dioxide 48, 104
sulfuric acid 104, 105
surface area (effect on rate)
    51, 54
sustainable
  metal extraction 81
  water supply 37
symbol equations 17
symbols 16
systematic errors 7

T
tables (of data) 8
tangents 53
tectonic plates 43-45
temperature (effect on rate)
    52, 55
temporary hardness 41
test for
  alkenes 93
  carbon dioxide 48
  halide ions 35
  hydrogen 35
  metal ions 35
  oxygen 48
  sulfates 69
theoretical mass 21
theories 3
thermal decomposition 56
thermochromic pigments 65
titanium 82
titrations 42, 67, 71, 72
tooth decay 37
transition metals 83

U
uncertainty 12
units 10
universal indicator 67, 109
unsaturated compound 93

V
validity 6
vanadium pentoxide 104
variables 6, 9
volcanoes 43, 45

W
water
  baths 111
  hardness 41, 42
  pollutants 37
  shortages 37
  softeners 41
  sources 37
  treatment 37, 38
wavenumbers 100
weak acids 68
Wegener, Alfred 44
  continental drift theory 44
word equations 17

Y
yield 104

Z
zero errors 7

The Periodic Table

Periods	Group 1	Group 2											Group 3	Group 4	Group 5	Group 6	Group 7	Group 0
1							1 H Hydrogen 1											
2	7 Li Lithium 3	9 Be Beryllium 4											11 B Boron 5	12 C Carbon 6	14 N Nitrogen 7	16 O Oxygen 8	19 F Fluorine 9	4 He Helium 2 / 20 Ne Neon 10
3	23 Na Sodium 11	24 Mg Magnesium 12											27 Al Aluminium 13	28 Si Silicon 14	31 P Phosphorus 15	32 S Sulfur 16	35.5 Cl Chlorine 17	40 Ar Argon 18
4	39 K Potassium 19	40 Ca Calcium 20	45 Sc Scandium 21	48 Ti Titanium 22	51 V Vanadium 23	52 Cr Chromium 24	55 Mn Manganese 25	56 Fe Iron 26	59 Co Cobalt 27	59 Ni Nickel 28	63.5 Cu Copper 29	65 Zn Zinc 30	70 Ga Gallium 31	73 Ge Germanium 32	75 As Arsenic 33	79 Se Selenium 34	80 Br Bromine 35	84 Kr Krypton 36
5	85 Rb Rubidium 37	88 Sr Strontium 38	89 Y Yttrium 39	91 Zr Zirconium 40	93 Nb Niobium 41	96 Mo Molybdenum 42	98 Tc Technetium 43	101 Ru Ruthenium 44	103 Rh Rhodium 45	106 Pd Palladium 46	108 Ag Silver 47	112 Cd Cadmium 48	115 In Indium 49	119 Sn Tin 50	122 Sb Antimony 51	128 Te Tellurium 52	127 I Iodine 53	131 Xe Xenon 54
6	133 Cs Caesium 55	137 Ba Barium 56	139 La Lanthanum 57	178 Hf Hafnium 72	181 Ta Tantalum 73	184 W Tungsten 74	186 Re Rhenium 75	190 Os Osmium 76	192 Ir Iridium 77	195 Pt Platinum 78	197 Au Gold 79	201 Hg Mercury 80	204 Tl Thallium 81	207 Pb Lead 82	209 Bi Bismuth 83	209 Po Polonium 84	210 At Astatine 85	222 Rn Radon 86
7	223 Fr Francium 87	226 Ra Radium 88	227 Ac Actinium 89	261 Rf Rutherfordium 104	262 Db Dubnium 105	266 Sg Seaborgium 106	264 Bh Bohrium 107	277 Hs Hassium 108	268 Mt Meitnerium 109	271 Ds Darmstadtium 110	272 Rg Roentgenium 111							

Relative atomic mass → (top number)
Atomic number → (bottom number)

The Formulae of Some Common Ions

Positive ions

Name	Formula
aluminium	Al^{3+}
ammonium	NH_4^+
barium	Ba^{2+}
calcium	Ca^{2+}
copper(II)	Cu^{2+}
hydrogen	H^+
iron(II)	Fe^{2+}
iron(III)	Fe^{3+}
lithium	Li^+
magnesium	Mg^{2+}
nickel	Ni^{2+}
potassium	K^+
silver	Ag^+
sodium	Na^+
zinc	Zn^{2+}

Negative ions

Name	Formula
bromide	Br^-
carbonate	CO_3^{2-}
chloride	Cl^-
fluoride	F^-
hydroxide	OH^-
iodide	I^-
nitrate	NO_3^-
oxide	O^{2-}
sulfate	SO_4^{2-}